FEM*ME*

Feminists,
Lesbians, and
Bad Girls

FEMME

Feminists,
Lesbians, and
Bad Girls

Edited by

Laura Harris and Elizabeth Crocker

Routledge
New York London
1997

Published in 1997 by
Routledge
29 West 35th Street
New York, NY 10001

Published in Great Britain by
Routledge
11 New Fetter Lane
London EC4P 4EE

Copyright © 1997 by Routledge

Printed in the United States of America on acid-free paper.

Library of Congress Cataloging-in-Publication Data

Fem(me): feminists, lesbians, and bad girls / edited by Laura Harris
  and Liz Crocker.
      p. cm.
  Includes bibliographical references and index.
    ISBN 0-415-91873-1 (alk. paper). -- ISBN 0-415-91874-X (pbk:
alk. paper)
    1. Lesbians. 2. Lesbianism. 3. Feminism. I. Harris, Laura, 1963- .
II. Crocker, Liz, 1971- .
HQ75.5.F46   1997
305.48'9664--dc21   97-1483
                                            CIP

CONTENTS

2. Generations: A Feminist Genealogy

3. Futures: "The Queerest of the Queer"

ACKNOWLEDGMENTS

We would like to thank: Barbara Cruikshank for asking Joan Nestle the question, "What about an anthology on femmes?"; Madeline Davis for her gracious and generous support; Heather Findlay for her numerous e-mail tips; Liz Kennedy for her advice; our interview subjects—Madeline Davis, Jewelle Gomez, Amber Hollibaugh, Mabel Maney, Joan Nestle, and Minnie Bruce Pratt—for their time and candor; Delritta Hornbuckle for providing information on Ethel Sawyer; Quang Dang and Alex Textor for their hospitality in San Francisco; Kris Kovick for opening her rolodex to us; and all our contributors for their faith, energy, and enthusiasm.

Laura Harris would like to thank: my family for their love and support, especially Marina Harris for her brilliant observations on lesbians, mothers, and what's hip or not; Maria Morales for her deter-mind-ded high-fem latina ways; and Alicia Harris for being sassy too; personal friends who asked, listened, and had faith: Thomas Harris, Lauren Wilson, Lynn (Lincé) Hudson, Jane Rhodes, Marilú and Lupé Valdez, Tomás Tamayo, and my girl-pals, Julian, L-Vee, Alicia M., Julietta and others, for gossip, dancing, distraction, and pleasure. Finally, I would like to thank Liz Crocker for her always generous friendship, her acerbic wit, her excellent editorial insights, and for dedicating her very smart self to the realization of this book.

Liz Crocker would like to thank: my family—Malcolm, Ruth, and Anne Crocker—for their support, especially my mother for her advice and affection; Marina Harris for pleasant interruptions; and friends: Aaron Schuham, Rhett Landrum, Alex Robertson Textor, Kimo Takayesu, and Jess Yuriwitz.

Acknowledgments

I especially thank Valerie Holladay for ten years of laughter, love, and late night phone calls. Finally, I thank Laura Harris for her enduring friendship, for her energy and vision, and for the gift of our partnership on this project.

An
INTRODUCTION
to Sustaining Femme Gender

Laura Harris and Liz Crocker

As we move through the nineties, conversations about butch-femme as lived experiences, as historical categories, and as a model of gender and sexuality have been increasing in number and fervor.[1] Our project arises from three concerns within these conversations. First, few histories have been written from perspectives that recognize and respect femmes. As a result, femme voices that could teach us much about the intersections of feminist, lesbian, and queer identities are often overlooked. Second, a mainstream feminism has not analyzed femme as a model of critical reshaped femininity and assertive sexuality. Such a model would be useful not only for lesbians but for many women. Third, queer theories have more often discussed femme identity in its relation to butch identity rather than focusing upon femme itself. At the same time, these queer theories about butch-femme portray femme as an aesthetic category rather than dealing with the ways that femme bodies are already marked by different intersections of identity. To answer the ways that femme has been elided, idealized, or not fully historicized, we in this introduction and the authors in this anthology, construct a theory of femme as a *sustained gender identity*. Such a theory allows a productive reconsideration of lesbian and butch-femme history, of feminism, and of queer thought.

In the eighties and nineties, there has been a surge of interest in writing the history of butch-femme communities from the perspective of those commu-

nities. In many lesbian histories, butch-femme life has been treated unsympa-
thetically: at one extreme ignored, at the other extreme denounced as pre-
feminist repressive practice.[2] Moreover, often these attacks were motivated
not only by a feminist distaste for butch-femme sexuality but also by race and
class biases.[3] As butches and femmes begin to more openly participate in—
and grapple with—the construction of lesbian history, they create revisionist
histories. Such histories of butch-femme are written as historical narratives
based upon oral sources, collections of personal narratives, and fictional representations set in historical contexts. In the groundbreaking *Boots of Leather,*
Slippers of Gold, Madeline Davis and Elizabeth Kennedy use oral sources and
conventional written sources to construct a detailed history of a butch-
femme community in Buffalo, New York in the forties and fifties. A more
archival project, Joan Nestle's canonical *The Persistent Desire: A Femme-Butch*
Reader, collects many different kinds of writing—fiction, personal narratives,
journal excepts, and critical perspectives—that contribute to a historical
record of butch-femme life. Finally, authors such as Leslie Feinberg, Chea
Villanueva, and Joan Nestle in *A Restricted Country* write fictionalized personal narratives which—in the dearth of historical narratives about butch-
femme—many read as history. Thus, rather than a single traditional history,
many different kinds of histories of butch-femme coexist.

Just as lesbians have struggled to write themselves into dominant cultural
histories, butches and femmes have fought to make their voices heard in lesbian histories.[4] It is ironic that the very visibility as lesbians that makes
butches targets of homophobia in public space also makes them more visible
as "real" lesbians than femmes in the context of a lesbian community. While
both butch and femme positions have been vexed within lesbian and feminist
communities, the visibility of butches has often empowered them to speak
for butch-femme. Thus femmes have been seen neither as "real" feminists
within feminist communities nor as "real" lesbians within lesbian communities. As doubly marginalized, femmes have been less able to articulate their
vision of lesbian history. One way of understanding this anthology is as a collection of femmes' stories—their histories—of living within butch-femme,
lesbian, and feminist communities. The focus on femme voices provides new
insight into previously written butch-femme histories, showing already existing connections between elided histories and liberation movements. Queer,
feminist, and lesbian movements could benefit from listening to these femme
voices as femmes occupy a vital space intersecting all three.

The history of femmes within feminism has been a tumultuous one. In
general, as women, femmes benefited from feminism's strides towards
achieving economic and legal equality for women in our society. However,

femmes—like other groups of women—were not always welcomed into a mainstream feminist movement that had as its primary constituency middle-class white women.[5] For femmes in particular, feminism's failure was its pejorative understanding of femme as equivalent to patriarchally imposed femininity, rather than alternatively a positive understanding of femme as a critical approach to femininity. In its (mis)recognition of femme, feminism denied femme its radical and critical nature. In doing so, feminism elided differences of class and race in relation to femininity, therefore not recognizing the range of femininities assumed for divergent purposes across different communities. While feminism's analysis of femininity as oppressive was useful for some women, certainly an understanding of the way that femme femininity is subversive and empowering seems crucial for many women. In reading femininity through femme, our project takes as its subject a femininity that is transgressive, disruptive, and chosen. For example, some women, who might otherwise reject dominant cultural standards of feminine beauty, graft a chosen and empowering femininity onto their bodies as femmes. Many femmes would not appear properly or conventionally feminine. Thus, femme identification provides for wide variations of femininities across differences of class, race, age, body image, and communities.

Often femme femininity, rather than being a way that one looks, is a set of behaviors used as codes of desire. Femmes have been marked as sexual objects especially when choosing to be part of a clearly sexual dyad of butch-femme. Due to this, femmes have a particularly troubled position in relation to the sexual politics around desire and practice that have plagued feminism.[6] In an attempt to liberate women from oppressive sexual regimes, feminism advocated an egalitarian model of women's relationships. Lesbian relationships in particular were seen as political unions rather than as based primarily on sexual desire.[7] For their clearly sexual codes of behavior that marked lesbianism as primarily sexual, butches and femmes bore the brunt of feminist disapproval.[8] The fact that the gendered power relations of butch-femme were premised upon reshaped masculinity and femininity further distanced them from a feminist movement that was intent on prescribing non-role-playing non-gendered sexual practice. Since gendered power relations are inherent to butch-femme sexuality, mainstream feminism failed and still fails to recognize butches and femmes as political precursors to feminist liberation.[9]

We believe that femme identities occupy a vital position in this debate over desire and politics. Femme sexual politics provide a liberatory model useful both for lesbians and for women in general. Femmes, through a reshaped femininity, exhibit an assertive sexuality that does not conflate desire with political practice. This very assertiveness can be politically empowering for femmes who like to play with the idea of power but are not disempowered by this play. For example, femmes with a bottom identification can renegotiate the dynamics of passivity/activity so that their feminine position is one of receiving pleasure rather than of being receptive solely for someone else's pleasure. What seems to be passivity is actually activity: she allows the butch to control her pleasure, but this control and the pleasure are exactly what the femme has demanded.[10] For the bottom femme as for other varieties of femme sexuality—top, s/m, bisexual, or others—her own female sexual agency is paramount. The femme who plays with power provides a model that *negotiates* rather than *ignores* power differentials in relationships. For feminists, lesbians, and women in general, this model of femme sexuality demonstrates that sexual play is not equivalent with a literal political position. In many ways, femmes' chosen pleasures rather than politically prescribed pleasures are radically feminist.

The radical sexual stance of femmes within feminism leads us to consider how femme identity intersects feminist and queer movements. However, femmes do not simply occupy a space between the two, half-feminist, half-queer; neither are feminist and queer movements discrete areas of thought.[11] Rather, we argue that the agitation of femmes within feminism was central to the formation of a sex-radical position out of which the queer movement grew.[12] One place to locate the historical connection between this sex-radical position and femme lesbians is the Barnard College Conference of 1982. Anti-porn feminists organized to protest the conference based on, as Carol Vance writes, "the anti-pornography movement's fetishized Big Three—pornography, sado-masochism, and butch-femme roles."[13] At the same time that anti-porn feminists ostracized femmes for being sex radicals, femmes themselves were proudly claiming a queer sex-radical identity. As Madeline Davis writes of femmes, "we are the queerest of the queer."[14] Davis links femme and queer in a primary way that is not often found. In queer theory, effeminacy, male masculinity, and female masculinity have been frequently analyzed; little has been written about women's use of femininity as queer, subversive, or radical.[15]

If queer has often been used as an umbrella term that can cover many types of difference, it often posits as its ideal a fluid and unmarked queer subject. In contrast, certain writers have articulated queer in a way that grapples with the intersections of sexuality with other differences of class, race, ethnicity, and gender. This produces queer theory that is premised upon the understanding that queer bodies are already marked by difference.[16] These different conceptions of queer produce variant understandings of butch-femme. Queer theory that emphasizes the fluid subject often depicts butch-femme as flexible, mutable, abstract, transitory, or purely aesthetic categories.[17] However, we feel that taking up butch-femme in the context of bodies marked by difference, by looking at femme as one of many marked differences, offers a more productive discussion. The authors in this anthology write about femme as queer by looking at how various regimes mark femme bodies not only in terms of sexuality and gender but also in terms of specific issues such as body image, class experience, national borders, bisexuality, incest survival, aging, bar culture, race or ethnic communities, heterosexuality, transgender and transsexual desire, activism, and feminism. Some of these identity categories are not always visibly marked on bodies; for some of the authors, femme can be both a way to mark your own body, as well as a way to strategically pass across, translate between, connect, and complicate various boundaries of identity. A femme understanding of queer, then, implodes the meaning of queer.

In theorizing femme identity, we in this introduction are setting forth a model of femme as a *sustained gender identity*, one that is carried out in this collection. An analysis of twentieth-century U.S. butch-femme culture shows us that not only did many women identify as femme through extended periods of their lives, but that femme identity has existed across generations. Moreover, while gender should not be understood as a biological imperative, what this history of femme shows is that femme gender identity is not simply role-playing in which certain sets of clothes or behaviors are on a daily basis easily assumed or discarded. Femme queerness is a sustained gender identity, a chosen rather than assigned femininity. As one facet of complicated identities that mark difference on bodies, femme not only names a gender identity, but is itself shaped by other aspects of identity. Rather than being defined by the outer trappings of femininity, femme gender is linked to a particular set of desiring relationships which occurs in butch-femme as well as other sites. By understanding femme as a sustained gender identity, we avoid the entrapment of femme in either too *stable*—one that sees femininity as biologically assigned—or too *flexible*—one that sees femme as one of many costumes—an identity category.

Understanding femme as a sustained gender identity allows us to return to some of the issues we have raised about feminism, queer theory, and femme histories. Whereas this anthology only begins to articulate a few of the complexities of femme, we provide some ways in which understanding femme as a sustained gender identity is productive. The difficulties queer and feminist thought have encountered with representing difference can be addressed by a model that theorizes femme in terms of the complexities of marked bodies.

Femme as a sustained gender identity allows us to re-envision feminist and queer models in ways that are productive across communities. This understanding undermines the myth of the apparitional femme lesbian who has disappeared into heterosexuality or lesbian-feminism. Femme as sustained gender identity is intersected by various historical contexts rather than subsumed by them. Even more than simply existing over time, femmes have been *causal* to shifts within feminism, the creation of queer theory, and the shaping of butch-femme and lesbian history. At this time, it is imperative to listen to femme voices as they speak to the intersections between—and push the envelope of—queer, feminist, and lesbian thought.

Histories: Creating an Archive

> Throughout the 1940s and 1950s fems were central to the building of African American and European American working-class lesbian communities. . . . Esther Newton's 1984 comment that the history of fems is yet to be written still holds true today.
>
> —Elizabeth Lapovsky Kennedy

Responding to Kennedy, we address the paradox of femme invisibility by creating an historical archive of femme experience in this section. We open with selections of femme voices from Kennedy and Madeline Davis's research on a 1940s and 1950s Buffalo butch-femme community. In "The Hidden Voice: Fems in the 1940s and 1950s," Kennedy argues that working-class butch and femme lesbians were essential precursors to the gay liberation movement. Her selections "highlight fem voices and bring to greater prominence fem roles in working-class lesbian history" (Kennedy 17). In our "Fish Tales: Revisiting 'A Study of a Public Lesbian Community,'" we re-read Ethel Sawyer's sociological study of an African-American fish-stud community in St. Louis, Missouri, in the 1960s. In doing so, we underscore her documentation of fish/femme sexual independence and community roles. In "Femme Icon: An Interview with Madeline Davis," Davis reflects on her femme transformations: "I have never thought of myself as easily transformable or mutable. And yet, in writing the history of who I am, I have transformed, there is no doubt about it. Yet, I have stayed categorically the same. I've stayed a femme." In the essay that follows, "'Articulate Silences': Femme Subjectivity and Class Relations in *The Well of Loneliness*," Leslie Henson addresses femme identity as it is paired with class suffering in this canonical lesbian novel, often read as a seminal butch text.

Like Henson's class analysis of femmes in fiction, novelist Mabel Maney discusses her classed representations of femmes in "Mysteries, Mothers, and

Cops: An Interview with Mabel Maney." A femme writer, Maney articulates how her novels as historically based parodies deal with femininity and butch-femme romance. In "Dresses for My Round Brown Body," Lisa Ortiz writes one of the quintessential forms of feminist narrative: tracing a history of one-self, of one's body, of one's experience. Ortiz names herself as Latina/Puerto Riqueña girl, as married woman, as feminist, as lesbian, as femme; she writes of passing and of claiming spaces between various communities. Finally, in our "Bad Girls: Sex, Class, and Feminist Agency," we theorize the "bad girl" role models that appear in femme personal narratives as well as fictional representations of femmes. We analyze the historical overlapping of the categories of working-class straight women, prostitutes, and femme lesbians, potentially a powerful feminist alliance. From the oral histories of femmes in the 1940s and 1950s (Kennedy) and the 1960s (Harris and Crocker) to the contemporary oral and written histories (Davis, Maney, Ortiz) to the essays analyzing current and historical representations of femme (Henson, Harris and Crocker), this section contributes to an archival collection of femme histories.

Generations: A Feminist Genealogy

> BC: What we have learned over the course of the last thirty years is that there are many genders of women. . . .
>
> JN: Yes, now I understand, but when I first wrote about butch-fem I was trying too hard to appease, so I did not address all the complexities of the experience. That is why I am so glad for friendships such as ours, for new decades of analysis.
>
> —Joan Nestle and Barbara Cruikshank

Spanning three generations of femmes, the authors in this section consider the slippage between being a woman, a femme, and a feminist. In "I'll Be the Girl: Generations of Fem," Cruikshank and Nestle trace the tensions between "the woman self and the fem self," and discuss how their own feminism facilitates the travel between these two states. Discussing Cruikshank's participation in welfare activism and Nestle's iconoclastic status as a visible femme feminist, they detail a cross-generational femme genealogy. Like Nestle and Cruikshank, Katherine Millersdaughter also takes up the difficulties of conjoining feminist and femme in "A Coincidence of Lipstick and Self-Revelation." Millersdaughter weaves together her experiences with incest survival, Nestle's writing, generations of feminist politics, lesbian identity, and femme desire. Marcy Sheiner uses her "Jewish-New York schtick" in "A Woman's Prerogative" to take a satirical look at sexual identity crises, tracing her own—and her generation's—changes over time. Sheiner discusses

the disjunction between identifying as feminist, lesbian, and femme, specifically discussing her relationship with a female-to-male transsexual partner.

Also discussing femme desire for variously sexed masculine bodies, Leah
Lilith Albrecht-Samarasinha, in "On Being a Bisexual Femme," invokes and
interrogates different generations of femme articulation to assert her own
femme bisexual identity. Searching to stake her femme independence,
Albrecht-Samarasinha explores the desires of her "South Asian-mutt's passing-slut 1996-New York-body." In "Fishes in a Pond: An Interview with
Jewelle Gomez," Gomez speaks to her own experience as an African-
American femme. In this cross-generational conversation, Gomez debunks
myths of femininity, asserting her own notion of femme gender. From conversations that consider femme as it is intersected by class, race, age, body
image, and links between political and sexual practice (Nestle and Cruikshank; Gomez) to essays that build on previous generations of feminists and
femmes to create new femme positions (Millersdaughter, Sheiner, Albrecht-
Samarasinha), this section is a femme genealogy of generations of feminist
and lesbian identification.

Futures: "The Queerest of the Queer"[18]

> I look at young femmes and marvel. They have sprung into the world like
> Athena, fully armored and stunning in the proud uncompromising
> strength of their spirits. They are the warriors I worked so hard to become.
> —Madeline Davis

Strengthened by their historical past, yet with their eyes on the future, the
authors in this section draw upon queer and feminist thought to figure
femmes as "warriors." We open with Davis's collection of vignettes, "Forever Femme," in which she traces her femme travels through lesbian feminism, butch-femme culture, and an s/m community. Writing the history of
her evolving femme identity, she closes by looking to her future and the
future of femmes. In "Passing *Loquería,*" Gaby Sandoval writes about the
meanings, the power, and the possibilities of border identities: *güera*, femme,
Chicana. In Sandoval's vision of the future, the border figures as a place to be
passed across by manipulation of identities. In "How Does She Look?"
Rebecca Rugg brings together her personal narrative as a queer nineties
"right-on white girl" femme with a critical analysis of actress Lois Weaver's
femme performance. Thinking in terms of race and class, Rugg criticizes the
"vile assimilationist politics" of various types of lesbians—pomo dykes, lipstick lesbians—who perceive femme as neither lesbian nor queer enough.

Also discussing the differences within lesbian communities, Minnie Bruce Pratt speaks of femme identification as her way of bridging lesbian feminism and the present and future activism of gender communities in "Pronouns, Politics, and Femme Practice: An Interview with Minnie Bruce Pratt." From her "upbringing in the deep South" to her current status as a femme "warrior," Pratt discusses femme as a queer site of resistance from which to fight a variety of battles against racism, homophobia, and sexism. Alex Robertson Textor's "Marilyn, Mayhem, and the Mantrap: Some Particularities of Male Femme" uses a lesbian model of femme to read eighties drag pop-star Marilyn's body and performance as male femme. Textor's essay delineates femme as a potential site for future queer male identification. Like Textor, Amber Hollibaugh theorizes femme across a variety of bodies by linking the genders of high femmes, drag queens, and transsexuals in "Gender Warriors: An Interview with Amber Hollibaugh." Speaking as a "gender warrior," Hollibaugh describes her work as an AIDS activist, as a sex radical, and as a transgendered femme. From writers who trace their femme histories with lesbian feminism and their nineties connection with queer (Davis, Pratt) to those who engage with the politics of visibility as nineties femmes (Sandoval, Rugg) to those who theorize femme gender across divergently sexed bodies (Textor, Hollibaugh), this section reads queer from femme to imagine femmes as gender warriors.

Conclusion

> Our history is made up of many histories—all the layers of identity that form our personhood, that connect us to legacies of love and pride and pain. . . . History will betray us if we betray it. If we do not learn the language of each other's historical truths, if we do not grow aware of the places where life has been stolen, our histories and our lives will be selfish things.
>
> —Joan Nestle[19]

In the three sections of this anthology, we map the connections between femme histories, experiences, and theories. Our methodology considers femme in relation to three interconnected topics—lesbian "Histories," feminist "Generations," and queer "Futures"—to consider femmes participation in, exclusion from, and transformation of each. In our title, *Femme: Feminists, Lesbians, and Bad Girls,* we speak to a misunderstanding of femmes as "good girls" whose femininities and sexual choices are not recognized as lesbian, feminist, or queer. Rather, we—and the authors in this anthology—understand femme as a contestatory lesbian identity, a radical feminist position, and a subversive queer model. Moreover, our title visually marks the historical transition from the "fem" of the forties and fifties to the "femme" of the eighties and nineties. Femmes—as bad girls—alternately titillate, threaten, seduce, rebel, please, speak out, calculate, and misbehave—but they never sit still and stay quiet.

Notes

1. Joan Nestle, ed., *The Persistent Desire: A Femme-Butch Reader* (Boston: Alyson Publications, 1992). Elizabeth Lapovsky Kennedy and Madeline D. Davis, *Boots of Leather, Slippers of Gold: The History of a Lesbian Community* (New York: Penguin Books, 1994). Lily Burana, Roxxie, Linnea Due, eds., *Dagger: On Butch Women* (San Francisco: Cleis Press, Inc., 1994). Lesléa Newman, ed., *The Femme Mystique* (Boston: Alyson Publications, 1995).

2. Sheila Jeffreys, *The Lesbian Heresy: A Feminist Perspective on the Lesbian Sexual Revolution* (North Melbourne, Vic. Australia: Spinifex, 1993). Lillian Faderman, *Odd Girls and Twilight Lovers: A History of Lesbian Life in Twentieth-Century America* (New York: Penguin, 1991). Charlotte Bunch and Nancy Myron, *Lesbianism and the Women's Movement* (Baltimore: Diana Press, 1975).

3. A brief list of many possible choices: Joan Nestle, *A Restricted Country* (Ithaca: Firebrand, 1987). Gloria Anzaldúa and Cherríe Moraga, eds., *This Bridge Called My Back: Writings by Radical Women of Color* (Watertown: Persephone, 1981). Tracy Morgan, "Butch-Femme and the Politics of Identity," in *Sisters, Sexperts, Queers: Beyond the Lesbian Nation,* ed. Arlene Stein (New York: Plume, 1993) 35–46. Jackie Goldsby, "Queen for 307 Days: Looking B(l)ack at Vanessa Williams and the Sex Wars," in *Sisters, Sexperts, Queers: Beyond the Lesbian Nation,* ed. Arlene Stein (New York: Plume, 1993) 110–128. Dorothy Allison, "A Question of Class," in *Sisters, Sexperts, Queers: Beyond the Lesbian Nation,* ed. Arlene Stein (New York: Plume, 1993) 133–155. Carol S. Vance, ed., *Pleasure and Danger: Exploring Female Sexuality* (1984) (London: Pandora, 1989).

4. For an example of a gay and lesbian history that does not include butch-femme communities, see Eric Marcus, *Making History: The Struggle for Gay and Lesbian Equal Rights 1945–1990* (New York: HarperPerennial, 1993).

5. For a general discussion of the problems around feminist sexual politics, see Ellen Willis, "Feminism, Moralism, and Pornography," in *Powers of Desire: The Politics of Sexuality,* eds. Ann Snitow, Christine Stansell, and Sharon Thompson (New York: Monthly Review Press, 1983) 460–467.

6. For a femme reaction to this feminist dismissal of butch-femme, Madeline Davis writes, "The Movement is a bit more 'liberal' with us lately, but they still don't seem to get it. . . . And it really makes me angry. Frankly, I don't understand not being role identified. Sure, I believe them when they say they are not, but it all seems so 'the same' to me and sort of boring. They're too busy holding hands and swaying and singing about 'filling up and spilling over' (or is that throwing up and falling over?). Well, there you have it. My reaction to being treated like a dinosaur by my 'sisters.' I'm fifty. I can afford to be mad!" Madeline Davis, "Epilogue, Nine Years Later," in *The Persistent Desire: A Femme-Butch Reader* (Boston: Alyson, 1992) 270–271.

7. Alice Echols, "The Taming of the Id: Feminist Sexual Politics, 1968–83," in *Sisters, Sexperts, Queers: Beyond the Lesbian Nation,* ed. Arlene Stein (New York: Plume, 1993) 50–72.

8. Carol S. Vance, "More Danger, More Pleasure: A Decade After the Barnard Sexuality Conference," in *Pleasure and Danger: Exploring Female Sexuality,* ed. Carol S. Vance, (1984) (London: Pandora, 1989) xvi–xxxix.

9. Elizabeth Lapovsky Kennedy and Madeline D. Davis, "'To Cover Up the Truth Would Be a Waste of Time': Introduction," in *Boots of Leather, Slippers of Gold: The History of a Lesbian Community* (New York: Penguin, 1994) 1–26.

10. Clearly, we are discussing femme sexuality within a butch-femme dynamic because we are framing our discussion of femme historically. Many femmes identify sexually along top/bottom roles, within s/m communities, in terms of bisexuality, and/or in terms of transgendered and transsexual gender communities.

11. For a discussion of this point, see Judith Butler, "Against Proper Objects," Introduction, *differences: A Journal of Feminist Cultural Studies* "More Gender Trouble: Feminism Meets Queer Theory" 6:2+3 (Summer–Fall 1994): 1–26.

12. For a discussion of this sex-radical position, see Gayle Rubin, "Thinking Sex: Notes for a Radical Theory of the Politics of Sexuality," in *The Lesbian and Gay Studies Reader,* eds. Henry Abelove, Michéle Aina Barale, David M. Halperin (New York: Routledge, 1993) 3–44. For a femme discussion of queer, see Joan Nestle, "The Femme Question," in *Persistent Desire: A Femme-Butch Reader,* ed. Joan Nestle (Boston: Alyson, 1992) 138–146.

13. Vance, *Pleasure and Danger* xxiii.

14. Davis, *Persistent Desire* 270.

15. On effeminacy, see Eve K. Sedgwick, "How to Bring Your Kids Up Gay," in *Fear of a Queer Planet,* ed. Michael Warner (Minneapolis: University of Minnesota Press, 1993) 69–81. On the gay male "clone," see D.A. Miller, *Bringing Out Roland Barthes* (Berkeley: University of California Press, 1992). On gay and straight male masculinity, see Mark Simpson, *Male Impersonators: Men Performing Masculinity* (New York: Routledge, 1994). For an example of the omission of an analysis of femininity from a queer lesbian perspective, see Nicola Godwin, Belinda Hollows, and Sheridan Nye, eds., *Assaults on Convention: Essays on Lesbian Transgressors* (London: Cassell, 1996). Their introduction defines a queer subversive lesbian position as contained within three possibilities, namely, "lesbian misbehavior of various kinds: sleeping with men . . . murdering them . . . and wanting to be a man" (1). For an example of the omission of femmes from a consideration of "resistant female identity" that only includes discussion of "self-defined mannish lesbians," see Eve K. Sedgwick, "Introduction: Axiomatic," in *Epistemology of the Closet* (Berkeley: University of California Press, 1990) 37.

16. A brief list of many possible choices: Phillip Brian Harper, "Eloquence and Epitaph: Black Nationalism and the Homophobic Impulse in Responses to the Death of Max Robinson," in *Fear of a Queer Planet* 239–263. Lauren Berlant and Elizabeth Freeman, "Queer Nationality," in *Fear of a Queer Planet* 193–229. Dorothy Allison, *Skin: Talking About Sex, Class, and Literature* (Ithaca: Firebrand, 1994). Gloria Anzaldúa, *Borderlands/La Frontera: The New Mestiza* (San Francisco: Spinsters/Aunt Lute, 1987). Cherríe Moraga, *Loving in the War Years: Lo Que Nunca Paso Por Sus Labios* (Boston: South End Press, 1983). June Jordan, *Technical Difficulties: African-American Notes on the State of the Union* (New York: Pantheon, 1992). June Jordan, *Haruko: Love Poems* (New York: High Risk Books, 1994). Esther Newton, *Cherry Grove, Fire Island: Sixty Years in America's First Gay and Lesbian Town* (Boston: Beacon Press, 1993). Leslie Feinberg, *Transgender Warriors: Making History From Joan of Arc to RuPaul* (Boston: Beacon Press, 1996).

17. For a queer depiction of butch as simply aesthetic, see Vicki Jedlicka, "Butched Up Barbie," in *Dagger: On Butch Women* (San Francisco: Cleis Press, 1994) 184. For an aesthetic depiction of femme, see Lesléa Newman, ed., *The Femme Mystique* (Boston: Alyson, 1995). Sue Ellen Case, "Towards a Butch-Femme Aesthetic," in *Lesbian and Gay Studies Reader* 294–306. Judith Butler, *Gender Trouble: Feminism and the Subversion of Identity* (New York: Routledge, 1990) 122–124. For a discussion of femme as a highly abstract category, see Lisa Duggan and Kathleen McHugh, "A Fem(me)inist Manifesto," in *Women and Performance: A Journal of Feminist Theory* 8:2 (1996): 153–160. For a disembodied (mis)understanding of butch-femme, see Elizabeth Grosz, "The Labors of Love. Analyzing Perverse Desire: An Interrogation of Teresa de Lauretis's *The Practice of Love*," *differences* 6:2+3 (Summer–Fall 1994): 274–295.

18. Davis, *Persistent Desire* 270.

19. Nestle, *Restricted Country* 186.

Part 1

HISTORIES
Creating an Archive

THE HIDDEN VOICE
Fems in the 1940s and 1950s

Selections from
Boots of Leather, Slippers of Gold:
The History of a Lesbian Community

Elizabeth Lapovsky Kennedy and Madeline Davis

Compiled and introduced
by Elizabeth Lapovsky Kennedy

T hroughout the 1940s and 1950s fems were central to the building of African American and European American working-class lesbian communities.[1] Since most lesbian relationships were based on the mutual attraction of butch and fem, social life was unimaginable without both. Fems sought out and patronized bars and house parties despite the risk of exposure. They avoided their families' attempts to control their lives, and resisted harassment by strangers on the streets. In the context of severe oppression, fems desired butches. They cultivated an enticing feminine appearance and embraced an erotic dyad that was predicated on fem sexual pleasure. They also helped build relationships that endured. Despite this central position in lesbian culture and social life, the contribution of fems to les-

bian history has generally been underplayed. With the exception of Joan
Nestle's work, in most existing documents and comments on lesbian history,
fems are not only less visible than butches, but also issues and problems of lesbian history are defined from a butch perspective. Esther Newton's 1984
comment that the history of fems is yet to be written still holds true today.[2]

Even though Madeline Davis and myself consciously worked to write a
community history which gave equal prominence to both fems and butches
in *Boots of Leather, Slippers of Gold: The History of a Lesbian Community*, fem
perspectives took a secondary position for a variety of complex reasons.[3]
First, our research was slanted towards exploring the emergence of lesbian
communities into public space. Such a view necessarily privileges butches,
for the butch was like the "magical sign" of lesbianism during the early and
mid-twentieth century. It was she, alone or with her fem, that announced
lesbianism to the public. Second, the structures of masculine and feminine
which assigned the butch to the public world and created butch solidarity
relegated fems to a more private world, and isolated most fems from
one another, making it difficult for them to develop their own voices and
to have confidence in their own stories. Third, fems had a somewhat
ambivalent position in lesbian communities of the past, in the sense that
many butches and fems questioned whether fems were "real lesbians." This
lack of a fixed identity did not belittle fem status in the mid-twentieth century, but it did undermine the legitimacy with which fems could speak about
"lesbian" experience. It also limited the ability of post-Stonewall lesbians,
who were looking for "lesbian" history, to hear what they had to say.
Fourth, the intellectual categories most lesbians brought to lesbian history
during the 1970s and 1980s were not helpful for crystallizing fem perspectives. By polarizing sexual experience into homosexual or heterosexual, gay
liberation was unable to offer creative frameworks for analyzing that many
fems had spent some part of their life as heterosexuals, and in some sense,
had chosen to be with women. The homophobic forces in our society were
even more limiting, because they prohibited the conception of human sexuality as fluid.

A fifth reason why fem perspectives were not as prominent in *Boots of
Leather* as we would have liked is that we had many more butch narrators
than fem narrators. We interviewed eight fems and twenty-four butches. The
structure of the butch–fem world, at least in the European American community of the 1940s and 1950s, made it more likely that fems would not be
interested in being interviewed. They were concerned more with taking care
of their butches and supporting them as they endured and challenged hostility than in being public about their role in community building. In addition,

from the beginning of the project in 1978, influenced by gay liberation's categorical distinction between gay and straight, we decided to interview only women who had remained lesbians throughout their lifetimes. However, our research showed that many fems who were lesbians in the '40s and '50s were now married and/or living with men. After several years of research we changed our research plan and decided to interview women who had been out in the 1940s and 1950s regardless of their current sexuality. Our late decision meant that we did not have the time that is required to track down fem addresses and persistently to coax them to be interviewed. One we did find turned us down.

Despite the limitations of the study in recruiting equal numbers of butches and fems and defining the issues from both perspectives, we nevertheless interviewed eight very powerful fems, seven European American and one African American, whose voices are essential to the story and make *Boots of Leather* a step on the way toward writing a community history of both fems and butches. This article is a set of edited selections from *Boots of Leather* which highlight fem voices and bring to greater prominence fem roles in working-class lesbian history.[4] In our work Davis and I not only attempted to document fem place and power in history but also to pose the questions that might move us toward a conception of lesbian history that is fully inclusive of fem perspectives and view points.

Fem Roles in Finding and Building Communities

In *Boots of Leather, Slippers of Gold*, Davis and I argue that Buffalo working-class lesbians—African American, European American, and Native American —are essential precursors to the gay liberation movement. Braving social hostility during the 1940s and 1950s, working-class lesbians took the risk of associating publicly in bars and in house parties. Together they built a common culture and sense of community that led to a developing consciousness of kind and a pride in being lesbian, all of which were essential for the gay liberation movement to grow and spread as rapidly as it did in the late 1960s and early 1970s. In Buffalo during the 1940s the lesbian community was almost entirely segregated. European American working-class lesbians along with a few Native American lesbians frequented bars in the downtown section of the city, while African American lesbians primarily went to house parties, only infrequently going to bars. In the mid-1950s, African American lesbians, fems and butches, desegregated the bars, creating in some contexts a larger community which encompassed African American and European American lesbians, while in other contexts the two distinct communities continued to exist.

Although butches and fems both agree that butches were more public in this role of community building than fems, in the sense that they were more visible, and that they fought for and protected their fems, fems were essential to the process. The simple act of taking oneself to a bar or a house party took initiative and courage, particularly in the anti-lesbian climate of the 1940s and 1950s. Once a fem found a butch partner her appearance with her butch in public—on the streets near the bar or near her home—stigmatized her as "lesbian." Families were not immediately accepting of a daughter who left home to live with a butch woman. In the European American community, fems were in the background for community building, providing support and love to their butches who were severely stigmatized by society. In the African American community fems had a more public role, taking leadership in desegregating the bars and in organizing house parties.

Selections[5]

Joanna [a popular and worldly white fem], who went to Ralph Martin's [in the 1940s] completely unaware that it was a gay and lesbian bar, was... enthusiastic about her experience, and couldn't wait to return. She was brought by a female high school friend who had been once before, but didn't tell Joanna until they were inside.

> Like I said we were supposed to go out bowling, right, so we wound up at this bar. Now previous to this I had never been to a gay bar. I didn't even know they existed. It was a Friday night and that was the big night you know, bigger than Saturday. And we walked in and I thought, my God, this is really something. I couldn't believe it.... [I] don't think there were any straight people in the bar that night.... There were an awful lot of lesbians.
>
> So we ... sat down. We had a drink. Oh maybe about twenty to twenty-five minutes we were sitting there. We were talking and watching, you're really in awe of all this.... And she and a friend wandered over, same thing, another lesbian. Asked if they could buy us a drink and I said, "Sure," didn't have that much money anyway. Actually if anybody asked us we would have had the drink because at that time money was scarce. I guess some people were making good money at the defense plants. We were too young to work in the defense plants. They sat down and started asking what our names were, you know, the first time we were there, blah blah blah. Well I could hardly wait to get back to that bar! We left in about an hour.... But I think it was only like a couple of days later we went back. Now it was a dull night so there were only a few people in the bar, a couple of gay boys and a couple of girls.... But, on Friday, we went back again. And there were the same two people, and they were so happy to see us, it was really funny.

Leslie, one of the women she met on this first night, soon became her partner for the next eight years. . . .

[After beginning her relationship with Leslie], Joanna was beaten by her brothers and then kept by her family as a sort of prisoner at home, never allowed to go out by herself. She, along with her butch, devised an elaborate and successful plan of escape and went to New York for a few years. Her family did not pursue her, perhaps because she was already eighteen years old. She did not take any chances, however, and changed her name while she was away. . . . Going to New York didn't immediately resolve Joanna's conflicts with her family. But over the years they came to accept her.

> I called my mother many times from New York and she'd always cry, and wanted to know, "Why did you do this to me, blah blah blah." You know, I felt horrible. But when I came back I didn't go to see her right away. I think maybe a couple of months passed and I finally said, "Well I've got to go see her." And I went to see her. She was all right. She was not as bad as I thought it would be, and I went there for dinner and sat around and talked with her and of course I had to leave. That didn't set too well. She wasn't really too happy about that, but she kind of came around, accepted [my friend]. . . . Yeah, she came to my house for dinner. She had to accept her. She got to know her, she liked her. My family still likes her. It's amazing. . . .

By the mid-1950s groups of Black lesbians began to patronize Bingo's and the street bars in the downtown section, and soon after, whites went to the bars which opened in the Black section of town, thereby ending the racial homogeneity of the lesbian bar community. After years of separate socializing in the context of a racist society, Black lesbians had difficulty achieving acceptance, but the reward of new places to socialize seemed worth the effort. Arlette [a stunningly beautiful and extremely competent Black fem], who took leadership in breaking the confines of segregated lesbian society, recalls when she and her friends first started hanging around Bingo's.

> Bingo's was the first gay place that really we found. . . . And somebody, I don't know who it was, came to say, "Listen, I found a gay spot," because the gay kids, really at the time, Black ones, had no bar to go to. Most of the time somebody would give a house party and we would go to that, but as far as a bar there was none that I knew of in Buffalo until I ran across Bingo's. So a whole bunch of us got together and went to the place. And it ended up we just kept going, we made friends with quite a few. And then there's still some that. . . . don't let one of the white girls like the Black girls and she was considered a nigger lover. . . .

[After desegregation] some Black and white tough bar lesbians interacted with one another frequently. Melanie, a white fem who has had several relationships with Black women, goes as far as suggesting that Black/white relations were better in the past than today. In the interview, when we ask her our standard question—what is the most important thing this book should tell about the past—she replies:

> Well, I would say that years ago there was much more communication between the Black gay people and the white gay people. Now they're more separated. . . . Before the Black kids used to come to the white gay bars all the time. . . . Black people used to have parties, after the bars would close. . . . And a lot of white people used to go to their houses and drink and that. Some of them had pay parties and some of them had free parties. Like you did find some of the Black people that were real friendly with the white, and they'd say "Well, come after the bar, come to my house and we'll have some drinks." Just socialize. It was more of that. Now everything's separate. . . . Years ago we used to dance with the Black kids and everything. We'd sit with them. . . .

In the late 1950s, and well into the 1960s, a weekend for many Black lesbians would consist of going to the bars and to house parties.

> Like we finally had a nice little place on Cherry Street, the Two Seventeen, and they would have a house party a few doors down, so everybody wouldn't come out till twelve or one o'clock. And we would go to this bar. . . . We would have a couple of drinks, and by that time the bars closed at three. . . . Then we'd go to the party, and that's where we would have our fun. We bought drinks and we bought food and we would dance till all hours of the morning. In fact, we really had a good time. And then we didn't have that confusion of anybody else coming in and bothering us. We had our own little set of friends. New people could come in, you could bring a guest, and they'd find out what was new. . . . And then somebody would have one this weekend, somebody would have one the next weekend, and somebody would have one the next weekend. It was constantly rotating. . . . (Arlette)

The parties lasted for several days. . . [and] food and drink were amply provided for a modest fee by the hostess. . . . Because of their size, house parties were quite visible, inviting harassment from hostile straights and from the police. Giving parties, therefore, required leadership skills for handling the community's relations with the outside world. Managing outsiders was as important as preparing food, drink, and music. In an interview with Arlette, who had given many parties, we comment that women must have done a lot of cooking and she immediately adds, "And answering the door," giving this task a place of equal prominence. The hostess had either to take care of the door herself or delegate the task to make sure no intruders came in.

> Usually there's somebody on the door that monitored the door, 'cause you would find people . . . trying to crash. They can't come in. . . . There are people and guys that find out, "Oh, we hear music, must be a party." Some people would stand out and try to wait for somebody to come in and make like they're with them. And then, if you know your crowd, "Who are you comin' to see? Sorry, it's a private party." They turn around and leave. . . . A new face that popped up, we'd ask them "Who told you to come here?" 'Cause sometimes people gave out the address. . . . (Arlette)

The tradition of house parties had a significant impact on leadership in the Black lesbian community. Like the tough bar community, with which it overlapped, it respected those butches who could take care of business in the difficult environment of the street. But unlike the white bar community, it recognized and respected fem leaders. One reason for this may be the structural significance of home life in the Black lesbian community. Home-based parties gave fems, whose role was associated with domestic life, an arena for contributing to the social well-being of the community. They were key organizers for the house parties, dealing with problems internal to the community as well as relations with the outside world. In addition, fems also opened their houses for visitors, nurturing those who needed a place to stay. Arlette, who was an important leader in the community, had the nickname, Mother Superior. When asked how she got this name, she explains, with a mixture of embarrassment and pride, that she always took care of people.[6]

> It was because of the fact that young kids liked to hang around me, and they were doing things, and I would try to tell them, "Look, if you work, go to school, [fine]. If you're not gonna do that you got to get out of here and do somethin' to support yourself." And I was always feeding kids, letting them stay someplace. But I stayed on their case to the point I would actually jump on them. And rather than call me a Mother Fucker they called me Mother Superior. . . . But the name just stuck. 'Cause I'm always trying to call myself lookin' out for somebody. I would tell them point-blank, "Look, I'll feed you but I'm not gonna take care of you. . . . You got a place where you don't have to worry about nobody bothering you in the middle of the night. You can sleep, you can get up and eat and you've got someplace to be out of the cold, so you better try to do somethin' to help yourself 'cause after that you're gonna have to leave here." And it got to the point where some mothers actually came to my house to jump on me. . . . It angered me for her to think I was a bad influence on her child. Then after they found out how the situation was . . . they'd call me, "Is my

daughter there, send her home." O.K., "your mother wants you, go home." But they found out that I wasn't making any kids do anything. I always felt like whatever you did it was a nice way of doing it and a bad way of doing it. If you're gonna do something, if you're gonna be a prostitute, be one with class. Don't be a bum in the street. So that's why I got the name Mother Superior.

Fem Sexuality

During the 1940s and 1950s, butch-fem roles functioned as both a personal code of behavior and as an organizing principle for working-class community life.[7] As the former they governed how a person presented herself in daily life, particularly in regard to image and sexuality. As the latter they structured lesbian relationships to the straight world, and to one another. The main way that lesbians announced their presence to one another and to the public was by the transgressive appearance of the butch, or of the butch-fem couple. In addition, butch-fem roles set the parameters of lesbian relationships; only butch and fem could be attracted to one another. Thus the concept of "role playing" is inadequate to describe the full complexity and power of butch and fem. Butch and fem were at the core of a complete and complex culture, one that both mimicked and transformed heterosexual culture. People followed butch-fem roles not simply because of their personal inclination but because it was a culture that offered significant benefits for building and maintaining lesbian community.

Although on the surface the butch-fem erotic system appears to imitate heterosexuality with the butch being the more aggressive partner and the fem the more passive partner, in fact butch-fem desire is much more complex. The butch as the doer is also the giver of pleasure. For most butches the main purpose in making love was to please their fems, a position usually associated with femininity. The fem was the more receptive partner; however, she knew exactly what she wanted, and was not shy in pursuing it, a position usually associated with masculinity. Although the butch was the leader in lovemaking most fems did not hesitate to express what they wanted. In many cases more experienced fems were instrumental in teaching younger butches about sexual performance.

This butch-fem erotic system which focused around female sexual pleasure developed at a time in heterosexual history when female sexuality was harnessed to male pleasure. The presence of a lesbian community gave women the space and support to pursue female sexual pleasure. In this context the fem's knowledge about and experience of her body's potential for sexual pleasure can be considered a precursor to the feminist exploration of female sexual autonomy in the 1970s.

Selections[8]

How was a community able to monitor the sexual activities of its members, and how might people come to know if a butch "rolled over"—the community lingo for a butch who allowed fems to make love to her? The answer was simple: fems talked! A butch's reputation was based on her performance with fems. What went on in bed with the lights out was not always completely private. Fems "talking" today confirm that many butches were indeed untouchable, though certainly not all. "Let's say a couple of the butches, they're what you call untouchable. They would not allow to be touched. At all, even if you wanted to. So they did all the work" (Annie). Fem voices also convey the satisfaction achieved in lesbian sex during this period.

Black and white fem narrators recognized and accepted the standard of the butch as the doer, the aggressor, in lovemaking with the fem the center of attention. All fem narrators felt comfortable with this erotic system and liked being pleased.

> I enjoy the feminine role better due to the fact it's not as much hard work; see, being a stud, that's a lot of work. I have a tendency to be kind of lazy. So I'd rather stay fem. Every once in a while I might want to act a little boyish and say "Lay down girl it's my turn tonight," but I couldn't stand a steady diet of that. No, that's kind of hard work. If [she's] anything like me, they gonna have a job. You just can't snap your fingers on me, boy. So I'm gonna stay like I am. . . . a lady. (Arlette)

The idea that pleasing a fem requires hard work on the part of a butch is widespread among fems. Curiously, no butches articulate it, which suggests that statements about work were the fems' way of affirming their control in sexual relationships as well as expressing their appreciation of butches.

Fems were divided over the rightness or importance of the ideal of untouchability. Like the stone butches who felt strongly about not being touched, some fems really disliked taking the more active role in lovemaking. . . . [Other] fems did feel moved to make love to their butches on occasion, although none wanted to do so regularly. Annie ventured into making love to her butch and met no resistance: "She wanted me to. . . . No, [she didn't ask] but she didn't stop me, O.K." Annie was surprised at her butch's needs but felt she could accommodate them because she cared for her a lot.

> Like the one girl I told you, she dressed very very butchie, she was an introvert, stayed very very much to herself, very nontalkative. She wouldn't mingle with the others, and tattoos on her arms, she really looked rugged. She looked rough. But when she got in bed she was just as feminine as any fem. . . . Well I happened to care for her, and naturally I wanted her

'cause I cared for her, so it really didn't bother me. It's not like something
was pushed on me that I didn't want. . . .

But all of these women who did make love to their butches were not critical of the stone butch. They appreciated the full attention focused on their
own satisfaction. Arlette confirms this:

> I've had some that I couldn't touch no parts of their bodies. It was all
> about me. Course I didn't mind! But every once in a while I felt like, well,
> "Hey, let me do something to you." I could never understand that. 'Cause
> I lived with a girl. I couldn't touch any part of her, no part. But boy did
> she make me feel good, so I said . . . "All right with me!" It kept me back
> though, 'cause I felt, "Hey, I want to do something to you tonight."
> "Nope!" Well O.K. Fine with me. I don't mind laying down.

It is striking that our fem narrators' discussion of sexuality is quite self-
concerned. It does not express the kind of intense sexual passion for their
butches—the passion of response—that is conveyed in the essays and stories
of fem writers and activists such as Joan Nestle and Amber Hollibaugh.[9] In
their life histories fem narrators frequently and straightforwardly affirm their
love for their butches. But we have no description of what excites them
about making love. There is no fem equivalent to the statements of butches
that describe how much they are turned on by their partners. We suspect that
the self-centered aspect of the fems' sexual life is correct but comprises only
one dimension of truth about the butch–fem sexual dyad.

Many factors combine to create this imbalance in fem stories. Fems' socializing together was not an institutionalized part of this culture. Fems might
have had individual girl friends, but there was no network of fem friendship
akin to the camaraderie of butches. Instead, there was a tradition of competi-
tiveness. Because of this, there was no safe and supportive place in which
fems could share reflections of their passion and learn from each other's joys
and losses. By extension, the interview sessions, conducted by women who
are self-identified fems or who have no role identification, might be suspect
and might easily have set up a defensive atmosphere surrounding delicate
issues of sexuality.

Due to the absence of a supportive environment, fems may have lacked
appropriate words. In reflecting on her relationships in the 1950s, Joan Nestle
points out:

> Fems may not have had a language with which to talk about sexual mat-
> ters. I don't remember fem women discussing sexual lust in the '50s. That
> was part of butch play. . . . Public sexual language [for fems] was one of

emotional need. . . . I also think that fem language was always coded language. . . . The loudest way of speaking was the offering of the woman's body to butch desire.[10]

Therefore, words of love, appreciation, closeness, and even flirtation could have been coded substitutes for expressions of passion. Fems may only have spoken about sexual passion for their butches, to their butches, in the privacy of their relationships.

From the writings of Nestle and Hollibaugh we learn about aspects of fem desire that might be applicable to Buffalo fems in the 1950s. A fem wants the feeling that the butch's most sought-after goal is to reach her femininity, the core of who she is. The fem also wishes to validate the butch's existence by being responsive to her butch's desire. A fem's self-definition, insofar as it includes the conscious giving over of sexual control to ultimate desirability, is a major component of her power. Hollibaugh writes:

> My fantasy life is deeply involved in a butch/femme exchange. I never come together with a woman, sexually, outside of those roles. It's saying to my partner, "Love me enough to let me go where I need to go and take me there. Don't make me think it through. Give me a way to be so in my body that I don't have to think; that you can fantasize for the both of us. You map it out. You are in control."
>
> It's hard to talk about things like giving up power without it sounding passive. I am willing to give myself over to a woman equal to her amount of wanting. I expose myself for her to see what's possible for her to love in me that's female. I want her to respond to it. I may not be doing something active with my body, but more eroticizing her need that I feel in her hands as she touches me.[11]

Fem satisfaction was at the center of the butch–fem erotic system. To give satisfaction was the butch's foremost goal, and the culture focused on her performance. There was social pressure for butches to attain the ideal of "untouchability" but no equivalent ideal of fem passivity. Fems upheld the standards of butch behavior in order to achieve their own satisfaction. This emphasis on their own fulfillment assured that fems developed sexual subjectivity, albeit differently from butches. It also balanced the power in butch–fem erotic relationships, making the pursuit of satisfaction legitimate for each partner.

Butch–Fem Relationships from the Point of View of Fems

Butch-fem relationships were gendered relationships without being fully integrated into a heterosexual system of male supremacy. As such they contained two contradictory forces: the gendered differences between butch and fem, and the similarity of women being together. Unquestionably butch and fem were different. Besides the differences in image and sexuality, the butch was responsible for taking care of the public world and protecting fems in a hostile world. Fems were responsible for the home, making it a comfortable refuge. At the same time butch and fem shared a tremendous amount in common, as women together. They both enjoyed romance and intimacy and both worked outside the home. These complex forces made the power balance difficult to define. Although the butch tended to be more controlling and more aggressive, her power was not backed up in the society as a whole. Fems tended to be less stigmatized by society as a whole and therefore to have access to better jobs than butches. Their more typically feminine appearance didn't conflict with the dress codes on most jobs. In addition to working in factories they could easily work as secretaries, clerks, waitresses, and prostitutes. In this complex context fems and butches created meaningful and satisfactory relationships based on mutual give and take. However, fem memories also have an undercurrent of resentment about butch control. Although fems recognized the limits of what was possible at that time period, given the oppression of lesbians, they also never stopped thinking of the possibilities of an even better life.

Selections[12]

Fems see the butch as stronger and more aggressive, but usually limit the areas about which this was true and complain about butches who were too controlling. Joanna had quite a bit to say about the suggestion that butches might be emotionally and/or physically stronger than fems and her views are common. "Well, that's a fallacy—I wouldn't say in every case, but I would say in the majority of cases, the ratio of stronger fem girls is much larger than those of the butchie girl, I think. [A butch girl identifies herself by] her clothing, her dress, her mannerism. . . . But certainly not the stronger." Several fems thought butches were stronger, more powerful, and liked it that way, but they are ambivalent about their control.

> I feel that, back then, role playing was very important. I still feel and always will that someone should be the more aggressive person in a relationship. I would say that I'm more of a type that is not a leader but a follower. . . . I'd like someone who would be a stronger person in the relationship, in terms of maybe managing the finances or stronger sexually also. . . . I prefer women who would be, not dressing real mannish, but just someone who would be a stronger person and sort of someone that I would be able to lean on and depend on. (Bell)

Nevertheless, she indicates later in her life story how much she valued her independence, and expresses her discontent with butches who asserted too much control.

> The only thing I didn't like about her was she was so damn possessive. I've always kind of been the type of person who likes to be very independent. I like leaning on someone for decisions, I like someone stronger in the sexual area of things, but I don't like being told what to do. I accept things better if someone will suggest to me, "It would be nice if you would do this or better if you do this," not say "You have to do this." Because it seems like from very early in my childhood I was being told . . . "You've got to do this" and shoving me here and pushing me there, and to this day I rebel against that very strongly, I can't stand it.

Butch-fem relationships encompassed these two contradictory impulses: the tendency toward butch control and the tendency toward cooperation. Most narrators look back with pleasure at their relationships and feel good about the closeness and time shared. There is an undercurrent of complaint, however, in the stories of fems about the bossiness of butches, especially their jealous control over fems' socializing outside the relationship and their selfishness. The tension was resolved differently in different historical periods, but also by different individuals within any one period. In some cases, the conflict led to personal growth and stability in the relationships, in others to extreme pain and, in some relationships of the late 1950s, to violence. The instability created by the contradictory power dynamics between butch and fem might be part of the reason for the avid interest of some of these butch-fem couples in the feminist movement of the 1970s. Its critique of gender offered insight into an ongoing, and often troublesome, issue in their lives.

The tendency toward butch control in committed relationships was unquestionably irksome to fems. In some part of their interviews, *all* the fems objected to butch bossiness or jealousy. Some found the limitations placed on them by the butches extremely unpleasant, and are filled to this day with anger. Joanna comments on what she considered the excessive constraints of her relationships in the 1940s and 1950s, due to jealousy.

> If two girls live together there's no such thing like you can say to someone, I'm going to stop and have a drink after work, with the people you work with or something. There's that routine of coming home . . . it's too domesticated, you know. I mean you become so involved, it's like being married then. This is what I fought against, I felt like I had never escaped my marriage and that was one thing I hated about my marriage, I felt like I was trapped. . . .

Curiously, fem narrators who were part of the rough street culture are no more critical of butch control, and, like the older fems, they emphasize their dislike of the possessive jealousy. A common complaint is about studs who stick too close so that the fems couldn't have any fun when they were out. Arlette still gripes about going to a new bar in Rochester that she had heard a great deal about, but not having a chance to enjoy it because she had to be so close to her butch.

> I don't like those kind of studs that feel like every time I step out the door [they] gotta go too. I don't need no shadows. We weren't Siamese twins. You take me out and expect I'm supposed to sit and look at you all night long. I feel like this, I had a girl I used to go with, take me all the way to Rochester to the Pink Panther. I heard so much about the Pink Panther. I get to Rochester and I said, "Umm, very interesting. Let's see what these kids are like here." The first day she came out to tell me, "Look at me." [She wanted me to spend the whole evening looking at her. I could have been home.]

In fems' memories, the possessive jealousy combined with the bossiness and sometimes violence created a difficult situation, something that fems would like to have changed about gay life.

Despite their complaints most fems evaluated their relationships positively. They were not sorry they had been in them, nor did they think they should have left them. The jealousy and bossiness were just an unpleasant side of an otherwise good relationship that they valued and cherished. Charlie explains that at the time she didn't know any better.

> Just like I was a wife. Well, first of all, she wouldn't let me work, which I wanted to work because I wanted to make money, but I did have my [child]. She still had a [child], and we bought this house and she was like the husband, she went to work, she brought home the pay. She was very demanding and commanding but we still got along. I didn't know any better or any different, I think that's what you'd call it. I think it's nice that people should be jealous, but not to the extreme.

Her girlfriend was very helpful and supportive to her, emotionally and financially, while she raised her child. To her mind, she was and still is a wonderful person.

> To this day she's one of the most wonderful people in the whole world. I see her [frequently. She] . . . tries to run my house. . . . Still tries to tell me what to do. . . . I mean you just can't take it out of her, that this remains in there, that she is the father. Demanding and commanding and bossy, but

. . . she only has about an hour and a half to do it. But she's really a wonderful person.

Fems from the rough and tough lesbian crowd also evaluate their relationships positively, appreciating the caring, closeness, and respect between butch
and fem. At many points in her life story, Annie favorably compares her
experience of being in a butch-fem couple to that of being married. To her,
everything is better about the butch-fem relationships, but she particularly
likes the cooperation and freedom.

> A husband is like a job. . . . It's like a nine-to-five job. Where with the
> same type of sex [in the gay life] you're more freer I think. . . .

Fem Identity

Fem identity is one of the most interesting and least explored aspects of lesbian history. Most fems did not internalize a deep feeling of difference from
other women at an early age, even if they experienced an early attraction for
women. In addition many fems spent some part of their lives in the heterosexual world, and many negotiated that world successfully. Nevertheless, they
chose to pursue their desire for women, and to be in relationships with
women for some part of their lives, and for many, the majority of their lives.
This evidence indicates that fem sexual identity does not fit a rigid
dichotomy between heterosexual and homosexual, suggesting that we recon-
sider the rigid opposition between these two categories that was embedded in
gay liberation thinking. This reconceptualization might produce the possibility of writing a lesbian history that can fully include the perspectives of both
butch and fem.

Selections[13]

Fem identity was different from that of butches. In general, it was not based
in strongly internalized feelings of difference, but rather in the commitment
to a different way of life—socializing in the gay world, and having a relationship with a woman. Whereas butches had two indicators of identity—attraction to women and desire to appropriate masculine characteristics—fems had
only one; logically, femininity did not set them apart from other women.
Fems had to have contact with a lesbian community or a lesbian relationship
to develop awareness of their difference. Most fems spent some time in the
heterosexual world and attempted to be happy, but it did not work out.
Moreover, they had more fun and better relationships in gay life. Although

they considered themselves gay, their gayness was dictated more by setting and circumstance than by a sense of fundamental difference. Being gay is what they liked, sexually and emotionally. They remembered that years ago gay was more of a descriptive term than a marker of fem identity. In the past, it was more likely that they would have been considered and referred to as fem, not gay.

Joanna had no conscious sense of being gay, lesbian, or different until a friend took her to Ralph Martin's on a night they had intended to go bowling. For two years, beginning when she was eight, she had had an intense erotic friendship with a girl two years older, but she had never interpreted it as sign of being "different."

> Because when I was quite young, like about eight or nine, there was a girl in my neighborhood and we played little games together. Didn't even know what we were doing. However, we were attracted to one another. . . . My mother knew there was an attachment but she didn't know what kind and she'd say "Why are you always hanging around with her?" And I said, "We have a lot of fun together." I knew that it was the kind of thing I could not tell my mother at eight years old. Couldn't possibly tell my mother that we were necking and fooling around. We used to take baths together. . . . Maybe that you would do with a kid sister. . . . I knew it was a different kind of feeling than I felt for my family, [or] for any of my other acquaintances. It was a tremendous attraction.

Joanna did not think at the time that she was different from other girls, or that she would not have the same feelings for boys later. "I really thought I was going through a slight infatuation. But I really couldn't fathom this. . . . I knew that it was not the thing that should be; however, I couldn't stop it and it went on for a couple of years."

When Joanna went into Ralph Martin's the first time, she immediately made the connection with her past experiences.

> And then [my friend] told me when we got in, she said, "Do you like it?" And I said, "Oh yeah, I do." I liked everything. I loved watching everybody. I thought that it was great. . . . I didn't think it [being gay] was odd so it really didn't strike me funny. Because don't forget I've already had that experience. . . . I thought that's what I felt for her. I never knew what I felt for her, except a lot of affection, admiration, and whatever that goes with someone you love.

When she saw butch-fem roles in the bar, she also "never thought that was odd." She knew right away that she was fem. "I mean how do you know what you feel? You know how you feel." Unquestionably, she "preferred it," and she stayed with that preference all her life. She remembers that same constancy was true for her friends, a core group in the bars of the 1940s.

> I have to tell you something. In this group that I first met, none of them ever changed. . . . Ever! That's funny. You know that you would think like maybe one of the girls who had been attracted like to another girl [who] had a little more masculinity in her. No. I never never have known one that changed. And as I said I'm still in contact with almost all of them that I was close to.

After eight years, Joanna left her first relationship and returned to live with her mother in an attempt to try heterosexual life. She attributes this partly to guilt generated by her family, who did not approve of her being a lesbian. She also thinks she was influenced by fear. At one point in her interview, she mentions that people have been afraid to tell the story of gays and to correct misconceptions, and includes herself as a person who has been afraid. "I was one too, I was afraid. Job, pain, whatever. . . . I was married a short time, you know. I was afraid."

In time, she met a man at work whom she was initially hesitant about marrying, but then changed her mind.

> I met this fella and I was working at [the Army Corps of Engineers]. He was an inspector, my age, and [we] started going out. Basketball games, sporting events, whatever, and he asked me to marry him. And I thought about it and I thought oh that's a bad idea. I went with him for oh about a year and a half and just dated, you know. I went home to my mother, you know, each night and, and then [all of a sudden] I said well maybe this is my salvation, you know. Never tried it, why not? . . . Lasted two and a half weeks. And I just couldn't. I knew that I had made the biggest mistake of my life. As I said if [he] had maybe been a different person but he was not the right person. He was a very weak person, which you don't discover until you're around someone. Then I said "Oh no, this is not my bag."

Several of Joanna's friends indicate that she was married slightly longer, more like six months, jokingly saying that every time she tells the story, the marriage gets shorter.

After Joanna left the marriage, she went back to her mother. "I just resigned myself to the fact that I'd made a mistake but I felt badly because I really did screw up his life, let's face it. . . . He's never remarried." At that time, she wasn't looking consciously for a man or a woman. "Because it really didn't make any difference. I think this is just the right person. There was no preference to gender, you know. I think it was just, I needed someone, I needed a friend. . . . I just needed someone that I could talk to and go out to dinner or whatever, you know, and enjoy."

The year her mother died, she started a relationship with a woman that lasted eight or nine years. She remained in the gay life from that point on, although a woman who knew her fairly well says that after a painful breakup, later on, she went out with several men again for a short period. She certainly was not opposed to such behavior. When imagining a future world where gays are no longer oppressed, she mentions there would be more gays, but, based on her own interests, she thinks there would still be heterosexuality.

> I don't think of a completely gay world as being utopia either though. . . .
> I think you should have your choice, why not? I certainly wouldn't want
> to see a completely heterosexual world or a completely gay world. I think
> we need the balance. . . . Because I think the reproduction is good, and I
> think relationships with, like even say men you work with, isn't that
> obnoxious to me. . . .

Joanna is very sure that she was not born gay, although she was aware that most butches thought that they were, especially the first two she was involved with:

> All of a sudden, my whole system changed, my whole chemistry changed,
> my body chemistry did. But I never felt as strongly about being gay at that
> time. . . . I thought that was something that happened to me. . . . But she
> [my first relationship], I know that she was gay from the time she was a lit-
> tle child. As far back as she can remember. She always liked boys' clothes
> and she was attracted to little girls.

Still, she doesn't really believe that they were born that way, but rather interprets their early feelings of masculinity in terms of family dynamics.

Joanna's gay identity is clearly based in attraction to other women. Although she was happy in her relationships, she had a struggle with living a life outside the accepted norms of her family. In addition, she had fleeting interests in men. Despite this, she lived most of her life socializing with the gay community and having gay relationships, and, in her mind, she was unquestionably gay. She was generally satisfied with this choice. "Let's face it, the gay life is not so terrible. . . ."

Corresponding with the shift in the definition of lesbian toward a basis in attraction to the same sex, fem identity as gay or lesbian became firmer in the 1950s. All fem narrators interviewed, without hesitation or qualification, considered themselves as gay, and some even felt comfortable calling themselves "lesbian." Just as in the 1940s, the formation of fem identity followed a path distinct from that of butches. In general, fems experienced less of an imperative to live the gay life, raising interesting questions about their choices. They usually did not experience gender conflicts at an early age, and contact with the community was essential, therefore, for forming their identity. They went through a long process of questioning if they wanted to live the gay life, often with actively heterosexual interludes.[14]

Arlette was and remains an important and respected leader in the black community. Before coming out she led an active heterosexual life. Although she was aware of lesbians from childhood because one lived in her neighborhood, and in retrospect, she can identify being attracted to women in adolescence, if not earlier, in her youth, she never considered herself different or gay. In her twenties, she became curious about gay women, and had her first affair with her boss, who was a lesbian. At the time, she was afraid because of all the negative things she had heard about lesbians, and therefore always got drunk.

> I thought it was terrible that women went together. I talked about her [my employer] like a dog. Oh hell yeah. You couldn't even convince me that was anything right about that. Because I used to talk about her bad when these lesbians used to come and pick her up, I said, "It's ridiculous, it's terrible" . . . But [my boss] ended up seducing me; she used to get me drunk off of some good Gordon's gin. Every time we turned out we would just about kill the whole bottle. And the next thing I know something happened, but I never knew what happened. Next time I came to her house she told me, you know, I'm getting tired of this drunk action from you, and I drank some more. 'Cause I would always get out of my mind so I didn't know what was going on. . . . I was curious, more than anything else. 'Cause they always told me lesbians would kill you. They were the wrong people to associate with. So I had a fear of lesbians. I forgot, the first time I walked in the club in [Detroit] it was the Club Rendezvous, this girl approached me in the ladies bathroom and demanded to kiss me. She scared me to death. And I didn't want to kiss her. She grabbed a whiskey bottle like she was going to hit me with it. And another girl snatched her out of there; and that was my first encounter with a gay lady. . . . I said well, I really thought they were crazy. She was drunk out of her mind. That same woman ended up killing a couple of people, though. . . . But it wasn't women, it was men she killed. . . . She was high in the bathroom. . . . And I said, oh my god, they're really like that.

Because Arlette was drinking, she doesn't consider this a full introduction to gay life. "I was always loaded . . . and like if you drink, you get loaded, you don't care what you do, but I always could never remember." Her curiosity continued after she moved to Buffalo, "But this time I tried to be a little sober." After her second relationship, which was with a young butch, she has primarily been with women, except for work, and maybe some short flings. She has periodically had an urge for a man, and thinks that is not exceptional. She appreciates partners who understand this.

Arlette is not sure what makes her gay. She can understand why other people can't understand gayness, because she herself finds it perplexing.

> Yeah, well, nobody's gonna understand that gayness, 'cause I couldn't understand it myself. But I realized when I was a kid, I'd think back, that if I saw a nice-looking girl, or a girl that attracted me, I could never understand, "Why am I attracted to this girl? Something's wrong with me. Why do I like her?" When I was coming up I liked fellows too, but there was some girls that I just had a funny feeling, that urge that I wanted to do something. And it was always pertained to sex, and I would shake my head, say, "What's wrong with you, you don't think like that." I can't say, if I always was gay or not, because maybe it was because that lady [in the neighborhood] used to come through my shortcut. But a lot of people try to make like family [is the cause]. No, couldn't possibly be family had anything to do with it. And then it could be because my family was really strict, too strict, that I could always be around girls but I couldn't be around no fellows. They were so old-fashioned. At that time . . . my grandmother had to go to a party with me. . . . I had to have an older person take me some place at all times . . . I always had to be chaperoned. I could go to a girl's house and spend the night if she had no brothers.

Consistent with not feeling different from straights at an early age, Arlette thinks that everybody has some homosexual inclination and therefore they should not be so judgmental about gays. She does not draw the line sharply between homosexuals and heterosexuals. When asked what is the most important thing we should tell people in this book, she responds:

> 'Cause Phil Donahue['s] show, those women made me so mad when they stood up and talking about, "Well I think it's terrible." I wanted to say, "You are a liar." If I was private you couldn't tell me you haven't looked at a woman or felt something for a woman, or you haven't ever had some type of experience. If you was in elementary school, you had a best girlfriend and you all used to play with each other. 'Cause we had a club like that and I didn't even know what we was doin', but me and my best, the only girl I was allowed to be round, we used to play with each other. Didn't know what we was doin' but we was doin' it. In fact, wait a minute, come to think of it, I had a very good friend of mine and I used to pick her up going to school every day. She grabbed me in the bathroom one day, she said, "Arlette, come in here with me," and threw me down on the floor and jumped on top of me, and she was getting her pubic hair for the first time, it was kind of sharp. And she leaped on me and just

rubbed away. I said, "What are you doing?" Sometimes I think about her, I wonder where she is and what's she's doin'. And I'd like to go over, run across and say, "Hey you, come here, we've got a job to finish here."

Despite the certainty with which Arlette considers herself gay, she does not consider herself lesbian. When first asked for an interview, she sent the message back that she is not a lesbian, but gay. In her mind, lesbian means the sexual aggressor, so she reserves that term for butches. This is true despite thirty years in gay life instructing many butches in how to behave. She claims that many fems feel this way, and many of the butch narrators remember the same. Her distance from the term lesbian seems a way of dissociating from the stigma. Arlette's thinking strikingly resembles the gender-inversion model, emphasizing the difference between butch and fem. But she also knows the similarities between butch and fem as gay women. She does not see the inclination to be butch or fem as based in physiology, but as a role someone chooses. "I don't know how they get their role because, I think it's a matter of choice, what they feel like they want to do, I suppose. It's hard to say. Because sometime, I feel like I might want to turn stud. Really!" She also knows that it is not only fems who sleep with men, either as prostitutes or by inclination.

> Like some of them end up, they don't want their woman talking to nobody, but they end up pregnant. How did you get pregnant? You supposed to be the stud. Can't no man speak to me but here you are gonna hand me a baby. . . . And you're telling me can't no guy touch me, you don't want no guy around, but you come home tellin' me you got a tumor and find out it's a nine-month tumor. Seen that happen too. These guys, most of the gay studs have the babies and the fems don't have no kids, and the studs are going around with the babies. One girl told me she had toilet paper and cotton in there. I said, "All that and you got pregnant? Don't tell me that. How did the man get in if you had toilet tissue and cotton in there?" "I have a tumor." The tumor came out with heads and legs. And I found a lot of that. You see a lot of studs, they got four or five kids, three or four kids, and the lady, where are your kids?

Annie also worked as a prostitute while she was in the lesbian community during the late 1950s and early 1960s. Her identity is slightly different, yet again, emphasizing the element of choice for fems, and the internal strength they have for finding and creating a good life for themselves. She grew up with a butch sister, so she had some idea about gay life, but she never thought about it for herself while she was young.

After she became a prostitute, she went with well-known underworld figures who controlled her strictly. To get away from them, she started hanging around a gay bar. She remembers being frightened the first time she entered, because of the stereotypes she had of gay women and their sexual appetites. "The first time, if you're straight going into a gay bar, you're petrified, everybody is. 'Cause you think that's all they want, is that they're like vultures, in which case they're not, right?" She was not thrilled by her first affair, but nevertheless continued going to gay bars. "They were always trying to make out with you, but I didn't want no part of it, 'cause I was straight." In time, however, she met other women. "That's how I got started. I'd periodically stop back into the bar. I wasn't gung-ho right at the beginning." She started to meet more women and fell in love with one.

After five or six years as a lesbian, she decided to get married. She left both the lesbian life and prostitution for fifteen years. It was a change she made for security and she thinks fems commonly make such decisions.

> I think I enjoy the gay life now, more now, that I'm older, than I did when I was younger. Because when I was younger, you really don't know if you want to get married, settle down, or what you really want, and you're very unsure at that point. Whereas a butch usually is butch and they usually stay butch. And you don't ever see them getting married. Where with fems, they'll be in the gay life for a few years or whatever, especially if they're young, and you can't really blame them. And then they decide to get married and have children, some of them. Or they'll marry for security. That's what they'll look for in a man is security.

While she was actively socializing with lesbians, she didn't think about the limitations of her carefree and exciting life, but slowly different goals surfaced. She didn't feel that she could achieve the kind of security she wanted with lesbians.

> I had to, I was young and I had to see what life was really about. I wasn't going anywhere fast, and I was getting older, and I wanted to do something with my life. . . . It's not that I couldn't do it [with women], I think I was looking for security. . . . Maybe because none of us worked. . . . We weren't looking forward or that. . . . No goals. So I went to beauty school . . . and I had a beauty salon for five years.

After making her way in straight life and doing the things she wanted to do, Annie came back to gay life. She prefers it, but she wouldn't rule out marrying again if the conditions were attractive.

> I might get married again, but he's got to be at least eighty . . . have to give him his vitamin pill in the morning and a sleeping pill in the evening. And at that point they've outgrown their jealousy and all that bit, and they just

want companionship. And that's what I would want out of a marriage. . . .
It would have to really depend on the circumstances. If he slept in his own
bedroom, I had mine, and strictly for companionship, why not. No sex,
why not?

Despite the fifteen years in straight life, Annie feels she was a lesbian when
she was younger in gay life, as she is now. When told that some people in the
community feel that fems aren't real lesbians, Annie is at first incredulous:
"Well what would you call them? I mean actually . . . if a woman's having a
sexual affair with another woman, she's just as much a lesbian. . . . They're
two lesbians, I would say." Annie has a modern gay consciousness that bases
identity in same-sex attraction. Like the butches who consider all women
who are attracted to women as lesbians, she went on to introduce the concept of the "purer" lesbian.

> Oh yeah. Not as much as, let's say, an untouched butch or a virgin butch.
> Now maybe that's where you're getting it from, these butches I'm assum-
> ing are the ones that you interviewed and said that they're the lesbians and
> a fem is not a lesbian. Right. Maybe because they've never been touched
> by a man. Maybe this is in the back of their minds. . . . Because with a fem
> woman, somewhere along the way, she's either had or will have, sex with
> a man.

She thinks butch and fem are not fundamentally different kinds of lesbians. If
a fem didn't have sex with a man, she would be as much of a pure lesbian as
a butch. "I would say she's very much a lesbian. Very much. Wouldn't you?
. . . And she's always been involved with the same sex, I would say she's very,
very, very lesbian."

Annie thinks that gender identification, rather than sexual interest, does
make a difference in a person's life, and that is what makes it more likely for
fems to go with men.

> I think with butches, I think this is something that overpowers them at a
> very young age, as far as being more masculine than girlish. Acting more
> tomboyish, than more girlish, that's what I'm trying to say. And I don't
> really think this ever really grows out of them, and when they start grow-
> ing up and they become that in their early teens and they start saying,
> "Gee she looks good, he doesn't look good but she looks good." And they
> start recognizing their problem. And I think with a butch, I don't think
> they could actually really take the domineering husband. Or the husband
> that wants to be the husband. You know what I mean. Where a fem is
> really adjusted to it. They're girl girl, and you find that it's very easy
> for them to adjust to a marriage more so than a butchie girl. Cause they've
> played the lead role all their life. . . . And then for them to step into a

marriage and have a man rule them, there'd probably be imprints in the wall. There would be the man's imprint.

In Annie's mind butches resisted female socialization while fems did not. Nevertheless, her clarity about the choices she made highlights the strength of fems and their will to live with women, despite the barriers against them.

Throughout the 1940s and 1950s, it was a problem for both butches and fems to articulate the construction of the fem identity in the lesbian world. Although fem identity has received little scholarly attention heretofore, it raises some of the most interesting questions about lesbian community. Most fems grew up feeling little difference from straight women in terms of their position in society. They realized their attraction to women at varying ages and did not feel that this made them either male or unfeminine. It also appears that they did not strongly internalize the stigma of being sexually different. Some were attracted to men for periods in their lives, others were never interested in men. Most had some heterosexual sex, at least in their younger years, and were conscious of making clear choices about how they would live their lives, rather than being led by some internal or biological imperative. They also shared a determination to be with the women they loved, to establish a viable place for themselves in lesbian society, and to defend their right to help structure a world that could comfortably accommodate the relationships they desired.

Notes

I want to thank Madeline Davis for her helpful comments on the penultimate draft of this article. I also thank my writing group: Betsy Cromley, Claire Kahane, Carolyn Korsmeyer, Isabel Marcus, and Carol Zemel for their insightful comments on the introduction.

1. It is likely that fems were central to the building of other racial/ethnic lesbian working-class communities, but the research has not yet been done to document this. The fullest sources on fems in lesbian community are from the Northeast where the major racial/ethnic communities were European American or African American during the 1940s and 1950s. For instance, during the 1940s and 1950s Buffalo had a minuscule Latina population and an even smaller Asian American population. At this time Buffalo had a significant Native American community; however, Native American lesbians did not form their own distinct social group; rather they socialized primarily in the European American lesbian community. The major sources on fems in history include: Joan Nestle, *A Restricted Country* (Ithaca: Firebrand, 1987); Joan Nestle, *The Persistent Desire: A Femme-Butch Reader* (Boston: Alyson, 1992); and Elizabeth Kennedy and Madeline Davis, *Boots of Leather, Slippers of Gold: The History of Lesbian Community* (New York: Routledge, 1993).

2. Esther Newton, "The Mythic Mannish Woman: Radclyffe Hall and the New Woman," *Hidden From History: Reclaiming the Gay and Lesbian Past*, eds. Martin Bauml

Duberman, Martha Vicinus, and George Chauncey (New York: New American Library, 1989) 293.

3. This end result is particularly ironic since Madeline is proudly fem; and I, as a staunch feminist, was completely aware of the way in which the feminine is devalued in western society and therefore should have been able to counter that process.

4. As selections they cannot cover the topics fully. For more information I refer people to *Boots of Leather* itself.

5. The selections about Joanna come from Chapter 2, "'I could hardly wait to get back to that bar': Lesbian Bar Culture in the 1930s and 1940s"; the selections about Arlette come from Chapter 4, "'Maybe 'cause things were harder. . . you had to be more friendly': Race and Class in the Lesbian Community of the 1950s," *Boots of Leather*.

6. The film *Paris Is Burning* suggests that the title "Mother" is used throughout the Black gay and lesbian community for those who show leadership in nurturing others.

7. This argument is developed throughout *Boots of Leather*, but particularly in Chapters 5 and 6. In some sense the whole book is an ethnography of a butch-fem community, and aims to take the reader inside butch-fem culture.

8. The selections for this section come from Chapter 6, "'Now you get this spot right here': Butch-Fem Sexuality During the 1940s and 1950s," *Boots of Leather*.

9. See for instance, Joan Nestle, "Esther's Story" and "The Gift of Taking" in *A Restricted Country*, 40–46, 127–130; Amber Hollibaugh and Cherríe Moraga, "What We're Rollin' Around in Bed With: Sexual Silences in Feminism," in *Powers of Desire: The Politics of Sexuality*, eds. Ann Snitow, Christine Stansell, and Sharon Thompson (New York: Monthly Review Press, 1983) 394–405.

10. Personal communication with Joan Nestle, January 11, 1992.

11. Hollibaugh and Moraga, "What We're Rolling Around in Bed With," 398.

12. The selections for this section come from Chapter 8, "'It can't be a one-way street': Committed Butch-Fem Relationships," *Boots of Leather*. Chapter 7, "'Nothing is forever': Serial Monogamy in the Lesbian Community of the 1940s and 1950s" also contains relevant information on fems in relationships.

13. These selections come from Chapter 10, "'In everybody's life there has to be a gym teacher': The Formation of Lesbian Identities and the Reproduction of Butch-Fem Roles," *Boots of Leather*.

14. There is very little research and writing on fem identity. See Louise Adams, "Disputed Desire: The 'Feminine' Women in Lesbian History," paper presented at the Eighth Berkshire Conference on the History of Women, Douglass College, June 1990. In addition, see Joan Nestle and Amber Hollibaugh's groundbreaking writing: Joan Nestle, *A Restricted Country* (Ithaca: Firebrand Books, 1987); and Amber Hollibaugh and Cherríe Moraga, "What We're Rollin Around in Bed With: Sexual Silences in Feminism," in *Powers of Desire: The Politics of Sexuality*, eds. Ann Snitow, Christine Stansell, and Sharon Thompson (New York: Monthly Review Press, 1983) 394–405.

FISH TALES
Revisiting "A Study of a Public Lesbian Community"

Laura Harris and Liz Crocker

As a contribution to the historical recording of femme lives and butch-femme communities, this essay offers our analysis of a compilation of excerpts from Ethel Sawyer's essay "A Study of a Public Lesbian Community," written in 1965 as a Master of Arts thesis for the Department of Sociology-Anthropology at Washington University.[1] Sawyer's essay is a sociological study of African American lesbians in a specific bar community that examines their gender identifications as fish and stud.[2] Specifically, Sawyer surveys and interviews the fish and studs about their sexual preferences, social behaviors, and "commitment to the life" (13). Sawyer's conclusions about the fish within this community reflect some of the historical stereotypes about femme lesbians that have circulated both in psychological or socio-scientific studies and within feminist and lesbian communities themselves.[3] One such stereotype of fish/femmes is that their lesbian identification is only transitory, and that the "real" lesbians among them are only fish as the beginning stage on a path to becoming studs. Another stereotype that influences Sawyer's work is that fish/femmes are sexually and socially passive. This stereotype leads her to negate their sexual agency by disregarding the difference between a chosen bisexual identity and socio-economic reasons for maintaining male partners.

It is important to situate Sawyer within the context of her historical moment, one in which lesbians were studied as part of the "deviant phe-

40

nomenon of homosexuality" (1).[4] One example of the study's datedness is Sawyer's claim that, for lesbians, "it is only through revealing oneself as homosexual that one can go about the job of converting others to homosexuality" (21). More subtly, the framework through which Sawyer examines this lesbian community is already tainted by a heterosexual paradigm that can best be seen in her emphasis on mate stability or long-term monogamy. Further, as she examines fish and studs, she only interprets their behavior in terms of stereotypical heterosexual masculine and feminine roles: "Studs are those female homosexuals who assume, both socially and sexually . . . the role modeled after the masculine role in the larger society. Fish are those who take on the feminine role" (6). As a result of this heterosexual paradigm, the conclusions that Sawyer draws about her sample group seem to the contemporary scholar inadequate in light of the depth and richness of the words of the fish and studs interviewed. Yet another indication of the historical limits of Sawyer's study is that, although she names the class and race of her subjects, neither are used to substantially forward her analysis. For example, Sawyer does not address the possibility that these fish and studs are involved in a radical contestation of sexual stereotypes of black women as immoral, aggressive, and oversexed.

Rather than dwell upon the limitations that Sawyer's historical moment imposed on her study, we read her essay as an important historical document. Written during a time in which little critical work was done on lesbians, her study provides a useful record of a lesbian community, specifically working-class African American lesbians who identified themselves as fish and studs. Although Sawyer often interprets her source material in a framework imbued with negative stereotypes, an alternative history can be read, one that shows fish as women who were making brave sexual choices and exercising sexual autonomy. Choosing excerpts from Sawyer's essay that focus on the fish-stud community, fish bisexuality, and fish sexual agency, we read between the lines to add to an archival history of fish/femmes in this period.

Fish-Stud Community

Sawyer's study includes interviews with her subjects from which she makes general claims about the fish-stud community. In this section, we choose excerpts from her analysis of "homosexuality" as a social phenomenon, the class status of her subject group, the class-determined dress codes of the fish-stud community, and the status of fish within this community. Sawyer writes:

> Granted that the defining characteristics of homosexuals are in terms of sex, homosexuality is also a social phenomenon. Gratifications are more

than just sexual, and sexual aspects may in many cases occupy a position of secondary importance. To be in the life means not just to engage in sexual practices with persons of the same sex. It designates a status vis à vis the larger society; a position within the homosexual subculture itself; a partici-pation in its round of activities; and an involvement in a way of living which for those who remain must be gratifying. (7–8)

Sawyer's understanding of homosexuality as both social and sexual frames her study's focus on her subjects as part of a subcultural group. Sawyer's emphasis on the social aspects of lesbian life appears many times in her study; ulti-mately, it serves as a hierarchical framework to judge fish as less lesbian since they have social connections outside their lesbian world.

Sawyer also chooses her subjects based on their class status. In the title of her study, she refers to them as "public lesbians" as they frequent a bar that she renames "Jim's" (3). Sawyer writes that her subjects are

persons of lower socio-economic status, though by taking occupation and income alone, a few could be considered more middle class. Some of those not actually belonging to the lower class, because of certain personal traits and attitudes are excluded from associations with other groups of Lesbians who might belong to a different class as is evidenced in the remark: "Sue is what you might call a Lesbian whore and has gone with damn near every stud in St. Louis. . . . The school teacher set cut her loose." (3–4)

Clearly, then, Sawyer draws class distinctions not simply in terms of occupa-tion and income but in terms of sexual activity and visibility. As we can see with the example of Sue, the "Lesbian whore," the study's analysis of sexual activity as signifying a debased class status means that this sexually active fish will be read, no matter what her actual income or occupation, as part of Sawyer's "lower class" community. Of this "lower class" community, Sawyer writes:

If a status hierarchy were to be constructed . . . Jim's group would fall at the fourth [lowest] level. . . . At the very bottom of the hierarchy would be those "loud and dirty ones who are boisterous and make trouble . . . a lot of them are down on Franklin Street." (4)

Just as Sawyer's study marks her subjects as "lower" class because of their sexual activity, this class distinction is also derived from their gendered lesbian visibility. The group of lesbians that frequents Jim's bar organizes itself along fish-stud lines made apparent in their dress codes:

Members of Jim's group are generally separated into the two categories of studs and fish. Studs dress similarly to males (slacks zip up the front, short hair cuts, no lipstick or make-up, men's shirts or women's boyish looking blouses, etc.) and attempt wherever possible to minimize their female characteristics, many wearing t-shirts underneath clothes to replace bras. Fish on the other hand dress as women in every respect, and to a casual observer might not appear to be in the life. However, aside from this obvious physical distinction (which serves at once to designate who is and who is not available as a possible mate), there are the matters of appropriate mannerisms and behavior, domestic responsibilities, attitudes towards homosexuality, the larger society and towards oneself which accompany each of the two roles. These two roles are complementary, i.e., a stud and a fish make up a homosexual couple. (6–7)

Furthering her description of these gendered appearances, Sawyer analyses the ways that status is conferred upon fish and studs:

Whether or not a person changes or remains within a particular role appears to be to a great extent a function of perceived rewards and gratifications accruing to these roles. To briefly mention a few, studs as a result of having attained the ultimate in homosexuality . . . are therefore privileged with a higher status within the subculture than that which is accorded the fish, who on the other hand enjoy the situation of marginality. (12)

If Sawyer's theory is correct that the stud is "the ultimate in homosexuality," and that it is possible to change roles at will to receive the "rewards and gratifications" that accrue to the stud position, we might wonder why she finds any fish at all. Sawyer moves from her claim about the higher status of studs and lower status of fish to claiming that fish have less "commitment to the life."

One knotty issue here is that there is really an ambivalence as to the actual overall status of a fish. On the one hand she is "definitely homosexual" whenever a particular situation calls for some clarification (most women would like to be if they had the chance or were not afraid), but on the other hand it occurs that upon asking whether or not a person is homosexual and if so, which role does she assume, the reply is sometimes, "she's woman, all woman!" Perhaps this situation reflects the marginality of the fish in the homosexual subculture. Their associations more frequently involve persons who are not homosexuals; their heterosexual relations are much more extensive; and in general, they are less committed to the life socially, sexually and psychologically. (13)

Overall, then, Sawyer analyses her lesbian subjects in terms of their participation in a social community that revolves around—but is not limited to—Jim's bar and grill. As she analyses them in this social setting, she gives higher status to those who are more "committed to the life," or, in other words, do not go outside the group for other purposes. Sawyer calls fish "marginal" and "less committed to the life" because they have connections, whether of employment, familial, or social, that take them out of the life. This, combined with their (to Sawyer) suspect femininity—"she's woman, all woman!"—further lessens their status in Sawyer's lesbian hierarchy.

"Commitment to the Life": Fish Bisexuality

In this section, we excerpt Sawyer's analysis that links the instability of lesbian relationships to her perceptions of fish as not "committed to the life" and, ultimately, as bisexual. Sawyer places mate stability as a primary concern in discussing

> mate instability which operates to a great degree within that homosexual subculture. In all cases except one persons do not have the same mate as they initially had during the beginning stages of research, and in most cases there have been at least two additional mates since first contact . (23)

Mate stability, then, becomes a criterion for judging lesbians in the hierarchical standards that Sawyer sets up.

> It appears that a system of ranking people who are homosexuals exists in Jim's group. . . . The single most important criterion for placing persons directly above them is that of the ability to get along with one's mate, having maintained a relationship through time. (To get along well together is not to associate with members of Jim's group.) (5–6)

Whereas Sawyer claims to see the group as setting its own standards that negatively judge those who do not have stable long-term relationships, she draws this conclusion from an example of one long-term couple who are not members of Jim's group. Rather than disagreeing with Sawyer's position, we understand the study itself as tainted by a dominant heterosexual model of a monogamous relation, ideally marriage. After all, many members of Jim's group as quoted by Sawyer mention the high rate of mate turnover; none of them expresses dissatisfaction or distaste for this practice.

Sawyer connects mate turnover with the fish's lack of "commitment to the life":

> One of the areas in which there appears to be a great degree of leniency operating in this homosexual subculture is that of commitment to homosexuality. To be committed to the life is not a prerequisite for belonging to Jim's group—at least not for fish. As was previously mentioned fish are less committed to the life than are studs. (14)

This statement further contradicts Sawyer's earlier claim that the members of Jim's group value mate stability. However, Sawyer's model that condemns non-monogamous activity serves to mark fish as culprits, the non-lesbian lesbians who are not "committed to the life."

Sawyer draws her claim that fish are less "committed to the life" from her observations that fish, although they still self-define as lesbian, have sex with men:

> To have sex with a man, while it is a clearcut case of dislike for the studs, it is one of ambivalence for fish. They both like and dislike it. While it may follow naturally from having a date with a man and getting married to a man (both of which they value), and it is also a necessary condition for having children (which they also like), their conception of themselves as being homosexual *perhaps* influences their attitude about having sex with males to the extent that they place negative values on engaging in sexual practices with persons of the opposite sex. (18)

These conclusions result from the questionnaire that Sawyer gave her fish subjects that asked whether or not they liked activities such as having a date with a man, getting married to a man, having children, and having sex with a man. From the data, Sawyer concludes that fish "both like and dislike" sex with men. However, the data also clearly reveal that, whereas the fish enjoy the social and economic benefits of dating or marrying men, and might like having children, only two out of her seven respondents claim to like having sex with a man.

Sawyer wants to define fish as bisexual because they engage in sex with men. However, as the numbers show above (and as the respondents discuss in interviews), most of the fish do not find sexual satisfaction with men. Thus, in order to deem fish bisexual, Sawyer must rewrite a definition of bisexuality that does not include sexual gratification, rather:

> The extent to which these persons really receive equal sexual satisfaction through heterosexual and homosexual activities, though it is not an issue here, is questionable, as motivations to participate in one or the other relationship may and do entail many non-sexual gratifications. Therefore, for present purposes, bisexuality will be defined as simply oscillation between heterosexual and homosexual mates, regardless as to what types of gratifications are fulfilled and will be viewed as a manifestation of non-commitment to the life. (16–17)

Once again, Sawyer's study has a contradictory position embedded within it, that fish have alternate motivations for participating in heterosexual relations.

As Sawyer speaks generally about the reasons for fish's bisexuality, she implies that social and economic causes prompt fish to have sex with men:

> Without the aid of systemic interviews, through observation and general conversation, the fact that fish tend to be more bisexual than studs can be established. Some of the fish date men frequently and openly ... some having switched from stud to male and back again two or three times since the research began ...
>
> One aspect of behavior on the part of the stud which has been problematic throughout the research is the fact that though stud-fish relationships are constantly threatened by males, their attitudes appear to be somewhat more than lenient with regard to fish and their relationships with males. This might to some extent be attributed to the fact that many of the studs are unemployed and fish-male relationships are functional in the sense that males provide income to the fish and her family, lessening the demands that the stud seek employment or contribute to the support of the fish, and secondly that many studs, despite their masculine role, are instrumental in their relationships with fish. They are inclined to view them as persons from whom they may gain favors, mostly money. It is not uncommon that the fish is often the sole means of support in a relationship, whether through the aid of employment, A.D.C. or other means. Some studs have resigned themselves to the fact that fish generally continue heterosexual relationships. (18–19)

From the quote above, we can see that certainly, in Sawyer's observations, there is no indication that fish are having sex with men as a part of a chosen bisexual identity. Instead, fish, as heads of households often including children, cannot rely on financial support from studs who are often chronically unemployed. One of the most glaring omissions in Sawyer's analysis of this point is her failure to take into consideration that, for these African-American working-class lesbians, finding employment and economic stability is a difficult struggle at best. Being women, black, and lesbians places them in a triple bind; for studs, their visibility as lesbians seems to offer an obvious reason why most, in Sawyer's study, are unemployed and rely on fish for financial support. Rather than having a chosen bisexual sexual identity, we would read the fish of Sawyer's study to be utilizing the economic structure of heterosexuality, in which men support women and their children, to live what the fish themselves call "homosexual" lives.

Further supporting our reading of the social and economic pressures that might cause fish to have sexual contact with men, Sawyer notes:

> The fact that Jim's group is composed of persons of lower socio-economic status also has its effect on mate stability and seems to operate particularly in cases where persons are living together as homosexual mates. Sometimes where there are children present, fathers contribute to the support of the children and will often visit. (28)

The above example of economic ties to men certainly does not demonstrate a fish bisexual choice. For the fish who Sawyer cites as self-identifying as bisexual, the many socio-economic pressures she cites for sleeping with men could lead us to question the "choices" available to fish:[5]

> This is the case of Marie, a woman noted by members of the group as being notoriously bisexual and who readily admits it herself. She is twenty-six years old, the mother of three children and lives in one of the housing projects . . . Marie has alluded to loving a man whom she claims is "really no good." . . . [As one stud recalls,] "When I would say something about it [the fish's contact with the male lover], she would always say "Go get a job." (33–34)

Similarly, the excerpt below can be read as evidence of the social pressures that, at that time, made it difficult or impossible to circulate freely as a lesbian couple. Sawyer quotes a fish who, breaking up with a stud, explains:

> "I'm fed up with going to Jim's. . . . I want to do other things and go other places like down in Gaslight—places where you can't take me [dressed as you are]." (28–29)

Fish Sexual Agency

From our discussion of the socio-economic factors involved in fish's sexual choices above, we now turn to excerpts concerning fish sexuality within the lesbian context of the fish-stud community. As we have discussed above, Sawyer's study often implies that fish are less lesbian than studs. Sawyer writes, "fish tend to be less committed to the life where matters not directly bearing on sex are concerned" (22). Also, Sawyer mentions fish's "general attitude that they can leave the life at will" (30). Clearly, we can see that Sawyer's statement that "homosexuality is also a social phenomenon," leads to a misreading of fish—who are primarily interested in lesbian sex and who have connections to the world outside Jim's group—as not "committed to the life" or bisexual. Fish desire for sexual gratification is misunderstood, both by Sawyer and by some of her sources, as signifying a "whore" (as in the example of Sue, the "Lesbian whore"). As one interviewed subject states, "the fish, many of them are whorish and flirtatious" (27).

The excerpt below is connected to the notion of fish as "whore." Sawyer writes that

> Another difference between fish and studs is that fish tend to minimize or under report the actual number of studs with whom they have been involved; whereas studs are less likely to under report. This practice on the

> part of fish appears to be to an extent a function of the social stigma
> attached to the situation of a fish having had "too many" studs. . . . The
> attitude of fish towards their own behavior is reflected in the statement
> made by a respondent while being interviewed on mate history. After hav-
> ing reported ten names of studs with whom she had been involved, the
> respondent sighed and replied, "that's enough." (10–11)

This returns to our earlier discussion of the way that Sawyer's heterosexual
model of the monogamous couple affects her understanding of her subjects.
Here too, the notion that studs—like "typical" men—would over report and
that fish—like "typical" women—would under report seems more her own
perspective than drawn from her sources. We could also point out that this
social stigma certainly does not stop fish from having multiple partners; it is
obviously an open "secret" that many fish have as many or more partners as
studs. This stud overstatement and fish understatement can also be read as a
group practice by which these black working-class lesbians subvert stereotypes of promiscuity that would affect each differently outside their black lesbian community.

Sawyer understands fish and stud sexual roles as clear-cut in terms of
aggression and passivity:

> Usually it is a stud who is the aggressor and the initiator in cases where fish
> are concerned. Studs on the other hand appear to vary a great deal in their
> modes of initiation, some having been introduced to homosexuality by
> fish, others by other studs, and mutual initiation between persons not pre-
> viously in the life.
>   *Fish do not always reflect the ideal type.* In cases where studs were initi-
> ated by fish, this occurred either at a very young age and/or by fish who
> were considerably older and had been in the life a number of years. (9,
> emphasis added)

Sawyer approaches the fish and studs with an "ideal type" of sexual behavior
for each in her mind. Clearly, the "ideal" fish is passive; the "ideal" stud is
the "aggressor." However, Sawyer also provides many examples of fish
aggressivity that seem to contradict her original model. Further, she explains:

> Cases of studs who were initiated by studs can easily be explained. At the
> time of their initiation they were fish and, like most fish, were introduced
> to homosexuality by studs. According to statements made by some respon-
> dents, most studs were first fish, and fish are the first to divulge this infor-
> mation. Often, one hears the statement, "she is going to be a stud before
> long." (11)

Sawyer's analysis is complicated and confused here by the fact that her model is so simple: fish passivity, stud aggressivity. Rather than deciphering a whole range of identifications we could imagine possible within fish-stud dynamics—baby stud, top fish, bottom stud, stud-on-stud initiation, or older fish-younger stud couplings—Sawyer flattens out the possible diversity of fish-stud coupling.

In the words of one fish:

> "A lot of people, after they stay in the life as a fish for a certain length of time turn stud. You know you have to get them young girls—you have to get them young girls who are coming out fresh." (30)

Again, rather than understanding this older fish's desire in terms of wanting an intergenerational relationship, Sawyer claims that there is a progression:

> This indicates a progression from fish to stud. One fish expressed the desire to turn stud but had certain reservations. Her reasons for wanting to turn stud were that she wanted "to be the aggressor, to pick and choose, and to do the protecting." On the other hand she felt that she could not live up to the idealized social role of a stud. "I don't feel that I would be able to support someone. I feel that a stud should be the provider and protector and right now, I'm not able." (11)

Both of the fish in these excerpts express desires to be "the aggressor," to "choose" their partners from the younger pool. We might speculate that, as one fish interviewed above stated, the older fish can tell which of the younger lesbians is "going to be a stud before long," and that these older women are not necessarily changing their role from fish to stud. Moreover, it is also possible that they are reacting to the constraints of their group in which it is only possible to be the sexual aggressor if you identify as a stud. However, Sawyer's claim that, from one example, there is "a progression from fish to stud," seems again not to recognize the potential diversity of fish-stud sexual desires.

Sawyer's interviews with fish at times offer insight into the independence of their lesbian choices:

> Georgia and Eunice are two fish who visit each other frequently, go out together and from all indications are good friends. Both live with their parents, have one illegitimate child (before entering the life) express some embarrassment about being seen with gay people in public, date men, and feel that they can leave the life and return at will. On several occasions (months apart) each of them has stated that they were no longer in the life.

> It has not failed yet that two or three weeks after each proclamation, they manage to show up at some social function on the arm of a stud whom they are dating or come alone and participate in other activities with members of the group. . . . Georgia's oscillation between being in and out of the life is to the degree that it has become a standard joke between her and the researcher. (32–33)

Although Sawyer does not emphasize the agency of the fish in the above example we can see their independence. Their choices to "leave the life and return at will" indicate, not a simple vacillation between lesbianism and heterosexuality, but rather an active negotiation of their desires. Moreover, Georgia and Eunice are not passive women seduced by aggressive studs; instead, they make choices to suit themselves. Finally, Georgia provides another anecdotal example of fish sexual agency:

> Georgia is a fairly attractive girl whom many of the studs at one time or another have expressed an interest in. She may establish a relationship with one for a few weeks and then it is over. Her excuse is that she "just does not like them anymore." (32)

We choose to end with Georgia's words, seeing in them an expression of sexual courage and autonomy that demonstrate why Sawyer's work is so important to revisit at this time. Ultimately, Sawyer's study offers us a new understanding of these fish femmes—not simply as heterosexual, bisexual, or "homosexual" (lesbian)—but as negotiating these markers of sexuality as well as the struggles they face as black working-class women, often single mothers, to pursue their own desires.

Notes

1. Ethel Sawyer, "A Study of a Public Lesbian Community," Master's thesis, Washington University, 1965. All subsequent references will be parenthetical.

2. Sawyer explains her methods thus: "The method of investigation includes a combination of participant observation, focused and structured interviews and the use of informants and discussion groups. The beginning stages of research which covered a period of approximately four and a half months consisted exclusively of participant observations during which time no attempt was made to interview any of the members of the group. Though this period of observation yielded some of our richest data, it also served to get acquainted and establish rapport with the homosexual subjects. As research has proceeded, observation on members of the group have encompassed a variety of settings including those where drugs are sold, distributed and used, parties, impersonators' balls, funerals, and occasional meetings at the investigator's home. In addition roughly one year has been spent in the process of focused interviewing" (7). "The subjects were seven studs and seven fish" (15).

3. For a discussion of such stereotypes in socio-scientific studies see Jennifer Terry, "Theorizing Deviant Historiography," *differences: A Journal of Feminist Cultural Studies* 3:2 (1991) 55–74.

4. John D'Emilio, *Sexual Politics, Sexual Communities: The Making of a Homosexual Minority in the United States 1940–1970* (Chicago: University of Chicago Press, 1983) 141–143.

5. While it is outside the scope of this essay, it would seem important to examine Sawyer's redefinition of bisexuality "as simply oscillation between heterosexual and homosexual mates" rather than as a chosen sexual identity premised upon desire for men and women. We also do not want to ignore the possibility that some of these fish might have chosen, if Sawyer had asked them, to identify themselves as bisexual; although we do want to point to the survey in which only two of the seven fish (28%) respondents answer that they like to have sex with men (17). It is in countering the Sawyer's desexualized definition of bisexuality that we emphasize the sexual desires of these fish which they often understand as "homosexual."

FEMME ICON
An Interview with Madeline D. Davis

Kelly Hankin

L et's face it: femme icons are hard to find. In a sexist culture that privileges masculinity and in a butch-femme culture that privileges butch
masculinity, finding a femme to pass the torch is no simple task.
Having read the available butch-femme literature, I have often used certain
femme voices as sources of inspiration, romanticizing them as role models
and icons. Driving to Buffalo (a city I had never visited but imagined as a
butch-femme Mecca) to interview Madeline Davis, I envisioned her in the
regalia of my imagined femme hero. As I walked up to Madeline's front door
and passed by one of her ex-lovers with a laundry basket, I realized that what
I would get was much more grounded than my femme flights of fancy imagined. Still heroic, Madeline Davis *is* a femme icon, but she is also a real
woman—passionate about her butch loves, articulate in her femme identity—who ultimately challenged and enhanced my own (sometimes very
rigid) ideas about femmes.

Femme Networks

KH: Reading "The Femme Tapes" and *Boots of Leather, Slippers of Gold* has
been very important for the validation and affirmation of my femme identity.[1] Do you have any thoughts on how important these writings might be,
not only as historical documents, but for femmes of a younger generation?

MD: It's hard. As an author and co-author there are things that I would hope
these texts might become for younger femmes, but what they have actually

become I don't yet know. . . . One of the sad things [about researching *Boots of Leather, Slippers of Gold*] was that many of the femmes that we had tried to find or hoped to find were gone. Of course, opinions as to why they were gone mostly came from butches. Some said that femmes weren't really lesbians to start out with, and that when things became difficult it was easier for them to slip back into the mainstream and heterosexuality. . . . I think femmes had difficulty staying "out" in the lesbian world because they lacked the group identity and strong friendship networks that butches had.

KH: How did you manage to stay "out" in the lesbian world?

MD: I'm younger than many of the femmes that we interviewed in *Boots*. A decade after I came out the women's movement began and support networks were being built. I started, little by little, having a non-role-identified, but at least women-positive group that would sustain me in the lesbian world.

KH: Were there femme networks and support for femme identity in these non-role-identified groups?

MD: There was not specifically femme support and, to this day, outside of a small handful of women in my life, I don't really have a femme support group—certainly not in my home city.

KH: Do you know any butch-femme couples in your age group?

MD: Most of the women that I am still friends with . . . who used to be in butch-femme relationships are butches who are now with women who do not self-identify as femme. . . . If you were to ask me about the couples, I might guess who is the butch and who is the femme. But I know that the women I would say are femme would never self-identify as such.

KH: Do you find it troubling that you cannot share femme identity with these women?

MD: I don't find it difficult until I look back at it from the perspective of having sat around that dining room table with Joan [Nestle] and Amber [Hollibaugh] making "The Femme Tapes," and I suddenly remember that there is nobody else in my life like that.

KH: "The Femme Tapes" is an amazing dialogue. I always get emotional when I read it.

MD: It was so emotional for us. That's an edited version, but we did a lot of laughing and an awful lot of crying.

KH: Do you receive the same kind of support from butches that you receive from self-identified femmes such as Nestle and Hollibaugh?

MD: I get a lot of support from the butch women in my life. They recognize my femmeness, and they love it and support it. . . . My lover and I are getting married this summer . . . there are four butches who are going to be ushers, one of whom is an ex-lover of mine!

KH: Do you think that there are femme friendship networks or support for femme identity within the younger generation of lesbians?

MD: I know that in larger metropolitan centers like New York, Seattle, and San Francisco, there are organized femme support groups. [pause] I can't imagine what that would be like.

KH: In *The Persistent Desire: A Femme-Butch Reader* there is a picture. . . .

MD: Yes, of the New York Femmes, with everybody showing off their nails. To be standing with a group of women showing their nail polish would be cute, but in some ways it would no longer be me. It certainly wouldn't be who I am every day.

KH: What do you think about the younger generation of butch-femme that you may read about or know personally?

MD: I look at butch-femme couples in Buffalo. . . . They have not gone through the same trials that butch-femmes couples went through in my early days. Perhaps they have gone through their own trials, but they have also come into the world at a time when choices are broader and when the queer umbrella is encompassing so many versions of who you can be. I'm having a horrendous time trying to figure out who I am under the queer umbrella.

KH: Much emphasis within the queer umbrella is placed on gender mutability and performance. Do you think that femme identity is mutable or transitory?

MD: I have never thought of myself as easily transformable or mutable. And yet, in writing the history of who I am, I have transformed, there is no doubt about it. Yet, I have stayed categorically the same. I've stayed a femme.

Femme Looks

KH: *Boots of Leather, Slippers of Gold* is an account of working-class butch and femme women from Buffalo. Being from Buffalo, how much do you think class has affected your femme identity—your own sense of it and how others perceive it?

MD: I think that the prevalence of the phenomenon of butch-femme may have a class connection. Buffalo is a very working-class city. It still is, even though many of the factories have closed. I was raised working class, and although all of my lovers were not from Buffalo and all of them were not raised working class, the people that I am used to and gravitate towards are pretty much working class. . . . My whole sense of appropriate sexuality, the way discussions are held about it, the way it is characterized, and the way I feel comfortable about participating in a lesbian dyad comes out of the fact that I am working class. And because I am working class, and because there is a fairly heavy emphasis in working-class families on role differentiation, that is very comfortable for me. I think as you move into the middle class the role differentiation is still there but it has a different look. It is more subtle, and where I come from it is not subtle at all—it's very "in your face."

KH: How would you describe yourself as a femme? Would it be "in your face?"

MD: First of all, I am going to be fifty-five years old in a couple of months, so I am a middle-aged woman. Who am I middle-aged like? Elizabeth Taylor is older than I am and I am certainly not her. [laughter] I admire her as an actress and as a beautiful woman, but that is not who I am. Who is the woman from that awful television program with the three women who live together?

KH: *The Golden Girls.* Which actress best describes you?

MD: I am probably more a Bea Arthur type. I am heavier than she is but I am probably visually more her type.

KH: That is interesting because Bea Arthur is often considered butch by both lesbians and mainstream society.

MD: It's funny, I've been doing a lot of theater lately and I've been playing butch roles. I'm doing a show pretty soon where I'm going to be wearing a man's suit and playing Perry Mason . . . part of it I think is because I am a large woman; part of it is because I am an older woman. There is something about aging and size that tends to masculinize women in a very strange way. It is because we have a vision of what feminine should look like and if you don't fall into that narrow range you then become masculine, which is the only "other" available. . . . Because of lesbianism's style differentiations and attention to comfort over impression, it has visually, and in some social way, masculinized me.

KH: I think that femmes have always had a problem being visually coded.

The butch women that I desire do not recognize me as femme unless I am in a lesbian bar.

MD: Do you think they assume you're straight?

KH: Definitely.

MD: I think they assume I'm a dyke. . . . Butch lesbians do eye signals with me in public "straight" places like airports, but I know that they don't know what they are seeing—they think they may be seeing a butch lesbian.

KH: Do you think they are eyeing you in a sexual way?

MD: No, as a comrade.

KH: Speaking of butch-femme visual codes, do you have any femme strategies for finding butches in a visual culture that simply defines butch as "masculinized"? For example, many lesbians write and talk about *Thelma and Louise* as butch and femme icons, but I have a hard time finding the butch or femme in that duo.

MD: I thought the person who was most attractive in *Thelma and Louise* was Brad Pitt, and I've known a lot of women who look like him. The woman that I was in love with when I was younger looked like Brad Pitt.

KH: Femmes never talk about their own desire for butch icons.

MD: My lovers, particularly in the sixties and seventies, would have thought it was perfectly normal for me to notice young men in the movies because they were more like butches. My lovers would have expected that. . . . If I went to the movies with a butch and said, "Oh, I'm so attracted to [the female movie star]," she would have said, "What are you, queer?" [laughter]

I think femmes are afraid to talk about it because these are men. On the other hand, they are very feminine looking men who have an androgynous quality about them. That's something we are attracted to—that interesting mix of masculine and feminine. Because we're lesbians we're turned off by the man, yet, we're attracted to a bit of the . . . "maleness," not the "manness."

KH: As long as they don't take off their shirt it won't break the illusion. . . .

MD: And certainly not their pants! [laughter]

KH: Speaking of clothing, what are you wearing to your wedding?

MD: We're wearing matching white silk outfits . . . and purple vests and yarmulkes that will match.

KH: Are you and your lover not wearing a dress and a tux respectively because you think it replicates heterosexuality or because it is just not who Madeline Davis is as a femme?

MD: My lover wanted to wear a tux, but I really didn't want her to wear one. I thought it was a bit too much play acting for us. I think that it's not too much play acting for some couples, but I do think that it is for us because our visual image in the world is not that dissimilar from each other.

KH: This suggests that butch and femme are not reducible to visual codes. What makes your girlfriend butch to your femme?

MD: She whines more than I do! [laughter] I know, you're asking about the visual differences. Well, I seem to care more about adornments like jewelry, make-up, particular types of clothing. She doesn't wear jewelry except for a ring, and she'd die before she would wear make-up. We also wear our clothing differently. She wears sleeveless undershirts. I wear bras. I wear skirts, she doesn't. Even if we wear the same clothing we look quite different. Our body language, the walk, the stance. Hers are all masculine; mine are clearly a practiced feminine. There is also an attitude difference. She treats me with a certain delicacy, a carefulness that she might find insulting if I showed it to her. She opens doors, carries packages. I am capable of doing those things, but I love it that she does them. On the other hand, I am more emotionally careful of her. I think most of the butches I have known have a fragility that may derive from a lifetime of alienation.

Femme Sexuality

KH: In "Forever Femme," you write about desiring a woman who wears a mini-skirt and fishnet stockings. . . .

MD: She haunts me. I have never touched her. Actually, I have touched her in my dreams, but I have always been afraid of her because in some ways she is me. . . . My sudden intense desire for her at that moment makes me feel so incredibly "queer." I've talked to Joan Nestle about this and she has spoken to me about some incidences in her life in which she has broken through that barrier and has touched a woman who is very feminine and is of "our" gender. And, in many ways it was very satisfying for her, but ultimately it was not what she could live with.

KH: Have all your lovers been butch?

MD: I had one lover who was not butch. She was my lover for ten years, and she is now one of my best friends. She is very butch looking, very butch acting . . . she is a carpenter, she has hair a quarter of an inch long, and she's got wonderful muscles, but she is not butch. . . . I drove us both crazy looking for the butch I was sure was in there.

KH: What makes her not butch?

MD: Well, sexually she was not butch. That was a major issue. I tried so hard to get her to be butch—the key didn't fit! It was so sad. And, at that point I was not into s/m so I had nothing to even vaguely substitute for it, like a top mindset which I have now.

KH: When you speak of having a top mindset, are you speaking of sexually being a top?

MD: I am speaking sexually. I am a sexual dominant, and that doesn't mean I don't like being made love to—I do. But s/m sexuality means that a power differential is set up that is for everyone's benefit. . . . The parties simply have different kinds of power.

    As a top I get what I want by saying, "This is what I want." [laughter] It is very up front, it is very clear. And, I expect to get it, there is no question. If my lover has a problem with that, I am open to discussion, but I have a particular set of expectations that are set up ahead of time.

KH: Do you give them a second chance? [laughter]

MD: Yeah, but I'm not sure about a third! [laughter] It is not as though things are not negotiable, of course they are. . . . In one way it is a style. In the morning I make my lover coffee. On the other hand, if I say, "This needs to be put away," she puts it away.

KH: Is sex for you always involved in s/m?

MD: Well, top/bottom is something you are, but it doesn't always have to be something you do. I think our dynamic is always polarized that way, although we don't engage in s/m "play" all of the time.

KH: Does a more dynamic or creative kind of sexuality lead to more frequency?

MD: It certainly can, but for me, some of this has to do with the aging process and the fact that I am going through menopause. . . . One of the things this means to me is that my desire level has lowered a little bit—not a lot, but a little bit. I also think that because I am in a relationship that is extremely secure, my desire has lowered. . . . I think in the past my sexual needs were often driven by insecurity.

KH: That puts a twist on supposed "lesbian bed death." For your life, not having as much sex has something to do with aging, but also with security. This is interesting because these days lesbians, for good reason, place so much emphasis on sex. Do you think lesbians are having more sex?

MD: I don't think we're having more sex, but I think we're talking about it an awful lot . . . because we're very curious. We are as curious about ourselves as heterosexuals are. All this business about "Don't ask me how I got this way. What difference does it make how I got to be a lesbian? Did anyone ever ask you how you got to be heterosexual?"—is bullshit. We're all curious; we all want to know how we got to be a part of this minority.

KH: In "Forever Femme" you write about giving a butch her gender. Many femmes write about butches giving them their bodies. Was this the case for you?

MD: I think so, in the beginning. My first long-term relationship truly put me in touch with my sexuality. . . . But I also learned a lot about butch sexuality from her . . . I learned just how far they could be pushed, how they could be satisfied without going over that line that would somehow undermine or destroy their own sense of butchness.

KH: Do you think that there is a stone barrier that exists within all butches that femmes know how to break through?

MD: I don't think that stone barrier exists in all butches. I think that many butches have trouble being vulnerable. But, having been up against that stone barrier, it's different . . . I also think that there have been an awful lot of femmes who have not learned how to properly make love to butches. I think that butches have been reticent to teach them, and that femmes have not been able to learn because they haven't had a support system.

KH: At this point in your life would you be able to have a stone butch partner?

MD: Absolutely not. Not anymore. Not that I don't have ultimate respect for it, but I need to be with someone I can make love to. I cannot be with someone who will not let me touch her. I am a lesbian. Part of being a lesbian, for me, means making love to women.

KH: What about femmes who are not tops, or femmes who are with stone butches? Are they lesbians?

MD: Many femmes are not tops. Butch/femme and top/bottom are not correlated at all. Are femme bottoms lesbians? Absolutely.

KH: Why do you think that stone butches, women who may not want to be on the receiving end of sex, are always perceived as lesbians, but femmes who don't want to "top" women easily fall into the category of heterosexuality?

MD: Because we only have the heterosexual model, which says that the straight woman lies on her back and has things done to her. . . . I think that's untrue, but that's what the model says. We have also come to believe the converse, which is just as false.

KH: Do you have any femme tips regarding sexuality that you want to share?

MD: I think it is tough to make love to butches. I think it is an art. . . . In terms of sexuality you have to be willing to listen, watch, and hone your senses to a fine edge, listen to the body.

KH: What about tips for butches?

MD: If you want your femme to please you, don't hide yourself from her, give her as many clues as you possibly can manage. If you want to please your femme, adore her, worship her, give her everything she wants and deserves. [laughter]

KH: I think that's a perfect place to end!

Notes

1. Madeline D. Davis, Amber Hollibaugh, and Joan Nestle, "The Femme Tapes," from *The Persistent Desire: A Femme-Butch Reader,* ed. Joan Nestle (Boston: Alyson Publications, Inc., 1992), and Elizabeth Lapovsky Kennedy and Madeline D. Davis, *Boots of Leather, Slippers of Gold: The History of a Lesbian Community* (New York: Penguin Books, 1994).

"ARTICULATE SILENCE[S]"
Femme Subjectivity and Class
Relations in *The Well of Loneliness*

Leslie J. Henson

Femmes are women who have made choices, but we need to be able to
read between the cultural lines to appreciate their strength.

—Joan Nestle[1]

In her biography of her life partner Radclyffe Hall, Una Troubridge
describes how Hall came to her and asked her permission to write *The
Well of Loneliness*, thereby exposing both Troubridge and herself to possible "condemnation." Troubridge claims to have replied "without so much
as an instant's hesitation: I told her to write what was in her heart, that so far
as any effect upon myself was concerned, I was sick to death of ambiguities,
and only wished to be known for what I was and to dwell with her in the
palace of truth."[2] Troubridge's words here manifest, in Joan Nestle's phrasing, "some of the enduring aspects of femme power."[3] Particularly, I would
add, the power to self-define as a lesbian. Even knowing that "it would open
their lives to turmoil and worse,"[4] Troubridge made the choice to urge Hall
to publish the book now considered one of the most historically significant
works of lesbian literature. Throughout her relationship with Hall,
Troubridge showed similar courage by dressing in clothing coded as feminine
when she was to appear with the more masculinely attired Hall. In this way,
she made herself visible as Hall's sexual partner, as what we would now call a

femme lesbian.[5] Given that turn-of-the-century sexologists equated true "sexual" lesbianism with the masculine woman's gender "inversion,"[6] for Troubridge to claim the power to self-define as a lesbian was a significant act.

In contrast to Troubridge's strong femme choices, Hall's important lesbian text colludes with the sexologists by marginalizing femme lesbian desire and agency. The dominant claim of the text is that the upper-class masculine invert alone represents the entire class of suffering inverts.[7] The novel does indeed construct a "palace of truth." However, it is one which includes the poor, working-class, and/or femme lesbian only as, in the words of the text's final scene, an "articulate silence." Yet if we follow Nestle's suggestion and "read between the [textual] lines," some representation of femme "strength" does indeed emerge. By using a femme critical framework in conjunction with a class analysis, my essay explores how the text dismisses, produces, and sacrifices femme desire and femme agency in the process of elevating the upper-class butch.

The text begins with a working-class woman, Angela Crossby, whose desire for the aristocratic butch, Stephen Gordon, the text dismisses as a product of Angela's class status rather than femme agency. Yet by "read[ing] between the lines," we can see how the text undermines itself by producing in the middle of the novel a strong portrait of femme desire and agency in the character Mary Llewellyn. However, at the end of the text, femme desire and agency are sacrificed to the dominant claim. By rejecting Mary, the upper-class Stephen imitates the suffering of Jamie and Barbara, an impoverished butch-femme couple, and thereby becomes the representative invert.

The opening of the novel sexualizes and dismisses Stephen's first femme lover, Angela Crossby, primarily for her working-class status. The text uses Angela's working-class status to explain away this feminine woman's willingness to experiment sexually and romantically with Stephen. In the novel, by means of her class, Angela comes to represent the by now all-too-familiar stereotype of the faux femme, the feminine woman who gets involved with other women but isn't "really" a lesbian. As a feminine woman, Angela is not supposed to experience active sexual desire, especially for another woman. Yet as a working-class woman who has taken jobs as a dancer and a prostitute in order to survive, she is also constructed as sexually promiscuous. Indeed, Angela embodies the classist stereotype of "working-class sexual amorality," as opposed to the asexuality ascribed to bourgeois women.[8] When Stephen confesses her passion for Angela, the text offers a classic sexological denial of femme desire. Thus, Angela allows herself to be swept away only because "Stephen's need was now hers, by sheer force of its blind and uncomprehending will to appeasement."[9] The text then uses Angela's class-based sexual "amorality" to claim that Angela allows the affair to continue not out of actual lesbian desire. Rather, she is motivated by "boredom" (147), the desire for "power" (147), "self-pity" (177), and, late in the affair, the need to throw her husband off the scent of her other extramarital affair with a man. In this way, Angela's working-class status is used to dismiss her as a faux femme who goes through the lesbian motions but isn't actually a lesbian.

In contrast to this depiction of Angela at the beginning of the novel, the middle of Hall's text produces a portrait of femme desire and femme agency. Reading against the novel's sexological discourse, we can see strong femme desire and agency in the character Mary Llewellyn. Echoing the sexologists, the text attempts to silence Mary's femme desire by claiming that Mary is "unconscious" of her "fundamental" sexual motivations towards Stephen (297). However, a femme critical framework allows us to see active femme desire in the scene in which Mary admires Stephen in the mirror, "noticing the strong, thin line of her thighs; noticing too the curve of her breasts— slight and compact, but of a certain beauty" (321). The sexologists might read this lustfully appreciative view of Stephen as Stephen's fantasy, since the description occurs while Stephen is watching Mary watch Stephen in the mirror. However, a femme reading recognizes the way in which Mary's gaze lingers on the "certain beauty" of Stephen's butch body. Mary savors the way Stephen's body combines "strong, thin" masculine "line[s]" with "curve[s]." While Stephen's body represents the butch who visibly usurps masculine "lines," Mary's *appears* to reproduce traditional gendered values when in the very act of lusting after another woman's body. Femme desire, it would seem, sees its love object but can't always be seen by the regulatory discourses that privilege the upper-class butch.

In the immediately preceding scene, Mary "[lays] her hand upon Stephen's knee" (297), "imprison[s] [Stephen's] nervous fingers in her own" (297), and asks Stephen to kiss her good-night (299). She then tells Stephen that she wants this kiss "'[m]ore than anything else in the world'" (299). After this, Stephen reveals herself to Mary as an invert who has been stamped with the invert's gendered "mark" (301), and the two women consummate their relationship. Contrary to the dominant claim that the upper-class masculine invert stands alone, these descriptions clearly indicate strong femme desire and femme agency. Mary knows what she wants—sexual intimacy with Stephen—and is not afraid to act on her desire. Like Una Troubridge, Mary is "sick to death of [sexual] ambiguity," and takes action to remedy that ambiguity.

From a critical femme perspective, Mary's passionate sexual feelings and assertive actions towards Stephen clearly indicate femme desire rather than

working-class "amorality." After Stephen and Mary become lovers, Stephen
is forced by her mother's homophobia to visit her ancestral home without
bringing Mary. Mary responds to the situation by writing a letter which
exemplifies femme desire and agency. The text describes the letter as "full of
many things which a less privileged pen had best left unwritten—loyalty,
faith, consolation, devotion" (338). The text thus indicates its alignment with
a "pen" other than Mary's. Yet the text also enables us to see Mary's writing
as based in desire for her female other, and hence as constructing an implicitly shared lesbian subject position. Mary's letter demonstrates the power of
femme desire in that it enables her to defeat "the world's first onslaught"
(338) on herself and Stephen by asserting lesbian desire in the face of aristocratic homophobia. In contrast to the dismissal of Angela, it is this
"onslaught" that appears morally problematic, not Mary's "loyalty, faith,
consolation, [and] devotion." Moreover, in coming from a woman whom
the sexologically-minded narrator designates as a "perfect woman" (314),
Mary's desire cannot be attributed to a biological or psychological error in
gender programming. Rather, it threatens the upper-class equation of masculinity with active desire, the equation of femininity with passivity and lack
of desire. Thus, the letter suggests that Mary's femme identity is a sexual one.

In the novel, unabashed femme desire troubles upper-class heterosexual
interests by encouraging the upper-class butch to rebel against the norms of
aristocratic womanhood. The femme lesbian's validation of butch masculinity—or what Pat Califia calls "the butch phallus"[10]—threatens to undo
upper-class gender constructs that ensure the perpetuation of aristocratic
privilege for the "legitimate" heirs.[11] Unlike Mary, representatives of the
upper-class social order perceive Stephen's butch body as monstrous. Lady
Anna, for example, sees Stephen's body as "a caricature of Sir Phillip
[Stephen's father]; a blemished, unworthy, maimed reproduction" (15).
Along with Stephen's inability to fit into the upper-class heterosexual social
scene, Lady Anna's perception demonstrates that the butch body is cast as a
"maimed reproduction" precisely because it threatens to "maim reproduction," the reproduction of upper-class bodies and traditional gender values.

Mary voices her resistance to upper-class gender values when Stephen says,
using the biologically deterministic terms of sexology, that she is an invert,
and that the world (upper-class society) scorns love such as theirs. Mary
replies, "'What do I care for the world's opinion? What do I care for anything but you, and you just as you are'" (312). It is only after this declaration
of femme desire for the butch woman "just as [she is]" that Stephen and
Mary are able to consummate their relationship. Mary's femme agency frees

the couple from the constraints of Stephen's aristocratic conscience and the sexological discourse which would deny the femme her active sexual desire. Femme agency thus allows the aristocratic butch to complete her rebellion against the norms of upper-class womanhood.

By the end of the novel, however, the text sacrifices femme desire and agency in order to allow Stephen to embody the moral values of an upper-class gentleman. Out of what the text presents as a noble, chivalric desire to save Mary from leading the low-class, dissipated life of the Parisian invert,[12] Stephen lies that she is having an affair with another woman. Mary then rushes, as Stephen had planned, into the waiting arms of a man, Martin Hallam. The text thus transforms the femme lesbian's desire for the butch into a pathetic displacement of every "normal" woman's desire for a "'real man'" (315). By presenting Stephen's lie to Mary towards the end of the novel as a noble one, the text takes away Mary's femme agency as well, denying her the right to choose to stay with Stephen. The text thus rewrites Mary's authorship of a shared lesbian subject position based on "loyalty, faith, consolation, devotion." Through this capitulation to upper-class heterosexual mores, Mary's self-authored lesbian femme identity is reduced to "an articulate silence . . . a jibing, grimacing, vindictive silence" (435). Stephen "brushe[s] aside [this silence] with a sweep of her hand" so that she can articulate *her* version of lesbian identity as necessarily coexistent with the aristocratic butch body (435).

This sacrifice of the femme allows the aristocratic Stephen to represent the suffering of "starvation poor" (358) lesbians. The deaths of the femme, Barbara MacDonald, and her lover, Jamie, at the end of the novel are used to support the text's dominant claim, its elevation of the upper-class masculine invert. The text claims that Barbara's death from double pneumonia and Jamie's subsequent suicide stemmed solely from factors related to their sexuality. Thus, the text de-emphasizes the economic determinants of these deaths, for example, the drafty apartment in which the two women lived, and their inability to afford "smart English doctors" (359). Once Barbara's and Jamie's deaths have been attributed to inversion alone, Stephen's rejection of Mary allows her to mimic Jamie's suicide, and thus to speak as a representative of the class of suffering inverts. The text describes how Stephen, in pushing Mary away, wounds herself (430–31). This self-wounding culminates in the lie to Mary that entails Stephen's metaphorical suicide: "Stephen Gordon was dead; she had died last night" (435). Through her metaphorical suicide, Stephen creates a discourse of identity that blurs class differences enough to allow "millions" of suffering inverts—but not the Mary

Llewellyn—to "become articulate through" Stephen in her final vision (437). As Nestle argues, the dismissal of Mary enables the text "to make a plea for greater understanding of the [noble masculine] deviant's plight."[13]

In the end, this cross-class discourse of lesbian identity privileges not just the butch's experience, but the *aristocratic* butch's experience, simultaneously marginalizing femme and working-class/poor lesbians. The erasure of Mary's femme desire and agency enables the text to marginalize working-class and poor lesbians by providing evidence that the emotional and moral aspects of sexuality-based oppression are primary. At one point, the text claims that even the material fact of Barbara's death is "as nothing" to the "shame" that stigmatizes homosexual unions (401). It thus emphasizes the emotional issues that Stephen finds the most fundamentally oppressive aspect of her inversion. Yet just as the text contradicts itself through its depiction of femme desire and femme agency, it undermines itself by maintaining the material, class-related determinants of Barbara's and Jamie's deaths as "*articulate* silences." By describing the material factors responsible for Barbara's and Jamie's deaths, Hall's text implies that it is upper-class moral codes that produce Stephen's pain, since it is her adherence to these codes (and not poverty) which finally separates her from her femme lover.

Thus, in *The Well of Loneliness*, the silencing/appropriation of class-based suffering travels hand in hand with the rejection of femme desire and femme agency. This double exclusion is replicated in the work of theorists of butch-femme such as Judith Butler and Sue-Ellen Case when they ignore the "raced" and "classed" material contexts in which butch-femme statements are made in order to celebrate a deconstruction of gender that the femme can participate in only when authorized by a butch.[14] In such theory, as in *The Well of Loneliness*, a notion of lesbianism that privileges the butch plays into the hands of upper-class, male-dominant interests. It is therefore crucial to reread traditional lesbian texts from a femme perspective in order to work against the relegation of lesbian femmes to second-class status in lesbian theories and communities. Just as importantly, critics need to extend our awareness of the larger systems of oppression we further when we perpetuate the symbolic banishment of lesbian desire from feminine women's bodies.[15]

Notes

I would like to thank Victorian scholar and class theorist Mary Ann Leiby for her insights on the role played by class in Hall's text. Without her discernment, editing, and friendship, this article could not have been written.

1. Joan Nestle, "The Femme Question," from *The Persistent Desire: A Femme-Butch Reader,* ed. Joan Nestle (Boston: Alyson, 1992) 141.

2. Una Troubridge, *The Life of Radclyffe Hall* (New York: Arno Press, 1975) 82.

3. Joan Nestle, "Flamboyance and Fortitude: An Introduction," from *The Persistent Desire* 15.

4. Nestle, *The Persistent Desire* 144.

5. Katrina Rolley, "Cutting A Dash: The Dress of Radclyffe Hall and Una Troubridge," *Feminist Review* 35 (1990): 56.

6. Esther Newton, "The Mythic Mannish Lesbian: Radclyffe Hall and the New Woman," from *Hidden From History: Reclaiming the Gay and Lesbian Past*, eds. Martin Duberman, Martha Vicinus, and George Chauncey, Jr. (New York: Penguin, 1989) 288.

7. See Newton 289–293; also see Sonja Ruehl, "Inverts and Experts: Radclyffe Hall and the Lesbian Identity," from *Feminism, Culture, and Politics*, eds. Rosalind Brunt and Caroline Rowan (London: Lawrence and Wishart, 1982) 20–23. Ruehl analyzes the role played by class in determining the relative meanings of "butch" and "femme" in the novel.

8. The quotation is from P.J. Keating, *The Working Classes in Victorian Fiction* (London: Routledge and Kegan Paul, 1971) 187. See Newton 291 for a discussion of the construction of bourgeois women as asexual.

9. Radclyffe Hall, *The Well of Loneliness* (New York: Doubleday, 1990) 146. All parenthetical page numbers are from this text.

10. Pat Califia, *Public Sex: The Culture of Radical Sex* (Pittsburgh: Cleis, 1994) 180.

11. For a description of the role played in nineteenth-century aristocratic marriages by strictures concerning reproduction and the transfer of property, see Joan Perkin's *Women and Marriage in Nineteenth-Century England* (Chicago: Lyceum, 1989) 50.

12. Ruehl 24-26. Ruehl argues that Stephen's lie exemplifies a "class-bound . . . *noblesse oblige*" (26), and that Stephen views the Parisian invert bar culture from which she supposedly rescues Mary "from a definite [upper-] class position" (25).

13. Nestle, *The Persistent Desire* 144.

14. See Lisa Walker, "How to Recognize a Lesbian: The Cultural Politics of Looking Like What You Are," *Signs* 18.4 (1993): 866–890. Also see Carole-Anne Tyler, "Boys Will Be Girls: The Politics of Gay Drag," in *Inside/Out: Lesbian Theories, Gay Theories*, ed. Diana Fuss (New York: Routledge, 1991) 53–58. Walker analyzes femme invisibility as it relates to race in Butler's and Case's butch-femme performance theories of the late eighties and early nineties. Tyler examines the lack of attention to race and class in these same theories.

15. An example of such banishment: a femme friend of mine told me as I was working on this article that she had been chastised by another lesbian for "dressing heterosexual."

MYSTERIES, MOTHERS, AND COPS
An Interview with Mabel Maney

Laura Harris and Liz Crocker

Author of the Nancy Clue mysteries *The Case of the Not-So-Nice Nurse* and *The Case of the Good-For-Nothing Girlfriend* as well as the Hardly Boys mystery *A Ghost in the Closet* and numerous short story publications, Mabel Maney began her career as an artist and bookmaker. We met Mabel one sunny afternoon in San Francisco, and after an unsatisfactory salad experience, we retired to a friend's flat where we might more comfortably unravel the mysteries of this femme novelist. Mabel, whose large blue eyes and translucent complexion merit mention, reminisced about growing up in Ohio, coming out in a lesbian-feminist setting, moving to San Francisco, and her new career as a novelist. As an originally nervous—but graciously mannered—Mabel relaxed and our conversation progressed, it became clear why she is achieving such success as a writer. Not only were the three of us in the room, but we could have sworn that Cherry, Midge, Velma, and Nancy were sitting right next to us, as Mabel's intimacy with and devotion to her characters made them palpably visible.

On Writing, Class, and Nancy's Transformation

LC: When I read your books, I understood them as butch-femme romances. I was surprised when I spoke to other people and they didn't have the same reaction—they just saw them as mystery spoofs. So when you are putting the books out there do you think that people are going to read these and think about butch-femme?

MM: I think of them as romances disguised as mysteries. I think all the romances are between butches and femmes because that is my primary personal interest. [laughter] Especially Midge and Velma. They are my favorite favorite favorite couple ever in the world. They are my dream couple, so that's why I write about them.

LH: I would add to Liz's question that there are codes that some people are going to pick up on and some aren't. When you are writing, are you thinking about the butch-femme codes—that you are putting out a code that only a certain kind of subculture is going to pick up on?

MM: Oh, absolutely. And I think the books are also as much about class as they are about those butch-femme codes. I have met people who say, "Oh, Nancy [Clue] can't be a butch, because she wears a dress." But I see her as definitely a butch. She is a sort of upper-class butch; she conforms to her culture. Although she is not Cherry's butch—she is not the kind of butch I think Cherry needs—which I think is really about class.

LH: You speak about Nancy and Cherry as not really being meant for each other and yet there is some sort of dynamic between them. They are from different classes so it seems to be a power dynamic. What do you think about power between butches and femmes, differences that are difficult to negotiate, and at the same time cause the passion?

MM: Right, that's a great question—how many hours do we have? The complicated dynamic between Cherry and Nancy is that they are from different classes and that they are used to different things. How that class privilege has made Nancy behave in the world is really the problem, more than the fact that she has access to more junk. I like to make little jokes about her consumption behavior. There's a scene in the third book where someone goes into the garage to get something and Nancy describes it as behind the powerboat next to her skis. Nancy's like a living Barbie, she has all these things. And Cherry doesn't have all these things, and Cherry has to work, and in fact loves to work. But the problem is how her class privilege has taught Nancy to behave as a human being. Her level of expectation is always too high, and she is used to being paid attention to—she acts as if the world owes her.

And really, on some level, I feel like the issues of class that I am writing about with Nancy have a lot to do with both my own economic background and with what I see going on in this country's division into corporate

America and the serving class. So, in my books, Cherry is a giver and Nancy is a taker, and that is what I feel like is happening in the culture is that some people are such selfish takers. . . . Sometimes I will write Nancy as the epitome of a selfish taker and then she is much too extreme. She really is a nice girl, but I get so angry with how much people think that they need, and how much they are taking from everybody, that I sort of dump it on Nancy.

LC: So how does Cherry being a "giver" factor in here?

MM: Cherry is the other extreme. I like to think that people would read Cherry and not behave like her, but she is also really adorable and darling. The thing is, who would you rather have on your side? Someone who errs on the side of being a little too giving, or someone who's incredibly selfish? So that is how I feel today's culture informs how we feel about these two characters.

LH: I think that is interesting; when I think about or write about butch-femme, class is a central issue. Butch-femme is certainly played out differently in different class cultures. For instance, that movie "Bar Girls" portrayed lipstick lesbians who seemed to be upper middle class, and the only butch portrayed is working class, dumb, slow, and Southern. That's such a stereotype which is not true; we all know there is such diversity.

LC: And the butch in that movie seduces a straight girl, right?

LH: But of course they are the only lesbian couple that lasts . . . [laughter]

LC: So—back to your books—why do you set these books in a mythic fifties? Why create this whole butch-femme universe where there are no lesbians who are not butch-femme, and then everyone in the world is either butch or femme or a housewife or a husband or a villain. Why do that—is there a kind of nostalgia there for something, or is it a creation, a fantasy?

MM: One reason for the setting is that it is just a mimicry of the originals; keeping it in the fifties keeps this layer of innocence that you could never have now. Let's take the character of Lauren, who is sixteen years old. In the fifties, a sixteen-year-old was innocent, still a child. There is no way that a ten-year-old would be that innocent today. So I wanted to be able to keep that sort of wide-eyed optimistic post-war attitude. Cherry would just be stupid today, but set in the fifties, she's just innocent.

There's another reason why everything is broken down into butch-femme couples. As a friend of mine said, to read these books, you just have to be willing to enter Mabel's brain for a while. She said, "These books are about your little world." I think that that's true, and in my little romantic world, everyone is a butch or a femme.

LH: In relation to your work, why Nancy Drew? How does she fit into this fifties romantic butch-femme culture?

MM: She is everyone's chum for that time. For many women my age, and I am in my late thirties, Nancy Drew was their favorite reading experience as a girl. Though there are people who have said that Nancy Drew ruined children's literature. I can see that—they are not very well written, and they are very predictable. And the early Nancy Drews are very racist and very classist and very judgmental. So there are a lot of problems with them, which I think that I address. I try to take the best of them—particularly the idea that there is this exciting world of girls who have this incredible freedom, and they're smart, and people respect them, and they give them all this power, and they get to go home and put on nice clothes. It's perfect!

LC: Recently, I looked at an original Nancy Drew book, and I realized that reading your books has changed the way that I see the original series. For example, there is a whole romance between Nancy and her father in the original books that seems really terrifying after reading your books where you depict their relationship as incestuous.

MM: Absolutely, I feel that there is a very incestuous subtext in the original Nancy Drew books. Her mother is dead and Nancy is paired with her father in a curious way.

LH: So were you originally interested in the Nancy Drew books because you wanted to write about this incestuous subtext?

MM: Well, I originally started looking at them because I am a book artist and I was doing work about my mother. See, I am very strongly identified with my mother. As a kid, I was just in love with my mother. My mother looks like Doris Day and she was one of those fifties-sixties-blonde-tan-little-white-linen-dress type of femmes. Very very femme. Cocktail parties, long nails, cocktail rings. I was very enamored of my mother; I thought of her as a movie-star type, very very glamorous, very very femme. And I started looking at materials that I read as a kid, or my mother would have read. I started thinking about my relationship with my mother and how she taught me about being feminine, about being a girl. It has always been a sore spot because my mother thinks I am very butch. She considers me some aberration of femininity.

LH: That's funny, my mother also sees me as not properly feminine.

MM: Which I think is very shocking. My mother thinks I am butch? God! But she does. She has a very narrow view of femininity. So I started looking at original source materials, and thinking about what I read as a kid, and what

I learned about being a girl. I started thinking about the idea of the missing mother in girl's literature. That brought me to Nancy. Her father is described as being young and handsome but he never dates, and her mother has been dead forever. There is someone else in the house but she is a servant, she is an older woman, and so essentially Nancy functions as her father's partner. And that is when I started thinking that there was an incestuous undertone.

LC: So then how does the Cherry Aimless character fit in?

MM: Well, at the same time, I was also reading the Cherry Ames books, the nursing books, which are written in the forties to get girls to want to be war nurses . . . I read them and I want to become a nurse. They are extremely stirring, and it is this wonderful world of women who are described in luscious detail. . . . They use this sort of uniform fetish to attract girls, and I have this uniform fetish, so I thought—oh! perfect!—these two should meet. Cherry is very very femme, she is a working-class femme. Nancy is this symbol of pure American girlhood, and I really wanted to subvert that somehow. That is when I decided that they would meet and fall in love. And the thing is that of course they are not meant for each other. They are just not. There's no way. So, in the end, my books are really spoofs of lesbian romance. They are really spoofs of all *my* romances. [laughter] That is why no one ever gets to have sex in them, because . . . hey, I am first in line! [laughter]

Competent, Lapsed, And Other Femmes

LC: What does it mean to write as a femme, or to publicly identify as a femme who is writing? When I read that interview of you in the *Advocate,* I noticed that you clearly identified as a femme writer. That's something that you don't see that often—we know that from working on this anthology.

MM: Right, you don't. It is a new thing for me to say that I am a femme. But I have always known it, because I have always been teased about it. I think that a lot of people have been influenced by negative images of femininity so that they think that femme is limiting, but, for me, it's absolutely the opposite. But, even I am influenced by those concepts of femininity that say that femme is about appearance. So then I think that, well, I am a femme, but I would never wear a dress, unless it was to a funeral, and then only to a funeral in the Midwest. I feel like a really specific kind of femme.

Once again I question whether that's about being a femme, or whether that's about the zillions of other issues in my life, like class, education, background. Being a femme is a physical hormonal thing. It's really sometimes just that simple. But just on a gut level, if I walk into a room, I know exactly who I think I am attracted to, it is just very very clear. So on one level, it is really just about sexual attraction.

LH: One thing that I hear you saying is that in fact you can't really extricate femme from your class, education, and other experiences.

MM: Right, or life choices. I always say I am a competent femme, which I think has something to do with my background as an artist. I have been an artist for years and years and years. I have only been writing—well, I have been writing my whole life—but really writing seriously for about three years. So I am used to being an artist and being in shows where I always show up with my work in a big box, I always bring my tool kit because there's things you need when you get there (you don't want to be asking the gallery assistant to run around as if they were your servant). So I always say I am a competent femme; I know how to get things done. I know how to take an idea and make it work. That's my training as an artist for years, which has nothing to do with me being a femme. But that training and experience makes me a particular kind of femme that is very different from someone who perhaps doesn't want to build something.

LC: In terms of literary representation, there is often an emphasis on one ide-alized type of femme, "*the* femme," rather than a depiction of lots of different kinds of femmes. Is opening up femme to multiple definitions important to you?

MM: Absolutely. I used to not call myself a femme because I thought that I wasn't pretty enough to be a femme. I thought that a femme had to be very slender and tall and wear women's clothes whereas I only wear really good bras. I have this obsession with really good bras, but otherwise I just wear men's clothes. Absolutely. Although there's degrees. I have this friend who calls herself a lapsed femme. She's just tired of doing her hair, and she's get-ting messier. She says, "I just don't take care of myself like I used to." So she's a lapsed femme.

LH: Are your friends butch or femme identified?

MM: I have a lot of friends, especially from art school, who identify as androgynous. I have this friend; we look a lot alike. She'll come to my house and we'll be wearing the exact same clothes. We look like lesbian Mormon missionaries—black shoes, black pants, white shirt—we look like we should be standing on a corner handing out pamphlets. She always asks me, "What makes you femme and makes me butch?" And I ask her, "What are you wearing under your shirt?" She says, "I am wearing a t-shirt and no bra." And I tell her that I am wearing a nice push-up bra. Sometimes it's just the underwear.

LC: Is there a specific way you relate to femme friends, as opposed to other friends?

MM: Sure, femme-bonding. I have my androgynous friends, and they are fun to hang out with, and I have my boy friends, and they are fun to hang out with, but there are just specific days that I have got to be with another girly-girl, whether she's straight or lesbian. We can go downtown, maybe get our faces done, buy some make-up, have lunch, and look at the bras. I have girlfriends that I only go bra-shopping with, which is a whole afternoon down at Macy's.

LH: I saw the movie "Heavenly Creatures," and I loved the relationship between the two young girls. That was me as a teen-ager, I just loved other girls—how about you?

MM: Me too.

LC: Do you think that, as you grow older, the way you present yourself as femme will change?

MM: I am already planning for my older age. I am going to look very butch when I am older. I was in the line at the library, and there was this gorgeous older butch woman. I guess she must have been about seventy. And we started talking, because I immediately ran over to stand by her, she was so cute. She had been on ships her whole life, and she had this great crew cut, she was wearing overalls, and she showed me her little sailing card. She was just adorable. Sometimes elderly women look very frail to me but this one didn't. I just thought, I am going to wear overalls when I am seventy and cut all my hair off.

LH: You were describing yourself as a competent femme. Your character Cherry—although she can seem naive or muddled—is also very competent. She's certainly not weak. I think that you are breaking the stereotype of femme as disorganized and helpless.

MM: Certainly. If you fell down and twisted your ankle, you'd want Cherry at your side. I like to write these scenes where someone hurts themselves, and Cherry just goes [snap] do this do this do this—you make me a stretcher, you boil me some water, you get me an icepack. She doesn't even bother being polite. You've got to be smart to be a nurse.

LH: And you've got to be strong to be a femme.

MM: Absolutely, especially in this culture where to be a femme, or feminine, is not respected. I see images of idealized women who don't even look like any woman I know, and they are always on display, or they are victimized. In a way, this culture has ruined femininity. I have to divorce myself from how I really am a femme as opposed to the culture's notion of femininity, because it's so absurd.

My Mother, My Lipstick

LC: Every time I see you, you are wearing that red lipstick; is that a trademark?

MM: All the women in my family wear red lipstick. When we went to bury my grandmother—who was ninety-six—before we closed the coffin lid, someone said, "She's not wearing her lipstick!" So we did her lips before we buried her. When I'm out at a coffee shop, and I look down, and I see a lipstick imprint on my coffee cup, I think, my mother's here! It's a very adult female thing in my family to do, to wear lipstick. It's one of our few family traditions.

LH: So how does this familiar lipstick ritual work for you as a femme?

MM: Well, I know I am a femme because I want to be the only one in the couple wearing lipstick. [laughter] To me, that is the definition for me. Just for me.

LC: Lipstick?

MM: Yes, lipstick. I *admire* people who wear lipstick. I am always asking people what their brand is, or their color, but I can't date someone who wears lipstick. I also see femininity as being a source of power. And I don't know where all of that comes from, but I think it comes from my mother. I have the kind of mother—should I talk about my mother?

LC: Please do.

MM: I probably need to go put lipstick on first. [pause] Anyway, I have this great videotape of my mother. My mother had five children. She's Catholic, a nice Catholic woman, married young. And the videotape is of Easter Sunday, every year there's another one of us, with our little bonnets, with this ribbon, and we're carrying our little bunny rabbits, and we are going into our little Falcon to go to church. And every year my mother is pregnant, but she's got her hair done up in the beehive, big dark glasses, big red lipstick, and she's smoking a cigarette. My parents smoked so much, all our home movies look like smoking commercials.

LH: That's hilarious.

MM: Unbelievable. I think of my mother as very powerful, so, by association, I think of femininity as being a source of power. For example, if you're Catholic, as I am, and you go to Catholic school where all the nuns wear black, then black is a power color. Well, that's how I feel about lipstick. And my mother always says, "As long as my hair looks nice, and my lips are done, I feel good." And I feel the same way, I really do. So even if I am writing all week and I am still wearing my pajamas at eight o'clock each night when my roommates come home, when I go out, I have to put that lipstick on. So it does seem like this costume, in a way, but it also is very comforting.

LH: Maybe it's your ritual?

MM: Absolutely, like in that scene in "Thelma and Louise" where Louise is going to do her lips and then she throws her lipstick away, I wouldn't have thrown my lipstick away.

LH: You say, I want to wear the lipstick but I wouldn't want to kiss someone wearing lipstick. In some lesbian communities, it would be hard to say that or it wouldn't be well received. But you are very good about stating your specific desires.

MM: There is so much shame built into our culture, which is what shocked me when Newt Gingrich was talking about shame as a new way of controlling people. And I thought, shame *already* controls people.

And so I think that for women to not feel ashamed about wanting a specific thing is really important. It is great that people are writing about this, because when I came out, someone said to me, in all seriousness, "You can't be a lesbian unless you like to camp." I don't like to camp. My family never took me camping. I don't know how to camp. Can I still be a lesbian? So I came out in a particular period of time that did not celebrate difference and now I see that there are a huge variety of lesbians, and I am so very grateful. Because I think being a lesbian is about sex—not camping!

LH: It is about sex—and I would add, it is about specific kinds of lesbian sex. Specific butch-femme sexual practices often get erased as if it is all about style—one person wearing lipstick and one not—and then everything being equal again in the bedroom.

MM: Which I wouldn't even want that.

LH: No, you wouldn't want that. I wouldn't want that.

MM: No, absolutely not.

Butch-femme Romance

LC: How do you understand your specific desires as femme?

MM: I identify as a femme, and I only date butches; people give me a lot of flak for that. They say, "You should date femmes," and "There's lots of femmes."

LH: Why would you want to do that!?

MM: I know! I don't want to! As if it is bad to have that specific of a desire. I came out in the late seventies, and everyone was supposed to look the same, and no one was supposed to talk about class. Everyone was supposed to have the same desires, and the same history, and wear the same clothes, and want the same things, and it was *so* oppressive. And when I moved to San Francisco ten years ago, in 1985, the first thing I did was drive to Macy's and open a make-up account. I had all my stuff in my car and I took it to the parking garage, and went to the make-up counter, and opened an account and bought all this stuff. What I really wanted to do was wear make-up, and I didn't want to be given so much flak for it.

LH: Is that acceptance of your cosmetic fetish important to you?

MM: Yes—as I was just saying—in the seventies, we couldn't wear make-up because we couldn't look anything like the general culture. I understand that notion of everyone joining forces to fight the greater culture, but what happened is that we oppressed each other. I remember going places and someone would say, "You're not wearing lipstick, are you?" ... Within a butch-femme relationship, there is this allowance for difference, because you are really different, and the way you approach the world is different. I had this girlfriend who was a butch athlete, and she used to call me (this was our big joke) a "high maintenance unit," because I go to the hairdressers and I get my hair dyed. I will have no money, and I will still have to go get my hair dyed. And she could go to the barber shop and he would zip it off for five bucks. I find that very sexy—*very sexy*—to be different, but we were still both women.

LH: So do you think femme desire can be a desire for masculinity but a differently contoured masculinity? For example, we just watched "Rebel Without A Cause" in which Natalie Wood tells James Dean, "Oh, you're so tough, but you're sweet."

MM: Yes, I think you can compare femme desire to the desire in old romantic movies. . . . I am a big sucker for those really romantic movies, and you just want someone who is going to act like that, who is going to be stable, steady, and very romantic and very very warm all at the same time. I have found a lot of young butches who think they are butch, but they are just *mean*. It is about behavior; not just mimicking bad male behavior. . . . It seems in the general culture (in the straight culture, although I have a hard time talking about straight culture) men define themselves as opposed to women whereas butches define themselves *with* women.

LC: So it is not oppositional?

LH: But rather taking from masculinity what works or what is attractive.

MM: It's what the culture always says men are supposed to be which I never see. I don't see men treating women in that really sweet gentle reverent way at all! I always say I want a girl who can build me bookshelves. So there is this sense of physical ability and strength which is very culturally masculine. But there needs to be this sort of kindness too, that I don't see in this culture. I don't see men treating women with kindness. This sort of kindness—reverence—which is a very knowing kind of thing.

LH: The weird thing that happens in straight culture now is that you get these "sensitive guys" who are really unattractive. [laughter] Straight girls that I know say that they don't go for these sensitive guys.

MM: Yes. People don't understand that being butch is not being male. Women do masculinity so much better than men, and on some level, men do femininity better than women. Being masculine has nothing to do with being male, at all.

LH: So do you have a theory about male femmes?

MM: The Hardly Boys are very femme. In *The Ghost in the Closet*, you find out that their father was a woman who passed as a man, and he taught them everything about being men. Gender roles are so limiting, and there are ways of being that are so much more interesting, like femme or butch. In my third book, there are many more men, and there are male butch-femme relationships.

LH: On an entirely different note, you mentioned your bra collection earlier . . .

MM: Well, I have to say, I have very nice bosoms. I have the best collection of push-up bras on the West Coast, and also the best collection of men's shoes.

LH: So do you look for a butch who's into breasts?

MM: Absolutely. You'd have to be, or you couldn't go out with me. Bosoms, oh God, now I am embarrassed. I do appreciate people who are specific. If you know what you like, you should just say what you like, and you should get what you like. I really respect people who just put it out there, and say "this is what I want." I put in that personal ad [in the San Francisco gay newspaper], "looking for sweet butch 35 plus." And I mean sweet butch, over thirty-five. Not, "I am kind of butch and I am thirty-one." No. I mean, read the ad. It's really particular.

LC: So how do you write about specific desires from a femme sensibility?

MM: Someone said to me, "You have to write more about sex." My response is that most of us have had sex, and anyway, it is all the activity leading up to sex that's so much fun. It's the chase, the teasing, the flirting, and the anticipation that I think is much more fun, or just as fun, as the actual physical act. And between butches and femmes it's really fun. Let's go back to Midge and Velma for a minute. There's a teasing way Velma bosses Midge that's very sexual that she does in front of other people. But Velma will only go so far; she would never humiliate Midge in front of someone else. So there's this trust between them, an agreement that neither of them goes too far even though they have the capability.

LH: And now you've answered an old question we asked about how to negotiate a power dynamic in a butch-femme relationship, and I think you're right that butch-femme is really about a kind of trust, to reveal these specific desires and to trust someone else to have that power.

MM: And not to have someone use it against you. But I think that trust is a slow thing in building. I have been out with people and I didn't know what they were doing. No one had given me the rulebook. For all the whining we did in the seventies about how men treated women, I ask, how do we treat each other? Once I dated this supposedly "politically aware" woman—and this is years ago—who was incredibly mean to me. Ever since that experience, I understand that what is important is the quality of how you treat people in your life.

LC: So, when you are writing about Midge and Velma or your other characters, are you writing your own femme rulebook for the way you want relationships to work?

MM: Absolutely. When I write about relationships, it is my desire for those kind of good relationships to happen, not just for myself, but for women. I hear stories of women doing the most amazingly horrible things to each other. Do you watch Melrose Place, where everyone is living in that apartment complex and sleeping with each other?

LH: We watch it!

MM: I always say, this must be written by lesbians! My God, the people on that show have a romantic attention span of ten minutes. Maybe it is something that happens with age—you figure out how it is you want to be treated and therefore you realize that you'd better treat people this way. Because so few lesbians come out in their teen years, we miss that adolescent development. In some ways, we are teenagers in our twenties.

LH: So, any bad dating experiences you would like to share?

MM: Well, I went out with this extremely beautiful butch cop recently who brought a gun on our date. It was just too much! She was just the meanest woman I have ever met. It was nothing to do with her being butch, she was just a mean woman. Visually she was my ideal, a big strong woman. But I just got out of that car so damn fast. I think that weaponry on a first date is just a little much—handcuffs maybe, but not a gun! [laughter]

LC: So, if that is the example of the bad date, what would be your notion of good treatment?

MM: When I walk through the world as a femme, I find that people are so needy. I want there to be a place where I can be taken care of. Even if it's on a physical level, I want to know that somebody can take care of me, or someone is willing to take care of me. That's why I always say that my next girlfriend is going to be someone who can build me bookshelves. Well, I can build bookshelves, but I want someone to want to do that for me.

LC: And for butches, I feel that in a lot of places you don't have the ability to make things work out well, for yourself or for other people. So if there is a place where someone is saying, "You're taking care of me, you're doing something that I can do for myself, but I'd rather you do it for me" then that's really great. It's not a feeling of being in control, but of feeling that you can fulfill someone's needs.

MM: One of the best things about butch-femme is that you have a role where you are needed. And I think that once you get home, that you should be needed, and appreciated for who it is and what it is you are. I like the idea of "playing house." When I came out in the way back when—feminist-lesbian era—we weren't supposed to play house anymore. The thing is that I want to play house.

LH: And play it, not have to live it in this oppressive way, but play it, have fun with it.

MM: Exactly, in a campy way. Gay men have such a great camp tradition, and lesbian culture doesn't seem to have such a tradition, which is just the ability to make fun of yourself. For example, when Nancy opens her purse, there's a flashlight and a bag of oranges and chocolate bars and a gallon of milk in there. That's where a femme tradition—keeping her secrets in her purse, or her purse as a source of power—is really pushed to the limit, and made a little silly.

LC: Exactly. We were talking about "playing house" which is where butch-femme gets campy. Even though it's a game that you play, it is very serious—and significant—erotically and personally.

MM: Sometimes I think it must be harder to be a butch woman in this world than a femme woman.

LH: Maybe in an everyday sense, but certainly butches and femmes feel different kinds of pain.

MM: But it's all pain, which is why we have to take really good care of one another.

LC: What I like about your books—that I also find in my own life—is that butch-femme is not just roles played only within romantic relationships but is important to lots of different kinds of relationships. For instance, the way that I interact with many different people, whether male or female friends, or in a relationship is part of butch-femme role-playing and identity. This happens also in your books; Cherry and Midge have that dynamic going on, but they are not a couple.

MM: Absolutely, the friendship between Midge and Cherry is really important.

LC: So it is a whole system of relationality, rather than just a way that you have sex, or *as well as* a way that you have sex.

LH: Look at us working on this anthology . . . [laughter]

LC: It's a good cop–bad cop thing.

MM: Don't even talk about cops!

DRESSES FOR MY ROUND BROWN BODY

Lisa Ortiz

Once I wore a tiny, frilly, shamrock-shake-green dress because it was so pretty. Forget that it was too tight to sit in and too short to keep from showing my "Monday" panties. I fantasized about being small and adored. Fawned over by teachers and kids alike. I felt pretty for exactly ten minutes before Larry Mac Donald called me a "tub-of-lard," successfully egging on other kids to join him and I ran home, feigning an illness that lasted until I thought everyone would forget.

I've always been eager to please. And even more eager not to disappoint. So with the exception of playing the boyfriend with my best girl friend at seven, I played the girl, the white girl: played with white Barbies; wore make-up, bikinis, nail polish; loved cats; wanted earrings so bad that I cried; hung out at the mall; and I wore dresses. See, I'm not one of the *machas*, never have been even in that first year out when I tried. I was never forced to wear dresses. Never had to take a stand to claim my Huskie Tuffskins. My whole life I've loved dresses and the frillier the better, but I wanted a little body to put in them.

My deepest thoughts do not escape my body. My round body, my strong body, my brown body, my femme body. My body that for so long belonged to no one, not even me. It was a disconnected thing. Divorced from both my emotions and my thoughts. It did what it was "supposed" to do even though no one ever came right out and said what that was. They didn't have to because I was a good girl and I had eyes and ears and was eager to please.

That eagerness is one reason why I kept my silence when in the fourth grade at a new school in a new town with a new stepfather by my mother's side, Lisa Mary Ortiz became Crandell, Lisa.

"Crandell, Lisa."

I almost didn't respond. I didn't know who she was for a moment. And for moments after my weak "Here," blood flooded my cheeks and ears hot as I made plans to set the teacher straight as soon as he finished taking role. The burning lasted all the way through the D's, E's, F's, G's, up to Ochoa, Rebecca, but when the teacher called, "Ortiz, Jimmy," my faced cooled with relief that I had been given this new name, this white name that set me far apart from the boy, Ortiz. At ten, the thought of being teased was enough to make me wish I was dead. Having crooked teeth was bad, but to be marked as the girlfriend of this Jimmy boy would surely have meant the end of me. I'd seen it happen once before at my old school. A new girl, Jeanette, cried and had to run home every day to escape the taunting.

"Oooh, Mr. and Mrs. Nichols!"

"I saw them kissing on the playground!"

"When are you gonna have a baby?"

Remembering this, I was grateful to my stepfather for having spared me a similar fate by hiding my name. But that's only because I was not aware of all that he had taken. And even now I'm not sure what was lost because Lisa Ortiz was aborted at age nine and replaced by Lisa Crandell. It's Lisa Crandell's life that I led and it's hard to tell what could have been. Maybe it would have been good, maybe it would have been bad. The latter is what I've clung to and combined with learned prejudices to justify his act.

Dresses for my girl body. I wanted to be cute and petite like Debbie or Diane Strong, the gymnastic twins who performed at the school talent show. Sun dresses, tennis dresses, short cheerleading and wrap-around skirts.

When I was in the sixth grade, I was taller and bigger than everyone else, including all the boys who hadn't yet begun growing into their feet. Except for Rayanne who had pins in her hips and couldn't exercise, I was the first kid to weigh 100 pounds. I remember standing in line after a tether-ball-recess when the "news" went public. I can feel myself even now trying to shrink as if I was in that moment, in that line, rather than here, seventeen years and 190 miles away from the desert that was my hometown.

Billowy gowns—like wedding dresses only in pink, lavender, yellow, baby blue— shooshed around their legs and feet. Pastel peach taffeta with spaghetti strings, and off-the-shoulder ruffles. Three scalloped tiers, like Cinderella, with little white bows and lace.

Quinciñera. I watched in admiration as one after another of the Mexican girls celebrated this rite of passage. Even Rebecca, my best friend from fourth grade, forsaked her uniform of khakis and Pendletons on this day. She must have been wearing twenty yards of material. And on her feet, replacing the black ballerina slippers that were a *chola* staple, were beaded white bride shoes. She looked beautiful and I felt honored driving with her and her mom to St. Joseph's. Remembering Rebecca I realize that *Quinciñera* was more than just a day of high-femme and celebration of womanhood. *Quinciñera* is the type of ritual I lacked and longed for. Initiation. Belonging.

Barstow is a Mexican town, an Indio town. I don't remember anyone calling themselves Chicana/o. I do remember being afraid of the gangs though. It's funny now to have even called them "gangs," let alone feared them. Seems in my memory that they were more like groups of boys or girls that hung around. Not linked to the drugs and violence like what I see today in and around where I teach.

For years I credited my white name with my successes. In part this placement of credit was valid. I know I was honored with a certain privilege because of that name. At least that's what I figure. The difference between the treatment I got and that of my Mexican classmates was impossible to ignore. Although *I* think it's obvious that I am Latina, others don't seem to want to see that in me. Because I was successful, they wanted to claim me as "their own." Or maybe it was the other way around. Maybe it was a combination of privileges—a white last name from an Aryan fire chief stepfather and a white-passing mother gave me an advantage. With the Mexican girls, folks were relieved if they graduated high school, but there was never any question that I would go to college. My family's priorities were different because survival was not an issue and society's expectations of us were greater. Class and perceptions of race and heritage all came together to set me apart and seemingly above.

For my part I've realized that fear fed my denial of my identity. I feared my similarities to those people that I was taught to believe were "the other." I feared that Lisa Mary Ortiz would have been predestined to a life like the women in *Mí Vida Loca*. It terrified me like my fear of cults. Only instead of long orange robes, a shaved head, tambourines, and a life of celibacy, I would have burned eyeliner on my lids, worn Pendletons, tweezed my brows, and fallen in love with a *cholo* with scars and tattoos in a hairnet. Then we would have skipped school, smoked cigarettes, drunk wine, and he would have gotten me pregnant in tenth grade and I would have kept it because I was Catholic after all.

In the minds of others, but more importantly, in my mind, Crandell protected me from these things. I had an excuse. I was white so I never had to say "No" to belonging. I was never asked. That's what the gangs offered, belonging, *familia*, and that's what I most desired. Rebecca belonged, but even she saw me as white. It's ironic how she and I wound up faced with the same types of situations and decisions. I look at the different choices we each made and, while they changed the outward appearance of our lives, we're really much the same. I hadn't realized all that I had lost or that most of it was just an even trade.

The summer before I started tenth grade, T-shirt dresses were the *fashion statement. If you were thin enough to tie a bandana around your waist, that was even better. My friend, Donna, had been made for these dresses but my thighs had not. Sometimes I'd try one on at the store, but I wouldn't even come out of the dressing room. They made me feel naked. Maybe that's because T-shirts were my sleepwear of choice. Most of the time I traipsed around the house in my stepfather's long T-shirt and my underwear.*

"So, tell me about your stepfather," my therapist asks, gathering evidence for her hypothesis that I seek abusive relationships.

It was the first time I'd considered my stepfather in a long time. Even now when I conjure up *his* image, I'm there too, always in a T-shirt and under-wear, either being spanked, on his lap, or sitting with my legs tucked up inside my long T-shirt.

"Lisa, you're so pig headed, you just don't know when to quit until you cry."

I don't know if this was meant to comfort me, but mom's lecture was as predictable as my losses. Noogies, wrestling, thumb fights, being poked in the chest. I recall much of my growing up as a series of wrestling matches, almost all of which I lost. Step-dad, step-brothers, and later, husbands. I only fought back twice. I'd like to think it's because I knew my power in being femme, that I didn't need to assert my brute strength, but I'm sure I had no concept. I suppose I just felt sorry for them.

"Stop, the both of you!"

Mom sounded frantic, but my stepfather didn't have the brains to quit and I was driven by something that would take me years to begin to understand. She yelled but, as usual, we didn't listen.

"Lisa, you never know when to quit until you cry."

Then one time it was different. I knew when to quit. I quit when he stumbled sideways and crumbled like a wad of paper in a fire cradling his right knee in his hands, tears streaming from his milky blue pig eyes and run-ning down his sweaty red face. I sat up, offending feet and legs tucked pro-tectively under my T-shirt, eyes dry and wild. He couldn't talk. He couldn't poke or noogie or hit. All he could do is hope neither my mom nor I hated him enough to finish him off. He was lucky. Two months more would have made the difference.

Dresses for my woman body. Yes, because that's what women wore. Prom dresses, mini-dresses, night gowns, office dresses, cocktail dresses, negligees, and wedding dresses. Wedding dresses.

When I use the word "wife," I use it in a very stereotypical, straight way because that's the type of wife I was, both times. After a year of beatings and a four-month marriage to Mr. Ford, I met Mr. Dobler, who seemed like a dream come true. So, at twenty-one, I married this cowboy and set out to be the kind of wife that poor Little Joe Cartwright never had.

For the first time in my life, I felt I had a heritage to claim. Country white trash may not seem like much to be excited about but I was hungry for family and whatever culture came with it. As a child I felt I'd been culturally deprived, now I understand that I had a rich cultural heritage, but it was devalued by me and my community.

Growing up Italian/Puerto Rican with the name Palmieri or Ortiz could have been filled with rich traditions, large family gatherings, loud talk, wine, Italian and Spanish spoken by and to the grandparents. If we had stayed in New York, some of the elements I've considered intrinsically part of culture—language, oral history, music, family—would have been available to me. Instead Mom and I moved three thousand miles away to find a better life when I was four. I went from being part of two very large minority groups to being an anomaly. I never even saw another Puerto Rican until I was fifteen and he was a jerk. I felt I was lacking something and sought it in the families of my friends and boyfriends. I compared and critiqued what I had in favor of families like the McKennons and Emorys, failing to see their problems as I idealized the family I'd never known.

Marrying into Matt's family offered me traditions like playing High Five and going to the family farm in Chino Valley. Food picked or slaughtered or hunted fresh then deep fried in lard and served with every type of starch we could find, creamed peas with potatoes, sweet corn, baking powder biscuits all smothered in lard gravy. Being part of them let me experience oral tradition like Grandma's twelve stories that she told and retold and the sayings passed down from children to their children to grand- and great-grandchildren. And their culture also taught me that white is right, the man is the bread-winner and to always ask before doing, where to buy Bud Light in bulk, and to never profess a different point of view or "make a scene" in public.

Christmas in Rockefeller Center. The wind whips through four layers of clothing including my wool skirt and thermal tights. Matt and I watch as the skaters dance on the ice below the enormous Christmas tree. Everyone is bustling, busy but friendly—it is the holiday season, after all, even in New York, New York. A woman in a white skating outfit trimmed in white fur glides past gaining speed as she rounds the curve.

She leaps into the air and my eyes follow her graceful turns across the frozen surface. As she stops, shards of ice spray from the edge of her blade, then she's off again. As she nears the far curve I see her gaining speed. I envy her grace and freedom, the way she defies even gravity.

Over the crackling of winter-weary cross-country phone lines, my aunts chat with one another.

"I just don't understand. We met Matt just five months ago at Christmas and we really liked him."

"Well, you know Matt was an alcoholic . . . and abusive, just like her first husband."

To give her the benefit of the doubt, my aunt was probably trying to keep my lesbian relationship a secret since I had confided in her, but her need to explain why I left Matt gave her permission to lie. Not that the accusations weren't true—or at least half true—but they weren't why I left. And that lie would later come back to haunt me as my sexuality was chalked up to poor relationships with men. Matt was an alcoholic and yes, *one* night he did beat me. Not to belittle the event, but to call him a batterer is just not accurate.

At the risk of sounding like a damaged woman who turned to lesbianism because of bad experiences with men, coming out as a woman who *has* had some pretty terrible experiences with men is important. I have always tried to avoid uttering the two subjects in close proximity to each other lest simpler minds come to the conclusion that there is some sort of causal relation.

One of the greatest conflicts I've faced is the necessity to exorcise the romance myth from my life. "Romantic love" is what kept me in my first marriage. I thought that struggle made love stronger. I thought that my love was so powerful that I could heal his wounds from childhood. I thought wrong and it was only after it occurred to me that he could kill me that I was able to leave, but then only with the protection of a new man, Matt. Then seven years later I found myself a prisoner in our bedroom, the only finished room in our recently gutted house. That night my mind was clicking as if the seven years since the last time I'd feared for my life were just yesterday.

Somehow I felt calm. I was older, wiser, and more aware. I'd been through the YWCA group therapy and convinced myself that I was not like *them*, hell, I'd helped train their hot line people. I'd read a book or two and Zippy taught me sixteen ways to kill a man. I'd listened while shaking my head— it'll never happen again—as Matt explained that if I was ever in a position where I needed to defend myself that I should "take out his knees." I'd flash on the scene of my stepfather lying on the floor in pain, my legs tucked up under my T-shirt. I knew I was capable of such action, but somewhere along the line, probably on a cop show, I'd been warned against using "excessive force." That phrase kept ricocheting through my mind, keeping me in check.

I tried begging, screaming at the top of my lungs, and I searched the room for some means of escape. The only door was barricaded by Matt's swaying drunken body. His face looked furious, and young, and desperate, and pathetic all at the same time. He'd fucked up and he knew it. If he let me out, I'd be gone. I could hit him in the head, but I didn't want to hurt him, I would if I had to, but wanted to try every other way first. He flipped me over on the bed and I drew my knees up to my chest for protection. "Take out his knees" whirled in my head. No. He would be unable to work which would kill him, and that definitely qualifies as excessive force. All that I'd been taught, by the YWCA, the books, even Matt, did me no good when being attacked by someone I loved. I think it goes hand in hand with the bizarre notion I have that I'm better equipped to deal with pain—emotional or physical—than anyone else. Matt glared at me and spit. Something snapped—not his knees, but my nerves. I didn't need physical force to take him down. I shouted, "You're just like your father! You need to hit a woman to feel like a man. You're just like him!" His moment of revelation gave me my chance at the door. "Dyke, cunt, bitch!" echoed through the empty house and followed me out as I slammed the door.

To me, "dyke," "lesbian," "jota," meant blue jeans, black bra, T-shirts, big boots, no more make-up, and whack off that hair. And this time, no man was going to say, "Well, it's OK. But don't ever cut your hair shorter than mine again."

Five years after my second wedding dress, I found myself knowing I was in love with another woman for the first time. Not the first time I had been in love with a woman, but the first time I actually knew and understood and had the power to act upon it. I didn't even bother to move the dresses from my husband's house.

My first year out I dressed and did my best to act the part of *lesbian* and to me this meant butch. It took me a long time to realize that my attraction to women who look "like that" is separate from my own gender. When I finally gained the confidence to be myself I had to contend with society perceiving me as straight, unless of course I was on the arm of a butch. I've been complimented for being "such a cute couple" while walking with a gay male friend, been given compliments in the form of "what a lucky man your husband is," had people make homophobic remarks when they find I teach in the heart of San Diego's queer district, Hillcrest, and been treated as straight even *with* a butch on my arm. Even some of my gay male friends claim that as a femme who is attracted to butches, I am just a closeted straight woman who can't deal with men. Society, whether queer or straight, judges my femme identity as heterosexual. I suppose this shouldn't matter to me, but it does. Coming out ten times a day because I don't look like a "real lesbian" is very tiring.

"Wow, Lisa, you really look nice . . . soft. More like yourself again. The last few times we've seen you, you were so . . . mannish."

I'm wearing a long teal-green skirt, a silk blouse, and a flowing autumn-colored jacket. It is a far departure from the jeans and black boots I'd worn for months, but what Sam doesn't realize, even though she too is a lesbian, is that my dresser is still stocked with blue jeans, T-shirts, and tube socks and I wear them often.

I have never considered myself "mannish." Though I'm tough, I think people are more worried about me when I'm in a skirt than jeans. And I feel my most powerful in dresses. It's some sort of odd paradox. What bothered me in talking to Sam is that she talked about my attire as if it reflected some sort of a phase I'd gotten through. It's the notion that my actions would ever be dismissed as a phase that strikes a painful nerve in me.

Some months prior, the family is "dealing" with my sexuality. The phone lines are clearer now, the distance between California's high desert and Long Island, New York, shortened by the nice weather of summer. My aunts chat.

"I'm sure it's just a phase."

"She never really had a father figure—well, unless you count Dave."

"I don't count that bastard. But she did have all those abusive relationships with men."

"Diane is her mother, you know, and she is very strong-willed."

"But she doesn't look like a lesbian. Every time I've seen her she's been wearing dresses. At Easter, she wore a long patchwork skirt and a purple silk blouse. I don't think that's the type of thing a real lesbian would wear."

When I embraced the label "lesbian," I knew the straight world would either dismiss it as a phase or translate the term to fit neatly into their pre-existing categories. To them, lesbians either are pathetic creatures who just haven't met the right man yet; perverts who eat pussy and fuck other women; or, at their worst, man-haters and possible child molesters. Femme is neither that simplistic nor easily ignored because the straight world isn't the issue, the queer one is. The queer world suffers from at least an equal amount of homophobia and misogyny as the straight world. Though we're "family," I find myself being offered token roles. It disturbs me because I think some of it is rooted in the community's perception of femme. I'm seen as sister or mom, so-and-so's girlfriend or maybe a safe fag-hag. Confusion over femme is within me and within our community.

Bali skirts are my clothing of choice. They work well sitting on the floor with my students and they look good on the dance floor. In my favorite Bali skirt, the purple one with gold threads, I set out for her favorite bar. Four months of working and flirting had worn me down to where age didn't seem to matter any more. I was on a mission. She sat straddling a bar stool watching pool. Soft butch, 23, Chicana, and cute. I pulled up a stool between her legs and asked her to dance.

And now that I've grown up and found my way back into the brown world my poorly developed cultural awareness, my *pocha*-ness, seems to glow fluorescent. I don't speak Spanish, never read all of Moraga's *Loving in the War Years,* dance salsa only fair and forget about maranga and ranchera. And with Latina dykes the roles seem to be so much more distinct. Stone butch butches and cha cha femmes. I'm not butch—that we all know—and while I identify as femme and present as femme, I'll never be a cha cha. It's just not me, yet being me gives me that feeling of in-betweenness. I find I'm often in an in-between state, negotiating space. Like the space between micro and mini hemlines. Not either/or but somewhere in between—either within myself or as perceived by others. Within the Latina community I feel my femme-ness is in question. Femme seems to be equated with femininity—short skirts hugging aerobicized legs, pushup bras, make-up, and high hair and heels. And when combined with the fact that I often feel uncomfortable in my old stomping grounds, with white dykes, I have no place that feels like home except with my lover.

The bar is packed and all the beautiful women of color are dressed for the occasion. On Saturday night, jeans will just not do—that's what I like and don't like about this bar. I wear my new favorite dress, low-cut, form-fitting denim, with a high slit in front. It's the closest thing I've got to cha cha in my closet and I'm feeling good about the way I look. A small group of us share a table and small talk in the Cool Room where they play old school music. Sittin' at the park, waiting for you . . . *Julia there. She and I have had our ups and downs, she's unequivocally butch but we're both high energy people and we tend to short circuit each other. We're doing pretty well tonight until the beer gets to both of us and feeling bold in my new dress, I flirt,* "Better watch out, Juls, or I might ask you out!" *And without a thought, her reply,* "No, I only date Latinas." *Suddenly my dress no longer mattered and with one off-handed remark she made it clear that neither did I.*

Femme and Latina are identities which I have to actively claim because I "pass" as straight and I "pass" as white. Other Latinas question my ethnicity and other queers question whether I will hang around when the going gets tough. I'm seen as someone who can potentially cross over to the enemy if need be. What hurts me the most is the patronizing treatment I've received from many butch women over the years. I'd say they don't even realize they're doing it, but that sounds too reminiscent of the excuses mothers, wives, and straight women have always made for men. I'd say that they just need to be schooled but I'm tired of having to educate straight folks about queer issues, men about women's issues, and butches about the difference between being butch and being male. As long as other *queers* question femme loyalty to the struggle because we can pass, we must divide our energy by combating stereotypes within and outside the gay community.

Being able to pass as straight is perceived as such a luxury or maybe the more poignant observation is that *not* being able to pass is seen as a badge of honor. I think it's the other way around, being butch is like being a person of color, they can't hide it, unless, of course they're mistaken for men. Otherwise people assume correctly that they're lesbians or ignore the obvious, but every time I am mistaken as straight, I make the decision whether to come out or not—to the butcher, the university secretary, my colleagues at a new school—sometimes I feel like it's just not their damn business, but not telling is passing and I don't do that. Being femme often requires an active commitment to be out and proud.

Femme allows me to embrace my body as female and Latina reconnects me with my stolen past. They are on and under my skin. It just seems as though they're difficult for others to see. For three and a half years I have lived and loved in the lesbian community. I have loved and hated butch women and in the process been reconnected with my body and my identity as a femme. *Femme* is a label put on me by casual observers and lovers alike. Being femme—like being a daughter, a Leo, a *pocha*, a lesbian—has shaped me but it's not all of who I am. Identifying as femme and identifying as Latina are very closely linked both in time and in meaning to me. My emergence into these identities is my reclamation of a body and name that were lost or stolen years ago. Comfort in my body—my round body, my strong body, my brown body, my femme body—is recent and tenuous at times. I am a large woman who was a large girl and I have scars from those years before I was equipped to defend myself. The beauty in maturing is that I no longer feel defensive. I am confident in my body and its capacities. I can stand naked in front of the mirror and love my curves—my woman hips, my *panca*, my breasts, and thighs. This confidence is my power in being femme *and* Latina.

The rebirth of Lisa Mary Ortiz has been a difficult labor at best. I look back to my Barstow days and my friend Rebecca and I feel I know femme. Whether in *chola* drag or high femme drag, she kept the look, the face, the *power* in being femme. She's a strong woman, a tough woman who was no less in a ball gown. It's not the clothes, although the courage to wear them is femme. It's not the make-up, although the look is femme. Femme is intrinsic power and comfort in your own body.

As a femme, I must define myself. Until recently, I was very happy with one butch's explanation of femme. She was trying to save herself after defining butch as strong, capable, powerful, assertive. I asked her what that made me since I was not butch. I was offended at the notion of being defined by what I am *not*, but she said, "Femme is subversive. It's taking all that they taught you to do/say/act/be for a man and directing it toward women." To that I add that femme is taking all those learned and innate characteristics and directing it toward ourselves. It is reclaiming the attributes associated with femininity that have so often been used against us individually and collectively and using them for our own benefit and pleasure. Femme is one element of my personality and gender that touches every aspect of my identity. Latina, switch, daughter, Leo, *pocha,* teacher, Puerto Riqueña, *mujer,* dog-person, lover, student . . . femme. I am femme and I wear dresses. I am powerful in spite of and because of it.

BAD GIRLS
Sex, Class, and Feminist Agency[1]

Laura Harris and Liz Crocker

Part 1: Lesbian Feminism to Femme Feminism

The lesbian is as fantasmatic a construct as *the* woman. There are women, and there are lesbian bodies—each body crossed by multiplicitous signifying regimes and by different histories, different technologies of representation and reproduction, and different social experiences of being lesbian determined by ethnicity, class, gender identity, and sexual practices.
— Cathy Griggers[2]

Looking at differences amongst women and amongst lesbians is the feminist, lesbian, and queer project of the nineties. If it seems impossible now to think of the feminist movement as a sisterhood, it seems equally impossible to define lesbians simply as women-loving-women. As Griggers argues in her essay, greater visibility of differences amongst women in the nineties leads to both freedom and loss. While visible differences contest a stifling regime of sameness, they also problematize identity politics which often rest upon notions of commonalities and stable identities. Lesbian identity politics, for example, were organized around the concept of an essential, common difference of sexual identity upon which political communities could be built. Investigating differences challenges the essentialism of these lesbian identity politics. It seems clear that it is partly from this complication of lesbian and feminist identity politics around issues of difference that queer politics and theory have grown.

The difference of butch-femme lesbians was seen as anti-feminist and anti-lesbian by lesbian-feminists who subscribed to the ideal that "lesbianism is the practice and feminism is the theory."[3] For butch-femme lesbians, the struggle to be recognized for their feminist practice has been a difficult one. For femmes, this struggle has been even more difficult. The path to recognizing butch-femme dynamics—and femmes themselves—as queer and feminist has been well trodden, yet remains a difficult terrain. As Joan Nestle writes in her introduction to *The Persistent Desire: A Femme-Butch Reader:*

> Many of the contributors, both butch and femme, document journeys of exile, particularly during the seventies, when the lesbian-feminist ortho-doxy, though still young, was at its most restrictive. But anger at an ideol-ogy is not rejection of it. . . . butch-femme women put the concept of "queer" back into the lesbian-feminist discourse, a concept that I believe can only deepen our discussions of women, sex, and gender. . . .[4]

Nestle suggests that the relationship between lesbian feminists and butch-femme communities could be a beneficial one; at the same time, she points to the difficulties that many butches and femmes encountered with lesbian femi-nism. Nestle's depiction of this troubled relationship is often echoed by other writers; Leslie Feinberg's *Stone Butch Blues*, for example, paints lesbian femi-nism as a threat to femme visibility.[5] In the first part of the novel, Feinberg draws a number of strong femme characters who are vital to the development of the narrator's butch identification and maturation. However, as the novel progresses, the appearance of lesbian feminism literally brings the disappear-ance of femmes. Only one femme character appears briefly at the end of the novel but eludes the grasp of the narrator. Thus, in Feinberg's novel, lesbian feminism separates the butch-femme couple and makes femmes invisible.

If Feinberg's novel does not imagine femme visibility after lesbian femi-nism, how does a femme author herself? Specifically, how does she represent herself as a feminist subject despite lesbian feminism's negation of this? In a contribution to *The Persistent Desire*, femme author Lyndall MacCowan writes of coming out in 1972 and joining a lesbian feminist group, the Daughters of Bilitis.[6] On DOB outings to bars, MacCowan describes seeing butch women and feeling "a depth of lust that surprises me" (304). Yet MacCowan did not identify herself as a femme until a decade later. She writes, "'femme' was not in our [lesbian feminist] vocabulary of options in 1972. . . . how is it that butch remained named, but femme became invisi-ble?" (305). While MacCowan's question might at first seem to echo Feinberg's depiction of femme invisibility, there is a subtle difference. MacCowan's desire for butches clearly constitutes her as a femme in her own eyes. She lacked not the understanding but the name for both her identity and her desires. Thus, MacCowan points to a linguistic lack: it is the term "femme" which is invisible, rather than femme desire or femmes themselves.

It is necessary to revisit this story of femme invisibility because it can provide us with clues as to why today femme is still often seen as a suspect category: accused of passing as straight, being passive lesbians or duped straight women, or used as an equivalent term for "feminine" or lipstick lesbian. Joan Nestle, responding to this common conception of femmes as somehow less genuinely lesbian than butches, named her anthology *A Femme-Butch Reader*. Nestle writes:

> The femme woman has been the most ambiguous figure in lesbian history; she is often described as the nonlesbian lesbian, the duped wife of the passing woman, the lesbian who marries. . . . I wanted to edit this book because I am a femme woman, tired of devaluation by myself and others, tired of past and present attacks on the integrity of our desire, tired of the penalties we have had to pay. . . . As feminists, we continue to fight back with a femme proclamation of independence. I subtitled this anthology "A Femme-Butch Reader" to herald this new voice in identity politics and break the traditional rhythms of the phrase and image. Femmes are the Lavender Lace Menace within our community. For my femme sisters—the queerest of the queer, as one contributor says—this book is only the beginning. (15–18)

Demonstrating the strength of her feminist analyses, Nestle skillfully and passionately articulates femme oppression, citing feminism as one means of empowerment for femmes while not collapsing femme into feminist or femme into lesbian. Historicizing the various appearances of femmes, Nestle points to the "past and present attacks" and "penalties" that femmes have paid for their queer desires. We cite Nestle here in order to frame MacCowan and Feinberg's depiction of femme invisibility. Understanding her "femme proclamation of independence" as a feminist statement begins to point to what is at stake in tracing a history of femme visibility: understanding femme desire and self-imaging as feminist agency.

Duped Women, Bar Femmes, and Sex Workers

Femme invisibility arises from the misreading of femme desire as either nonexistent or as easily transferable to heterosexuality. In this section, after examining how femme identity has been disparaged, we consider how femme desire mobilizes butch-femme dynamics thus exhibiting femme agency and utilizes class identification thus subverting gender identity. We use as a focal point specific representations of femme desire in "The Femme

Tapes"—a taped conversation between three femmes: Joan Nestle, Madeline
Davis, and Amber Hollibaugh—and *Stone Butch Blues*.[7] In these texts, femme
desire reinscribes female sexuality and gender in resistant ways; such rein-
scriptions can be read in femmes' self-images, in the acts of describing themselves and naming their desires. For example, in their personal narratives,
Davis and Nestle speak of their sexual mobility in a bar scene, implying that
femme desire motivates an active femme agency. In Feinberg's novel, we
examine the representation of femme sex workers as they negotiate gender
role constraints, breaking down the virgin/whore dichotomy. In doing so,
femmes both initiate and give direction to butch-femme dynamics in this
novel. In different ways, both texts foreground the feminist agency of femme
desire in a way that contests the historical denigration of femme desire and
erasure of femme identity.

Historically, femme desire has not been acknowledged as active lesbian
desire. Such an image of the femme lesbian can be found in sexual-scientific
nineteenth-century discourse in which the duped feminine woman, due to
her weakness and confusion, falls prey to the dominating mannish woman.
While that is certainly a fantasy worth indulging, other images of femme exist
that do not depict femme as the image or victim of another's gender and
desire. In fact, a better understanding of the subversive or queer nature of
femme self-imaging can be gathered from reading femmes' own articulations
of their gender and desire. While these self-depictions are subversive, often
femme lesbians express the difficulty of finding images of themselves. In
"The Femme Tapes," Hollibaugh says:

> I don't have any images of femmes. I don't get it. I know I am one . . . I
> am not straight. What am I? I don't get as oppressed on the street in the
> same way [as butches], but it makes me confused in terms of gender. Am I
> a real woman? It just really blows me away. No wonder femmes don't
> know how to talk about it—there is no imagery. (255)

Put into the context of the nineteenth-century sexual-scientific discourse
which portrayed femmes as the "real" women seduced by mannish lesbians,
Hollibaugh's question "Am I a real woman?" reverberates historically, suggesting a connection between a lack of femme imagery and a historical mis-
representation of femme desire as feminine weakness.

Like the historical misunderstanding of femme desire as feminine weakness, Feinberg's *Stone Butch Blues* at times conflates femme desire and heterosexuality. In the letter that opens the novel, the narrator Jess asks Theresa, her
lost femme love, where she is now: "Are you married . . . lying with an
unemployed auto worker who is much more like me than they [lesbian fem-

inists] are?" (11). While the unemployed auto worker may be more like the butch than the lesbian-feminists are, we might imagine that for many femmes he would be a poor substitute for butch masculinity. Moreover, the narrator's question repeats a common perception that there is a slippage between femme desire for the reshaped masculinity of butch lesbians and heterosexual desire. The narrator's assumption of Theresa's heterosexual transformation—coupled with our earlier discussion of Feinberg's portrayal of femme invisibility after lesbian feminism—makes femme desire and visibility dependent upon butch recognition in her text. However, turning from Feinberg to femmes' personal narratives, we see that their femme desire is a queer gender desire, not a desire for masculinity in any old body.

In "The Femme Tapes," Madeline Davis speaks about the specificity of femme desire for a queer masculinity:

> Some of my partners were very feminine men. They were Sal Mineo when he was a pretty, big-eyed, soft-looking baby-butch type. . . . [I] wondered why my girlfriends were into muscle and macho . . . I went with a couple of guys who were faggots and were quite effeminate. . . . I loved that combination of toughness and softness, that combination of masculinity and femininity. And then I began looking for it in women too. . . . I started going to gay bars when I was eighteen. . . . The first butch I saw tending bar . . . turned my knees to water. I knew it was a woman, but it was this combination . . . so powerful, so scary. (256)

Davis's description of her desire for the sexually attractive combination of masculinity and femininity shows the difference between her femme desire for masculinity in a butch and other women's straight desire for men. In contrast to Feinberg's description of femme desire as interchangeable with heterosexual desire, Davis is turned on by gender-ambivalent bodies or subversive constructions of masculinity produced by butches. Identifying herself as coming from a working-class background, Davis speaks of recognizing her femme desire in a bar before being part of any lesbian or butch-femme community. The activity and mobility required of Davis in a bar setting provides another contradiction to femme passivity: femme cruising.

Lesbian bars are the setting of many femmes' narratives about recognizing and acting upon their desire. While middle-class lesbian identity might have more often formed in various lesbian-feminist venues, working-class lesbians often practiced their lesbianism in community bars.[8] Like MacCowan and Davis, Nestle describes how bars relate to her femme identity, furthering this topic by linking class identification and the sexual autonomy of femme desire in a bar.

> So when a person says to me, "How can you say you were a femme before
> you went to the bars?" I know we have a big difference in our back-
> grounds. I went to the bars with a sexuality, but some women never give
> me that autonomy, because they think, No, your sexuality didn't happen
> until you were twenty. I think class and protected backgrounds enter here.
> (257)

As Nestle describes in this text and in many of her other writings, her class
background prompted a very early identification of her sexual desires.
Coming from the home of a single sexually active mother, Nestle was not a
child raised on sexual myths or protected from the often harsh ramifications
of her mother's sexual exchanges.[9] The class necessity that Nestle develop
economic independence at an early age also influenced the necessity for her
to develop sexual autonomy from an early age. We might hypothesize that
Nestle refigures her gender for a better female advantage, one not available to
her in terms of class privilege. For femmes from a working-class background,
such a reshaping of sexuality can be a form of empowerment in relation to
gender norms.

In Feinberg's *Stone Butch Blues*, the representations of femme sex workers
echo some of the claims about femme agency and desire made by the partici-
pants in "The Femme Tapes." Feinberg's sex worker femmes have agency as
they renegotiate the role of the whore in relation to gender role constraints.
Whereas the femme in Feinberg may be a stripper or prostitute, she is also
the desired, respected, and protected damsel of butch desire. The
virgin/whore dichotomy is refigured as the femme occupies both spaces at
the same time. Simultaneously, the femme's ability to support herself—coupled with her desire for sexual fulfillment from butches—gives her a certain
autonomy that subverts cultural surveillance and control of female behavior.
For example, the main character, Jess, has a relationship with a sex worker,
Milli. However, the relationship breaks down because Jess refuses to accept
her femme's reality: that the female gender role is imbued with sexual service
and that often female survival necessitates manipulating this sexual role.
Ultimately, Jess realizes her mistake, understanding that the butch-femme
pact is about a mutual respect for the outlawed sexuality and subversive gender performance, one that valorizes femme as a gender warrior.

Feinberg's text offers many examples such as the one above in which
femme desire shapes butch-femme dynamics. In the novel, the economy of
desire between stone butch and pro femme rests on an axis of pleasure given,
not taken. The stone butch gives physical pleasure to her pro femme and the
"stone" femme gives her "untouchable" emotional pleasure to the butch. In

her very first sexual encounter Jess makes love to Angie, a pro, as a stone butch. Angie comments on their connection, "Don't be ashamed of being stone with a pro, honey. We're in a stone profession" (73). Whereas not all femmes are pros or sex workers and not all butches need be stone, what Feinberg's depictions of sex workers affirm is the autonomous sexualized power of a femme woman who has the agency to manipulate her surroundings just as often as she is oppressed by them. We can return to the image that began this section: the weak and confused feminine woman who falls prey to the seductive power of the mannish dyke. If we re-read femme identity as a location of feminist agency, then perhaps we should pay very close attention to who falls prey to whose seductive powers.

Bad Girls: "Beep Beep"

Reclaiming Joan Nestle, an iconoclastic feminist, as feminist icon, we investigate one thread that runs through her writing, the prostitute as femme bad girl role model. We can understand Nestle's use of the prostitute image as femme fantasy as enabling the femme to choose to be a woman on her own terms rather than those prescribed for her. Understanding the fantasy in the context of butch-femme dynamics revises the heterosexual ideal of feminine pleasure giver by empowering the femme as feminist pleasure seeker. This fantasy arises from Nestle's identification with culturally stigmatized and sexualized straight women, from Pat Ward to her mother. Naming Pat Ward, a well-known prostitute involved in a much publicized trial in the fifties, as her role model, Nestle states in "The Femme Tapes":

> I used to come home from school—I was around ten or eleven—and play that I was Pat Ward on trial, because I knew she was sexual and so was I. I had already been masturbating and I had sexual feelings. I remember seeing pictures of her, wearing a white blouse with a Peter Pan collar. She looked very prim in the middle of all this sexual discussion about her, and she became the woman I wanted to be. I used to play-act that I was this prostitute who had a public sexual image but no one really knew her. (255)

As a young, sexually aware girl, Nestle identifies with Pat Ward's juxtaposition of an outlaw sexuality with a "prim" and proper femininity. Moreover, Nestle reads Ward to produce a femme role model who combines a visible, seemingly proper femininity with a female sexuality that satisfies her own desires, not someone else's. We can understand Nestle's femme role model as both virgin and whore, publicly known yet unknown, sexually active yet not a sexual victim. Thus, the power of this bad girl role model arises from her negotiation of these dichotomies that often entrap women.

Whereas Nestle discusses the Pat Ward image as a bad girl femme fantasy, in her written work, it is the realities of her mother's working-class life that shape and form her femme identity. Nestle states in "The Femme Tapes" that her sexually savvy mother helped her articulate her femme difference: "My mother gave me a legacy of difference. I felt different because I was the daughter of a woman who did not have a husband, who had lots of lovers" (259). The theme of this "legacy of difference" appears many times in Nestle's writing about her mother as a Jewish, single, working-class woman in a hostile world. In her volume of essays, *A Restricted Country*, Nestle imagines her mother's response to Andrea Dworkin's anti-penis diatribe:

> They called you freak and me whore and maybe they always will, but we
> fight them best when we keep on doing what they say we should not want
> or need for the joy we find in doing it. I fucked because I liked it, and
> Joan, the ugly ones, the ones who beat me or fucked me too hard, they
> didn't run me out of town, and neither can the women who don't walk
> my streets of loneliness or need. (122)

In this imagined mother to daughter message, the femme is aligned with a sexually active straight working-class woman against a feminism that would recognize neither of their sexualities as feminist. The search for sexual pleasure, shared by mother and daughter, is their strongest weapon against both those who dismiss them and those who threaten them with violence. Between the woman who has been the victim of sexual violence and the woman who has many lovers, femme agency negotiates sexual danger and sexual pleasure, one of feminism's most divisive dilemmas.

Finally, in this discussion of femme bad girl role models, it is also important to take into consideration the very real historical connections between lesbians and prostitutes, between femmes and sex workers as sexual outlaws, and between their shared battles with feminism. In "Lesbians and Prostitutes: A Historical Sisterhood," Nestle traces a history of lesbians and prostitutes from ancient Greece through the twentieth century, a shared history that is broken by lesbian feminism's class-based denigration of "whores and women who look like whores." Nestle writes:

> Whores, like queers, are a society's dirty joke. . . .The shared territory
> broke apart, at least for me, when I entered the world of Lesbian-femi-
> nism. Whores and women who look like whores became the enemy, or at
> best, misguided oppressed women who needed our help. . . . A much
> closer connection came home to me when I . . . discovered that at differ-
> ent times in her life my mother had turned tricks to pay her rent. . . . And
> finally, in my own recent life I have entered the domain of public sex. . . .

I have taken money from women for sexual acts. I am, depending on who is the accuser, a pornographer, a queer, and a whore. (158–59)

Whereas we have discussed Nestle's identification with the image of the prostitute, here she writes of her actual experience in "the domain of public sex." To a predominantly middle-class lesbian feminism that was preoccupied with sexual danger, "whores and women who looked like whores" seemed too visibly different to be included in this feminist community. This visible difference is both a class difference and a sexual difference; working-class lesbians as well as prostitues were willing to and had to risk sexual danger in their everyday lives. Reclaiming this "shared territory" is an important feminist project that offers an alliance between straight working-class women, lesbians, and prostitutes, a connection that feminism has previously passed over.

It is not a coincidence that many femmes self-image as bad girls; rather, the prostitute as independent sexual agent offers a role model or fantasy for femmes of feminist sexual agency. It seems evident that the sexual outlaw image of the prostitute, among other bad girl images, is compelling for a femme as she perceives her own desires as conflicting with gender norms. The image of the prostitute is one of sexual aggression in the guise of seductive and passive female subservience; this image could enable the femme to script the sexual scene. The fantasy of a prostitute is a woman who consciously manipulates the economics of heterosexuality and, in doing so, establishes control over her status as a sexual object. In this way, femme bad girl role-modeling is a strong expression of a feminist consciousness that allows women to break down the virgin/whore dichotomy, among others, and produce female roles for their own transgressive and pleasurable use.

Notes

1. We are borrowing the phrasing of the title of the essay as well as section three from Donna Summer's popular song in which Summer sings of identification with "bad girls." Donna Summer, "Bad Girls" (1976) from *Endless Summer: Donna Summer's Greatest Hits,* Polygram, 1994.

2. Cathy Griggers, "Lesbian Bodies in the Age of (Post)Mechanical Reproduction," in *The Lesbian Postmodern,* ed. Laura Doan (New York: Columbia University Press, 1994) 119.

3. Joan Nestle, *A Restricted Country* (Ithaca: Firebrand, 1987) 105. All subsequent references will be parenthetical.

4. Joan Nestle, ed., *The Persistent Desire: A Femme-Butch Reader* (Boston: Alyson, 1992) 17. All subsequent references will be parenthetical.

5. Leslie Feinberg, *Stone Butch Blues* (Ithaca: Firebrand, 1994). All subsequent references will be parenthetical.

6. Lyndall MacCowan, "Re-collecting History, Renaming Lives: Femme Stigma in the Seveties and Eighties," in *The Persistent Desire: A Femme-Butch Reader,* ed. Joan Nestle (Boston: Alyson, 1992) 299–328.

7. Madeline Davis, Amber Hollibaugh, and Joan Nestle, "The Femme Tapes," in *The Persistent Desire: A Femme-Butch Reader,* ed. Joan Nestle (Boston: Alyson, 1992) 254–267.

8. For a discussion of class in relation to bar culture, see Lillian Faderman, *Odd Girls and Twilight Lovers: A History of Lesbian Life in Twentieth-Century America* (New York: Penguin, 1991).

9. See Nestle's *A Restricted Country* for a description of her childhood.

Part 2

GENERATIONS
A Feminist Genealogy

I'LL BE THE GIRL
Generations of Fem[1]

Joan Nestle and Barbara Cruikshank

Thank You for Letting Me Be the Girl

Joan Nestle

T he large hall of New York's Lesbian and Gay Community Center
was dark in preparation for the night of benefit readings for ILGO
(Irish Lesbian and Gay Organization). After pushing myself up the
four flights of stairs, I quietly slipped into the room and introduced myself to
the young woman behind the table as one of the readers. "Oh, I know you,
Joan," she whispered. "Look," she said, coming from behind the welcoming
table and holding up her stockinged leg. "I wore these in your honor."
Green pumps flashed in the darkness. How beautiful she was, in her black
short dress, its hem hitting just above her knees.

Later in the evening, just as intermission was coming to an end, the room
darkening once again, a young woman appeared before me. Bending down
so she could whisper her words to me, she said, "I had to come speak to
you and thank you for what you have written about fems. You gave me the
right to be myself." I looked up at her, at her neckline swinging away
from her body, at her softly swelling breasts, such tender assertions, rising
above a black lace bra, her dark curly hair framing her face so earnestly
turned towards me. For one moment, I felt we were making love, the whispered voices, the darkened room, the revelation of the body, but this time
I was the one struck by the gift of what she could offer. "Thank you," I

105

mumbled, "but you are beautiful. You did not need any permission to be yourself."

The tensions between artifice and self, between enacting and being, between alienation and integration, between innocence and judgment were all present in these whispered words. I have emphasized youth in the retelling because two fem generations were represented that evening. How strange it was to be thanked for a return to the "natural" state of celebrating a young woman's body, adorned in celebratory clothing. I think these younger women take play for granted, that it was "self" that was the exciting creation.

I, on the other hand, am just beginning to understand that my fem desire, born in the fifties or better said, expressed in the fifties, can be explored in terms of performance as well as gut-wrenching need. My fem self is both an identity and a performance because I have outlived the decades of risking all for a touch—meaning the vice squads, the police, the doctors—and now have the breathing space of some autonomy, both intellectually and politically, though I know how precarious this relief is. Because of my history, I have both a fem identity and a fem persona.

I'll Be the Girl

Barbara Cruikshank

Things were beginning to slow down just a little. A few hours might lapse between her demands for some "fresh." Fresh pussy that she would dip into with her fingers and then spread over her lips; it ran down her chin as her fingers ran up my thigh for more. After six weeks of complete immersion in sex, I was catching on to something I had to figure out.

I wanted the lust to be even fiercer, nastier, and to gear up for it, I suggested we go out for a dance and a drink. Later, in a tight dress perched behind a drink, I chirped right up with it.

"So, we do it like you're the boy and I'm the girl, right?"

She nodded. Picking up that I had something nasty to say, she gave me just the look I needed to finish what I had started. She leaned forward and glanced down at her biceps exposed by a sleeveless ribbed tee. Her arm muscle seemed to grow more definite and she stroked it taking in my response. Glancing back down at her own masculinity, then directly at me, I knew she was ready to hear all I had to say.

The mood was right, now where were the right words?

"Well," I began in a lowered voice, sliding my chair closer to hers. But before I knew what to say next, she held my eye as she reached up and stroked my jaw line. Her lips moved to say, "You are beautiful." I saw the words, but in my mind she held me up with those big arms and penetrating eyes and said, "I will hold you up forever. Stick with me and you will always be beautiful." I believed every word of it.

Now that my imagination was in motion and the future was bright, I had only to say it. But there weren't enough words. My hand moved up to pet her masculinity. It flexed under my hand. "So, you told me about fucking with dildos [we hadn't done that yet], and you call what you do on top of me 'being in you.' It seems like you are making love like a man with a penis. I used to think you had penis envy . . ."

She winced and then smiled sheepishly, straightening up her shoulders and leaning back.

". . . but now I know that you have nothing to envy because you really do have a penis. You might say that it is all in your head, but I know that it is all hard and thick when it gets between my legs." She spit out a laugh and I giggled, ready to go on. I had a lot more to say, so I leaned forward close to her ear and went straight into it before she thought that was all there was to it.

"I don't want you because you are like a man, but because you act like a man. You put on masculinity as a show for me like male birds show off their plumage to get the girl. Your dick is more real than any man's because yours gets made up every time we fuck; we make it real. It is never taken for granted or left to fend for itself. You do have a dick, so let's just go ahead and call it that, O.K.?"

She stared at me. I knew I had to do something quick to keep her confidence up; these were words and notions we had been taught were "imitating heterosexuals." I leaned closer still, clinging and tugging on her biceps, I whispered, "I can feel it when you get big. I love your big cock in me. Do you like me to call it that?"

She silently assented. After some pause, she bounced in her seat, "Yes, yes, yes." Then she looked sincere. "This is so nasty," she said, eager to take it all seriously.

"You don't even like to use a dildo that much, you said. I think that is because it gets in the way of your real cock." She nodded. There it was then, settled, she was the boy.

"Now what do I have?" I asked. "Now let's say that I am the girl. I know I already am the girl, *really*. But I mean how do we make me being the girl just as nasty and sexy as you being the boy is?"

She stared at me; I could tell that she didn't know what to say.

"You are the girl; you're all girl," she said, giving me the once over. "You don't have to do anything different." Her reassurance deflated my nerve. I didn't need a compliment, I wanted to do something different; I wanted her to give words to my fem the same way I made her butch. I wanted her to make me being fem as nasty as her being butch.

I knew there was more to say but I was distracted by the next six weeks of fucking with her new penis. We experimented with all the possibilities of her being the boy both in and out of bed. The rest could wait. And it waited.

Back at the bar in six more weeks, I lost my nerve. Falling back on politics just at the moment I could have revived all that lust and nastiness, I complained, "I feel invisible. You're the boy in every way and people treat you like you define our relationship. Because you are butch, it's like you are the 'real' lesbian. You set all the terms and everyone gives you all the power."

I needed something from her. "We act just like heterosexuals, you're the boy and I'm the girl. You are butch against my girl/female, not my fem. I need a new identity and there isn't a narrative for it."

The next six weeks I complained and tried to tell her that to just assume I was the girl, just because I am a girl, was sexist. This was truly no better than heterosexuality; I was "just a girl." I wanted to be a fem, and to find a way to do it that didn't depend solely on being seen with a butch. I felt dependent. If her boyness was an act, I wanted my girlness to be an act—not in the sense of play acting, but in the sense of enacting, accomplishing something. It was the acting that made the sex sexy to me, but I didn't know how to say it. Those six weeks ended the relationship. We broke up.

Generations of Fem: An Ongoing Discussion Between Joan Nestle and Barbara Cruikshank

JN: "I'll be the Girl" takes things that I have written about four steps ahead. Which is . . . a construct of reality. It makes sexual artifice very erotic; the gender creation itself really faced head on . . .

BC: It is what I call an analytical fiction. Not very entertaining really, because the point is so heavy-handed. I was trying to figure out a way to tell a story about how difficult it is to grapple with what I used to call "fem invisibility." That ending is just a bunch of notes to myself. What happens now, do they break up because politics got in the way of desire?

JN: I think what makes your piece so interesting is the nature of the fem quest. At this point, the questions that you cannot answer are the heart of the narrative. In real life, we manage to reach our pleasure in the midst of a butch-dominated moment, but here in a text, we can look at ourselves without the danger of loosing our orgasms. It has taken me all these years, fifty-five to be exact, to find your questions.

Sometimes the obvious nature of the inquiry is stunning. A few years ago, I was in a small room with Jewelle Gomez, another fem-identified woman, and two butch women, Mary Alice and Amanda. We were getting our thoughts together for a panel discussion. Mary Alice said even if she was on a desert island, she would still be a butch. Then she asked me could my fem self stand up to the same isolation? Did it have to play off a butch? I was among friends, so I didn't need to give a defensive answer. I had never really thought about fem autonomy that way. My answer now is that I would be Joan on that island, therefore I would be fem, but I wouldn't be having much fun—that's where the performance part comes in. Because I was queer first, that is a freak, without gender and without a stage, I have had to work hard at creating any stable gender. Ironically for me, fem came before woman.

I think it is important for your narrative to get derailed at the point that it does. Fems, meaning myself, must also be exciting to themselves, be as fully into their performance as a transgressive act as they are into their need to be fucked.

BC: They break up then. She goes off looking for it somewhere else.

JN: That's the whole thing: where is she going to look for it? Where does it exist?

BC: Well, she's got to make it up herself. What a chore. There isn't a clear and visible butch-fem culture out there. The only truly intergenerational culture exists in texts like *A Restricted Country*. Every generations seems to reinvent butch-fem and perhaps that is just fine, but it would be nice to make it all less painful for the next generation.

JN: I have been lucky enough to create scenarios for my fem self that allowed for safe exploration of some of its edges. For a short while I became a fem whore, making assignations with butch women who sometimes pretended to be traveling salesmen in need of a lay. I traveled to their apartments with my sex clothes in a large bag and always felt uncomfortable until I changed to my working clothes. Then standing in my black slip and my pink sling back heels, I took a careful look at them and said, "what is it that you would like me to do?" Usually, they were sitting on a couch or chair and I occupied the center space in the room. At that moment I was enacting one side of fem power, not the domestic, supportive fem that had held so many lesbian relationships together back in the old days, not the pretend whore for a night for the delight of one's partner of twelve years, but a fem on her own, doing something complex and highly personal, for her own erotic journey. Now this experience certainly involved butch women, but the story I was evolving was my own.

Fem/Female

JN: If we leave behind, as your story asks us to, the butch relationship to masculinity and focus on our own gender complexities, we come up against the difference between woman and fem. I can make, at times, a really clear distinction between the socially constructed woman self and my fem self. My woman self is perhaps the more masculine self, the woman self that I move through the world with, that I go to work with, the much more guarded self.

BC: Independent, strong, brave . . . ?

JN: I feel that way in my fem self as well, but my woman self is a functional bargain in some sense. I do not bring my fem self to work. And the fem self plays. When I was younger I was always stronger in many ways than any butch woman I was with. I don't mean physically but I mean emotionally, and in how I relied on myself to hold my daily world together economically. This is one way class enters my erotic formation. I had to support myself from a very early age. For example, I could not play with drugs that threatened my ability to get up every morning. In the same way, I had to have my desire under control to keep a roof over my head. But I was also full of need, so I created an erotic sense of dependence. Do you know what I am saying?

BC: Absolutely.

JN: I find it hard to discuss some of this; this is what the sex wars have done. I have all these accusing voices in my head . . .

BC: Which words are hard to use?

JN: Saying "dependence" or "vulnerable" because I hear the—I want to say lesbian feminists, but I don't mean it as a betrayal of *my* sense of lesbian feminism—but a certain voice of lesbian feminism, you know, saying that this is pathology. The early condemnations of butch-fem were so simplistic in their assumptions about historical resistance and the experience of gender. In the name of one liberation battle, the complexity of another was sacrificed. In my own way, I was part of this over-simplification when I wrote things like, "I never knew a butch who wanted to be a man," as if such a desire was an unthinkable thing. It is just very hard for me to make my way through all of this honestly. The shifting ground of what some call "postmodern" thinking has allowed me to look at desire with a much more seeing eye. I don't feel as apologetic as I did when I wrote *A Restricted Country.* There is definitely a distinct fem self that I create in bed, that I worked on for a very long time.

BC: Are we making fems sound schizophrenic, girls with multiple personalities? Anyway, is that fem different from what you call your woman self?

JN: Yes, because I don't have sex as a woman. I would only be a woman with a man. I have sex as a fem. When I was younger, I thought that a woman and a fem were the same. I was just exploring everything, men and women. I was learning, sorting out, discovering that the desire I felt with a woman was a hundred times greater than I ever felt with a man. I desired penetration with a woman and felt nothing when a man penetrated me. Oddly, what was interesting with a man was not the moment of entry, but their cocks all by themselves. I liked to play with a cock because I liked to see all the things it did. But with a woman it was the point of entry. Now I can have it all, lesbian cocks and lesbian hands.

BC: So if you don't have sex as a woman but rather as a fem, at what point in your day is this transition marked? Is it when you walk through the door and you come home from work? Or, is it when Lee walks through the door? Is it dependent on your butch or is it dependent on a whole way of life?

JN: It's dependent on outside cues, like I could put on certain music here by myself, and I am a fem. I can put on certain clothes and no one else has to be here, and I am a fem. This all means a certain kind of self-knowledge of one's own repertory of responses. When I was younger, I was much more confused about how deep penetration really could go, about how much of myself I had to trade for that deep deep entry of a butch's hand. Now I have a much stronger sense as a self-possessed fem that my partner needs me as much, and even more, that I can live with my own need in my own skin. I can lie in bed and feel self-contained in my own fem desire and fem appreciation of myself when no one is touching me. There was a time I could never have done that.

BC: Let's think of becoming fem as a kind of garment. If you are making this transition from woman to fem, what do you have to first take off in order to put on your fem garb? What is it to take off being a woman?

JN: All the garments of public responsibility as symbolized by my work clothes. For the last thirty years, it has meant putting down my satchel with all my student papers, all the memos and requests of college teaching. It means divesting myself of pantyhose, slacks, pumps, bra. It means giving my body its own time when it is dressed only in garments of surrender.

BC: Could you balance your checkbook as a woman or as a fem?

JN: (Laughs) That is so smart. I don't want to do it as a fem. But as a woman of course I have to do it—in my own way which is more impressionistic than Lee's. I know exactly when to stop writing checks. The way I think about money when I am a fem is exchanging it for sex. I never think about it except as something I can manipulate in an erotic way, but I don't think about it as a daily responsibility. Fem for me is an escape from that.

BC: When you eat too much chocolate, are you a woman or a fem?

JN: By the way, what did you do with the candy?

BC: It's on top of the fridge, I didn't eat it!

JN: Oh no, you can eat it. It's just that Lee would make me throw it away as if I was an alcoholic, and the chocolate is scotch.

BC: Is eating too much chocolate fem or woman?

JN: Eating is a problematic area for me, so this is all new thinking for me. Eating things that drip and are sweet and full of sun. Eating potatoes and rice, that's a woman. Eating meat in a way is a woman. Eating too much chocolate, I hate myself for it. It's hard for me to feel like a fem when I feel like an out-of-control eater. But I do feel like a woman, like a typical woman who can't control her eating.

BC: And a fem can control her eating?

JN: What I do as a fem is not contaminated. What I do as a fem is a wonderful erotic traveling, so there is no punishment connected to it; but as a woman I feel very punished.

BC: And you punish yourself by beating yourself up for eating too much?

JN: Right. Being a woman is being in a world of external judgment. The fem world is one of accomplishment which is freeing, which is not how I always experienced it as a younger woman.

Fem/Feminism

BC: How is occupying this other place of fem, then, not just abandoning women of the world. If we abandon our womanness when we dress right and eat fruit and so on, when we take on fem, how is that feminist? How is that simply not abandoning women or our womanness? Here we have carefully created this entire artifice to support ourselves as fems, including other people, clothes, hair, food, a whole culture of fem. Does this culture of fem leave other women behind? And say, well, fuck you, you are the work horses of the world anyway . . .

JN: I think there is travel back and forth between these two states, or stories, the fem story and the woman story. And perhaps I wouldn't have survived many of the things I did as a woman, if I hadn't had the other story.

The fem part may look like it's betraying the woman part—I wanted to say it the other way. I have often felt that women betray fems, but fems don't betray women. The women I work with form a comradeship with me as a woman, but they wouldn't as a fem. They wouldn't even know what to do with it. And the minute I say that I know this is not the whole story. The risk of desire has been a shared bond with some of my straight women friends at work, especially the women who are looking for the touch they desire.

I don't assume that because I have one world of erotic realness, that has to be every woman's. But I think perhaps that straight women, in their own desire, experience their version of what is my fem place. I mean if I know that I myself have two stories that take me through the world, then I think that other women must too.

In my writing and public speaking I try to listen to women, rather than saying, "Now, this is who you are supposed to be." One connecting link is the sense of respect for straight women's desire. To create a sexual politics, to create spaces for sexual desire, that is part of the feminist struggle. That is for me a profound way of building solidarity that leads me not to betrayal but to a different kind of territory. I have taken the position of defending pornography and prostitution because I feel that women get abused so terribly *because* they are desiring beings and when they connect to sex in a public way, they endanger their lives. The whore in all women, the girlfriend who says yes to another man, the wife who has an affair, the woman who says no or yes in her own voice, is what patriarchal society wants to beat down.

BC: Clearly placing desire at the forefront of one's ambitions, then, is an abandonment of women who play by the rules. Those good girls. In your own history as you tell it, you have an allegiance, a solidarity, with bad girls of all kinds, sex workers, whores, queers. It's not just that fem abandons women. But we do abandon certain kinds of women, women who aren't interested in placing their desire at the forefront . . .

JN: And we abandon domesticity. When we were sitting in that room yesterday with all the babies and all the lesbian moms, I felt like a different creature. And I looked around and even though X is in a butch-fem relationship, at that moment in that room, what I saw were women, "good" women. Doing the good woman thing. Here were two socially constructed narratives clashing against each other. I don't conceive of lesbian parenting as the same as woman parenting. They occur in a different historical and communal context, and yet, of course, diapers are diapers.

BC: It was so unsexy. You took a stab at it though, you tried to talk about the baby, licking the baby, and so on. You tried to sexualize it but it sort of flopped didn't it? No one really picked that one up. Oh, babies, you can't . . .

JN: You just can't combine babies and sex. But I know that to some of those women who were also fems having a baby was an erotic experience.

BC: The only person I know of writing about the sexual incentives for reproducing ourselves is Susie Bright.

JN: How do you face these issues of solidarity with other women?

BC: I come and go. Feminism demanded of me that I become a woman and that I fight within the domestic sphere for women's rights. That I take up the issues of childcare, reproductive rights, that I take up basic issues of fundamental social inequalities between men and women. That fight was my fight and I did take it on, but at the same time, I didn't achieve any kind fulfillment of my own sexual desire in that fight. I was always too nasty. "Oh Barbara, you bring up sex all the time. You're always talking about sex." And I would get very passionate and insist, often only to myself, that if we're not having great sex, this is wrong. It would get turned into a joke.

So when I got into my first butch-fem relationship, when I started out, I was incredibly powerful. It was like, oh my god, I can do anything, I am this totally potent fem. My whole world changed. But as time went on, a script kind of took over, the script of the dutiful wife or something. I gave up more and more of that power. The butch was out sleeping around, I was doing all the cleaning. I was doing all the things I thought I was supposed to do, and it wasn't sexy. I gave up my femness for another narrative, I felt unattractive and gained a lot of weight. I wasn't having sex.

I experienced all that as giving up my femness and in that transition, I had a kind of rebirth of my own feminism because here I was again occupying the position of woman as opposed to fem. When I occupy the position of fem, feminism can seem like a straight woman's cause.

I became a welfare rights activist and hung out almost exclusively with single mothers. It was wonderful. I am still committed to the welfare rights struggle but it wasn't my struggle you see. I had family members on welfare.

A lot of the activists were dykes on welfare of course. But here I was fighting for who I would have become had I been straight.

JN: One of the most complex intertwinings is the relationship between feminism and fem. In the early seventies, when I first heard Monique Wittig say, "I am a lesbian and not a woman," it made perfect sense. Then as our thinking developed in different directions, I realized all the shifting territories: I am not a woman, I am a lesbian, I am not a lesbian, I am a fem. But of course, life and politics demand that I be able to reintegrate these spheres when I must. Being a fem does not mean turning back on the choices or struggles of other women, for fems are women from all societal places. What is surprising, however, is how feminism can reverberate in different women's lives, the different kinds of autonomy it can give. Feminism has given me dignity as a worker and as a citizen, it has given me an understanding of the totality of male power in the world, but it also gave me a deeper fem self, a courage to push my explorations of loosened gender beyond what I had allowed myself. In other words, it gave me the strength to overcome the stigma of my "freak" desires. "My Woman Poppa," the first story in which I wrote about taking a woman's cock into my mouth, could not have happened without feminism. How perverse is liberation!

BC: You've been talking about your fears over your own possible essentialism and "postmodern" criticism of your work this weekend. You were saying that there is woman, there is lesbian, and then there's fem. Are these all three different genders? Feminism insisted that we were all one gender, we could all join together in a single struggle for liberation. That's essentialism. What we have learned over the course of the last thirty years is that there are many genders of women. When you refuse Sheila Jeffrey's vision of a lesbian movement and lesbian culture, you are refusing a narrowing of scope. There are many gender-female roles to occupy. Poststructural critics try to get us to see that and to articulate how we perform those genders.

JN: Yes, now I understand, but when I first wrote about butch–fem I was trying too hard to appease, so I did not address all the complexities of the experience. That is why I am so glad for friendships such as ours, for new decades of analysis.

Fem/Feminine

BC: You said the important thing about your femness is that it is put on every day, it is something that you have to craft and recraft all the time. Isn't that precisely what distinguishes fem from feminine? Isn't that why fem is to butch what butch is to fem, that is, something that is performed, that is a ploy, and self-conscious?

JN: I never used the word "performance" before. I've written about the shortcomings of calling butch-fem "role-playing." Here again is that historical contradiction I spoke about in the beginning.

For me, fem has been as natural as breathing, but I also understand that all systems of desire have artifice built in. I also believed and still do that the historical butch-fem community from which I come demands another kind of analysis than we are doing here. Now I live and struggle in a world where nothing feels natural but all feels real. Maybe breathing is the only "natural" thing and nothing else is. Maybe everything else is created every day. You know, one of the differences between straight society and queer society, queer culture or queer consciousness, is that we have a recognition that we form ourselves. At almost every crucial moment of our lives we have to construct ourselves, construct other ways of being.

But I am still a little uneasy with the glib and highly abstract language of some queer theory. I think we have to have the sense to know when to fall humble before the sincerity of lived lives. Play with the texts all you want. For me, femininity is a text. I never thought of it as natural, not in the fifties and not now, but if those young women at the gay community center [in Joan's introduction] were celebrating the feel of what they call their femininity, then my own historical positioning must not be turned against them.

BC: I came away from your earlier writings with the idea that butch-fem is not an imitation of heterosexuality. That was a very devastating charge against butch-fem when I came out.

I learned the difference between feminine and fem from your writing. The difference was power. I treated your works as fem handbooks. I was inspired by two ideas in particular. One was that sex cannot be left out of any story, life, or liberation movement. The second was that to get good sex took courage. That is repeated in the writings of Audre Lorde and Dorothy Allison.

To be feminine in the working-class culture I grew up in was, in my mind, to be a victim of men, to be vulnerable in horrible ways to violence, poverty, screaming kids, and consigned to a life of housework, factory work, and dependence.

What I learned from your writing is that fem is an identity that is carefully thought out. It is a way of setting standards for yourself, a way to demand great sex and never settle for bad sex, a way to get a hold of freedom. By articulating fem as an identity, as something you sat on that barstool and thought about as a way to get the kind of sex you wanted, your writing created the possibility for me to leave the feminine behind and get on to fem.

We don't wake up one day and discover that we are fems. I got pressed up against a wall by a big butch and the sex is what made me want to be fem. That is when I read your book, *A Restricted Country.* I went looking for ways to be fem, to be a bottom. It was very confusing and it took forever to figure out that to be a fem bottom in bed didn't mean that I had no power. Figuring out the power of my own sexual practices was slow and painful; I had to learn the hard way.

I fantasize now about creating a fem culture that will make it easier for wanna-be fems to distinguish between fem and feminine. Maybe it is no longer important though. Riot Grrrls and rowdy rockers seem to get it.

JN: I understand your wish to make the distinction between femininity and femness very clear. The lesbian chic image is an example of how the fem can be depoliticized, but fems have a long history of being subversive. That is why our stories need to be told. How do we hold out against all the created visions of us?

What gets confusing is the self-presentation. I wasn't taught how to be feminine when I was growing up, that which many women have to rebel against, to become another kind of woman. I didn't get any of that. What felt essential to me was my desire. That I didn't feel I had to learn, I mean I knew I wanted to be fucked by a certain kind of woman, but who I was around that fucking, how I would encourage it, what I would do with it, that is what I was creating.

Now the desire itself, I know, had to come from someplace. My image of it all was that if I could just get them home, if I could just get them to my bed, if I could just take off all my clothes, then all the things that don't give off the right signals because I don't have a bouffant hairdo and I don't have the right clothes, then my hips, ass, and my tits will tell them everything I want them to know. That is, I thought when I was stripped of artifice, they'll really know how much of a fem I am. So in that time and place, artifice, the outside dress of desire, was my enemy.

BC: Well, you probably know a lot of butches with the same hips and the same breasts that don't speak the same language.

JN: Now I see also that I worked very hard in bed. What I felt to be a natural expression of self, was actually an attempt to get back to a body. The body seems to be a natural thing, but to get to my body, I had to go through the layers of freak, woman, lesbian, fem. As you said so well, we had to find a way to change what being a woman meant. I had to find a place for my body that did not promise destruction. In my earlier years, being a fem made it bearable for me to be a woman. Now at fifty-five, the questions of survival are posed in different ways. My fem self may be the only solid ground under my feet in this changing unhappy historical time.

Now ask me how do I watch football, as a fem, as a woman, and I'll tell you that I have another form. I have this place between fem and baby-butch . . .

BC: There you go. Ha.

Notes

1. We are using the vocabulary of "fem" rather than "femme" in order to evoke the working-class and gendered identities we each inhabit. Moreover, we choose "fem" to highlight the distinction between fem (a sexual identity) and feminine (an attribute of gender, lesbian or not). The difference is both subtle and highly charged. While some lesbian feminists are still uncomfortable with the sexual and gender difference marked by fem, we are interested in how the performance of the fem gender can be distinguished from gender-female.

A COINCIDENCE OF LIPSTICK AND SELF-REVELATION

Katherine Millersdaughter

It is Tuesday afternoon, and I am at the grocery shopping for chocolate. I have a pint of fudge brownie ice cream in one hand and mint chocolate chip in the other. Though I should be heading for the register, I am aimlessly wandering the aisles until, finally, I decide to check out the make-up section. So it is, with lipstick on my mind, that I lay my eyes like hands on the body like text of butch: blue jeans and work boots, a green employee's tee-shirt, short, dark hair and a distinctively round swing in her strut. Just a few yards ahead of me, walking toward me, she casually glances at my two pints of ice cream. When her eyes finally glance off mine, her walk eases into a slow unmistakable swagger, and I look down, really flattered and thinking, "Now she is lesbian": wearing her clothes and her walk like no one else can, running her hands through her hair, her eyes down the lines of my body, my stanzas, my in-between spaces.

Wherever I am, at home furtively nosing through old family photos, in front of a classroom, at the coffee shop, biking up Broadway, I am always looking for lesbian. This woman in the jeans and green tee-shirt, she was definitely it: that full-bodied, beautiful word, lesbian, and not incidentally, that strong-bodied, sweet word, butch. "Not incidentally": this is a problem, this equivalence between lesbian and butch. It is an equivalence that has had me shaking in my own jeans and work boots, a lesbian drag that, as pleasurable as it is at times, can work against the flesh that would curve here and swivel there. It is an equivalence that has hoisted on me a wardrobe of stiff, heavy lines that, in turn, have cast my identity into suspicion: "You're not really a lesbian: your body doesn't fit." It's true, the same moment that found me triumphantly staking a claim and finally naming myself also found me suddenly harassed by a painful, gut-centered suspicion that there are degrees of lesbian. I have worried that I fall into the suspiciously metallic, unfiltered dregs of not-straight: not exactly queer, or bisexual, or lesbian, just "not-straight." Rationally, defiantly, I have defended my self as absolutely lesbian, but that defense has found me abandoning my swish for a swagger, my pretty tilt of ass for a mean stance. And it has always found me rejecting the name, femme, as shorthand for feminine, for straight girl. With my hand to my heart, I have sworn, "It does not name me. I am not femme. Sure, I'm not butch, but there are other lesbian ways of being." There are better lesbian ways of being: according to too many, the "world of butch and femme" is "ultra-stratified" and, in affect at least, indistinguishable from "heterosexuality itself."[1]

"Better" aside, there are, of course, a variety of lesbian identities or postures, and, intimidated by the stigmas attaching to femme, I have leaned toward androgyny. Certain it was the correct thing to do, I threw my make-up away and resigned myself to short hair; I shoved my "straight girl's" clothes far back in a bottom drawer and costumed myself in tennies, shorts, a tee-shirt and baseball cap. However, I remained equally certain in my penchant for red lace undies; I allowed myself the excitement of rare nights in heels and a little dress; and I hung on breathlessly to the fantasy of a butch's hand on my side, guiding my oh-so-nicely clad body into a room, any room would do, a living room, a restaurant or bar, a kitchen. My point is that I looked but did not feel androgynous. I felt sexy in a particularly gendered way, and, every time a softball-dyke put her hands on my hips to move me out of her way (so serious she was about the game and in a hurry), I wondered if she could feel the lace under my shorts. I would sit down on the bench, watch her hit the field, and, with my own hands on my hips, I would think to myself, "Surely red lace feels qualitatively different under shorts than white cotton."

Finally, fortunately, I discovered Joan Nestle. I have laid my hands on *The Persistent Desire* as though it were my lover, as well as my own self and body, sucking us up past my lips and across my tongue.[2] How many of us post-Stonewall dykes have come into our own and other women's bodies through other women's writing? It's true, my first lover fucked me in the margins of her text and, afterwards, dressed me from the wardrobe of myself.

> I might've tried to reply, or wanted to wriggle away, but I couldn't hardly, because she was holding me down and covering my mouth with her lips, her kiss, and one of her long, sleek legs was sliding up between mine, so that my belly had begun to shake. Escape was even harder when she slipped her fingers under my panties. "Take yo' drawers off, sugar babe?"[3]

The Persistent Desire empowered me with the power of my swish and pretty tilt of ass. It brought me into a fuller understanding of my self and body: it brought me into my own ways of getting and wanting sex, my own ways of experiencing my body and other women's sex, my own ways of refusing heterosexual norms and asserting the "sexy" of lesbian sex. Now, I admit I am extremely wary of anything capitalist, consumerist, and glitzy, I hate mall-shopping, I have but one pair of high heels, my hair isn't that long, and I rarely ask for a chair, I'm fine sitting on the floor. Nonetheless, there is a power and familiarity of Nestle's "Gift of Touch" that brings me immediately into myself, that highlights in the sound of femme an explosively nuanced lesbian sexuality, a near ineffability that turns me on.

For too long femme sounded too much like "feminine," that which signified my worthlessness and marked my self as sexy only in my powerlessness. I learned early on that my world's interest in making a "lady" out of me meant midnights and random afternoons under my father's body on the bedroom, bathroom, or basement floor. I was three and a half years old when I knew my father had made a hole between my legs that would never heal; I knew this and more and all of it in terms of "feminine." Femininity was synonymous with a painful penetrability that had torn my body open.

When beyond the gaze of my father, I turned my back on that feminine body and forged a space/self in between "boy" and "girl" that others named "tomboy." Years later, I would forswear calling it femme. And still more years later, I would insist on calling it femme, tomboy femme. I can swagger across a street if I need to, I can wear jeans and work boots and very often I want to, and my body can turn as impenetrable as any other, it is entirely my own if I say so. As Gayle Rubin notes in her contribution to *The Persistent Desire,* there are many ways of being butch, rich in a conscious engagement with the languages of masculinity, "gender codes and symbols" specific to class, race, and decade.[4] Likewise, there are many different ways of being femme. Those of us who call ourselves femme have varying needs for the several languages of femininity, masculinity, and lesbianism in the expressive production of our identities. I am always and consciously engrossed in a whittling away at the available languages of gender and sexuality, tracing and re-tracing the unpredictable contours of the individual and collective femme.

I grew up afraid of my body, as many girls do. I grew up despising anyone feminine, women and men alike. But still, my young, tomboy self took secret pleasure in a woman's drag and held pretend tea parties and picnics, where all my guests and myself sat around in beautiful dresses with big, beautiful hair and parasols. I was all contradiction, imagining my jeans and tee-shirts into sequined evening gowns as I dug my knees into the dirt and played marbles with the best of them. I was the fastest runner in the fourth grade and dressed myself in golden wings and silver streamers as I bolted across the field and beat the boys. I lived two selves: the impenetrable tomboy in my world of classrooms and playgrounds and the beautiful but not-female, not-feminine woman in the impenetrable space of my mind. And I un-lived that other self, the not-me, the girl who was neither impenetrable nor beautiful. Ugly but very sexy, he said, very sexy . . . I was not her. She was someone else, suffocating beneath the weight of her femininity and all that it inspired: her father's rage, her mother's distance, and her own self-contempt. I was not her,

> straddled on your bed
> palest pink legs forced apart
> arms held down: your
> fucking hand
> fucking violently
> inside brown vaginal folds
> to
> the palest pink. [5]

I did not suffer the hands of that father but wrenched myself free, yet again and again and imagined his body and voice into storms overhead. I turned the cement of the basement floor into the cool dirt of the cornfield. I raised my solid, tomboy's frame from the earth to the tips of the cornstalks where I walked like Jesus with my eyes to the dark depths of god's outrage. My tomboy's body took shape in my mind only when it could not take shape in my world, and I walked the water of a shimmering cornfield in worn tennis shoes, shorts, and a dirty white tee-shirt. I did not grow up with religion, but I did believe in Christ. He was my self, not a man at all but a girl, not a girl at all but a body, split in two: I was hung up to dry from bedposts and moonbeams and crucified on bedroom, bathroom, and basement floors.

When I have sex, I have to concentrate really hard on keeping my body whole, because too easily it splits into the two halves of my childhood. I focus on the feel of her skin on mine; I close my eyes and turn the feel of her fist inside my body into the vision of her long, slim fingers and delicate knuckles when she turns a door knob, grips a pencil, lifts her coffee. I listen for her voice and wrap it around me as I imagine the lines of her palm, the texture of her fingers. I save our sex from my splitting in two: one still like death beneath her, the other floating in high places, watching, my chin to my chest, my eyes to the bleeding hole at my side.

Somewhere in my early twenties, when my college years introduced me to the word, sex, and politics of lesbianism, I turned away from the self-image of Christ that never quite proved my savior. I became intent on making myself in my own image, intent, in other words, on discovering a better image that I could make my own. From looking up to his bleeding body, I turned toward my own flesh and forged the bodily lines and stanzas that would signify me in the safety, strength, and desire of a truer self. I needed a name, and lesbian came close to re-sounding the feel of my body as I walked into another woman's arms; femme lesbian, however, has done this and more. Finally, in knowing myself femme, I assert a poetics of my own sex, gender, and desire, a study of the infinite excess of my body, the title, the frame of clean space on my page, my margins dripping with the orgasmic, critical trace that bears the tumultuous meeting of my body with hers, our sex.

I picked up *The Persistent Desire,* and, suddenly, my predilection for strong-bodied women skilled in throwing me up against the wall made sense. It's true, as hesitant as I have been to take up the name femme, I have loved butch, worshipped butch:

> M: Worship.
> A: Complete worship.
> J: I can spend hours looking at the side of Deb's face as she drives the car; there is adoration, there is thank-you for making things safer. [6]

So there in the store, a pint of ice cream in each hand and a sudden decision to check out the lipsticks propelling me toward the make-up aisle, I find myself red in the face and turning my eyes to the floor, so shy I am in admiration of her oh-so-nicely clad, swaggering body. As we pass each other, I resist the urge to turn my head and watch her. Instead, I turn the corner, and, dumping my ice cream on the floor, I begin testing lipsticks on the inside of my wrist. Making unabashed use of the aisle-length mirror, I try a few colors on my mouth. I am having a good time, pouting my lips in the mirror and giving myself long, sideways glances. I decide on the Cafe Au Lait, but the glass case is locked. So it is, with an uncharacteristic unreserve, that I go in search of the dark-haired, swaggering beauty. She is two aisles over squatting on the floor, butch-handling slim plastic bottles of lotion into line on the lowest shelf. I say, "Excuse me? I've just come from the make-up aisle." I am suddenly flirtatious, opening my eyes really big, looking at her sideways and through my lashes; I am turning the toes of my right foot toward my left foot and sliding my hands into my pockets. I am speaking in mock seriousness: "And I'm wondering if I have to buy a tester, or if I can get my very own, never-ever-used-before stick of moisturizing lip color." She looks directly at me, and I make the most of the moment by smiling really big. I move my hips to the left and rest my palm on the up-turn.

My femme is about being taken. Within my kind of femme/butch romance, there is a possessing/being-possessed that is the loving, re-visionary performance of our difference: rather than relegating sameness to spectral back-drawers of disavowal, our sex is a constant eroticization, articulation and negotiation of our difference as it meets our sameness and as it affords both of us the means of control and abandonment.

> The reality, for me and my kind, whatever we told you and whatever you believed, is that fucking between equals is passionless. Penetration without context is meaningless. Sex that is gentle, passive, egalitarian, and bloodless does not move us. Lesbians were right to be so suspicious about penetration back then. There really is, in fact, no equality in penetration.
>
> When we fuck, we possess. When we are fucked, we become the possession. For some, the only time in our lives we can give up control or achieve total control is as we are taken or as we take. [7]

But there is a taking involved in the being-taken, in the giving up of oneself into the control of another. The radical revision lies not only in the change of context, what I believe is a profound shift from straight to lesbian, or from the violent foreclosure of (hetero)sexual difference to a sexy juxtaposition of difference with sameness. This revision lies also in the instability of the very dyad, femme/butch, that delivers into language our difference: it is the consciousness of our bodies and roles as never fully discrete but unpredictably interchangeable in the intimacy of skin, legs, arms, lips, and words. A femme finally 'fesses up: there is an aggressive being-taken that takes and commands the butch in turn: confide in her, "You are so powerful," and you bring her to her knees. In other words, there is in my kind of femme/butch romance an explosion of the very binary relation between equal and unequal, making of our desire the way out of the aggressivity of difference. Into the clean heat of sun, we enter close, intimate spaces wherein difference is all pleasure and far more passionate than to ever find articulation in opposition.

She is leaning into one hip, slowly moving her eyes like tongue over the curves and corners of my painted lips, and I feel an intensity of sun rivering up between my legs. She is running her hands through her hair and asking me, "So, you want the color you got on right now? It's pretty." I am blown away by the combined triviality and power of the moment: she has called me pretty, and I will never be the same. I am handing her the tester, and she is smiling, reading the label, "'Cafe Au Lait,' hmmmm." She is kneeling down, now unlocking the glass case, now peering into the lowest shelf. Reaching in and moving a few things around, she murmurs, "hmmmm," puts the tip of her tongue to the corner of her mouth in concentration, taps her fingers against the glass, squints into the dark depths of the make-up case and repeats herself, "hmmmm."

Finally, she tilts her head up, looks at me sideways and says, in a slow, low and practiced voice, "I hate to break your heart, Honey, but we're all out. How about I take your name and number and give you a call . . . when some more of it comes in."

There is a long pause, and then I blurt out a choked, panic-stricken, "Oh."

You see, it occurred to me she was flirting in return and suggesting we see each other again, outside the grocery. I was cold with fear, embarassed by the extremity of my response, and afraid she would notice something was a bit off. So I reached down for my ice cream and walked away.

My life has taught me that sex is dangerous, and sometimes, still, I am afraid. Once, years ago, the moon was shining in through my bedroom window. It should have been beautiful, but my father's face was grey as any corpse. He was death itself, sitting on the edge of my bed, but they were my eyes sown suddenly shut, my lips sown suddenly shut, and my body on display in the open casket of his embrace.

The kind of sex I like can terrify me, split me in half. It is about power, about giving it all away and finding it again in the slow, commanding turn of her fingers, the turn of her voice as she works my self back into my body, the turn of events as I begin to ease her into my taking-over. However, it is also about risk, hazarding a return to twenty years ago, where I still lie choking on the basement floor.

Once home from my strange trip to the grocery, I brainstormed several forms of penance while slamming around the kitchen and muttering, "She was really great and I ruined it," "I should be better now, I'm twenty-six years old for Christ's sake, almost twenty-seven," and "It is very possible that I am incurably, insanely unpredictably frigid." Finally, however, it occurred to me that those who claim I desire women because of what my father did to me are incontrovertibly wrong: my lesbianism cannot be an attempt, pathetic or otherwise, to escape remembering my father's wrongs in the faces of other men; I am remembering my father's wrongs in the faces, postures, and gestures of other women.

> No trauma 'makes' someone
> homosexual.
> I'm not a lesbian because of . . .
> I'm not a lesbian in spite of . . .
> I am lesbian.
> It is that simple:
> I am lesbian because I am lesbian.
> I am INCEST SURVIVOR
> I am LESBIAN
> I am WOMAN
> I am.
> Alive. [8]

I am not a lesbian because of . . . nor am I a lesbian out of spite. But I am a lesbian despite . . . I cannot separate my lesbian from my raped self. Each soaks the skin of the other and other selves still, they touch at points, intermingle, grapple. I am of and through my world, a place of father-daughter incest and compulsory heterosexuality. But this does not mean I am equal to my victimization; this does not mean my gender and sexuality are reducible to my father's, my family's, and my community's wrongs. The relationship between my sexualization and sexuality is a complicated dynamic of revision, resistance, desire, and love. The bedroom, bathroom, and basement floors of my father's house were schoolrooms, and the curriculum was a specific heterosexuality in which I would never be anything but some man's sexy little girl. I am what my father tried to ensure I would not become, a woman who makes openings in her body to inspire and embrace the lust of other women.

I am multiple, and in too many intractably singular spaces my multiple self has not found welcome. Too often, I have been told, "Oh, I wouldn't say that if I were you, they'll think all lesbians are victims who've been fucked over by their fathers or fucked over by some man."

> i would like to write here that i have found the lesbian community and that lesbians helped me heal and it was wonderful but i am not ready to write the "they lived happily ever after" story. i may never be ready to write that. i don't believe that is my story. there is a story that needs to be written though. i have found certain womyn who are as committed as i am to destroying the lies that have served as our lives.[9]

A friend of mine found *Loving in Fear* in a used-book store. She bought it for me as a gift through which to communicate her respect and concern for the lesbian and incest survivor in me. I appreciated her gift, but almost a year passed before I was able to read the book, because I did not yet share that respect and concern. Within the place of my own consciousness, then, I have known the refusal to acknowledge both selves at once. I have been afraid of implicating the lesbian as only, centrally, a victim. I have been afraid of confronting the same suspicion in others, afraid of confronting the charge, "You're not really a lesbian, you just think you are because of what he did to you, you're avoiding men until you get over the trauma, women are a temporary fix." Not incidentally, my femme, what they usually call my "feminine," has been used to substantiate the charge: "And besides, you're not nearly butch enough, honey. Lesbian? No, we don't think so." Finally, I have been afraid of my femme as the surest sign of a false consciousness constitutive of my self, and I have forsworn the femme in order to affirm my self as both a lesbian and, incidentally, as one who was raped by her father.

Loving in Fear is the anthology I first came across that affirmed my need to be openly lesbian as I openly give voice to my experience of father-daughter rape. And it is the first text I came across to give so much voice to the experiences of incest specific to gays and lesbians, experiences complicated by the violence of homophobia. Most analyses of sexual child abuse assume the heterosexual identity of the survivor; at best, the analyses label a particular percentage of their study homosexual or bisexual but do not propose, let alone explore, the particular ways in which we experience memories of the abuse. Diana Russell, in *The Secret Trauma,* goes so far as to suggest the usefulness of work that theorizes lesbianism as a consequence of sexual child abuse. She proposes that, if true, this theory substantiates her argument that incest is indeed traumatic, for what besides trauma might induce one to embrace lesbianism? Russell does not insist upon the validity of the theory, but neither does she acknowledge, let alone challenge, its anti-lesbian underpinnings. Furthermore, this one reference to lesbian incest survivors is the extent of her consideration of sexual identity as it might inform experiences of intrafamilial rape.[10] We need to consider how lesbians' practices of foreclosure might be troubled by the predictable dismissal of their sexuality in terms of the sexual abuse; moreover, we need to ask how the prohibition against telling on our fathers infects the prohibition against "telling on" or naming ourselves, how we might, because of that infection, experience our desire for women as analogous to our fathers' violent misdeeds. This last issue describes my own sense of fear toward my desire for other women and the way in which my two terrible secrets have "swapped juices": the one is too close to the other; the enforced, protective silence about my father is too close to the silence and invisibility demanded of me by institutionalized heterosexuality.

The Queer Press Collective's *Loving in Fear* is a refusal of the silence that Russell and others maintain on the relationships between sexual identity and sexual child abuse; further, it is the vital re-articulation of the interconnected experiences of homophobia and memories of abuse.

> We are all meant to be loving in fear—kept in our place by the lies and myths surrounding our existence. The people who tell us that abuse is the cause of being queer—now that the problem is identified they can work to fix us—or say that queers are all perpetrators of abuse, want to keep us loving in fear. . . .
>
> Whenever we break the silence, as survivors, lovers, friends, and as queers, we are fighting for the right to love as we choose.[11]

The sexual abuse of girls and women functions to keep us in fear of, and bound to, particular constructions of our bodies; similarly, homophobic violence functions to keep us in fear of our bodies, our desires, and our voices. To be sure, the articulation of lesbianism in terms of what our families did to us is a hateful mis-speaking of our love and sex, a mis-speaking that soils the powerful meeting of our bodies with memories of blood and shit. Together, childhood sexual abuse and heterosexist violence have too many of us afraid of the sex we need and the women we desire.

And they have us insisting upon our normalcy, insisting upon our silence. We are too often shutting each other up, concerned someone will get the wrong idea. Too frequently we are searching out and projecting clear-cut identities, concerned someone will use the fluidity of shifting, signifying boundaries against us. It's true, as a femme lesbian, my experience has been that I hesitate before speaking about the incest because already I am so sexually suspect, among straight, bisexual, and homosexual people alike.

> [F]emme lesbians are seen somehow as the ultimate example of the hetero-sexual woman gone astray. Perhaps she was abused once too often or had a terrible father. We all know the reasons we have been given for why women choose other women. It's never that there are women who want to be with women, who are absolutely lesbian. It's never that we have our own symbols, our own ways, our own deep attractions.[12]

I have a stake in being queer: it is saving me, or it is me, the self my father tried to straight-jacket in the dress of hetero-patriarchal relations wherein a woman's husband is nothing less than her father. And though I have denied it, I have a stake in being femme, in the symbols, ways, and deep attractions that allow me a particularly gendered, sexually strong body that betrays no one in its way of moving but, rather, initiates two bodies' meeting, anointing us in the re-visionary power of femme-butch sex.

The voices have been chilling, insisting upon my silence, questioning my desire and turning me away; however, it is fair to say many more have offered the healing that has brought me entirely into my self. But I am cursed with shyness, as many of us are, afraid of my materiality and yours. I prefer, sometimes, the sexy, textual relations that have me all ear-marked and under-lined, annotated; that have made of me a slew of steamy metaphors, a slow turn, and return, of your pages; that have brought my tongue to your theory, the sleek length of your narrative, the curves of your poetry.

I am a femme lesbian, twenty-seven years old, and I am a girl, only three and a half, my father's erection searing the length of my right forearm. I am many selves. I am all words, madly looping letters and scantily clad margins inscribed in the white of my flesh. I am complicated, a shifting intersection of meadows and gates and you, treading the green length of me.

I have had an overwhelming need to find a name for myself that respects how I am different from and similar to others. Finally, I discovered that name in Joan Nestle, then Leslie Feinberg, then Cherríe Moraga, who once told me as I sat in an auditorium filled with queer academics, "The butch-femme dance is really (pause) hot." My femme is not "feminine," and the strange day at the grocery finally made that clear. After leaving the gorgeous butch in the make-up aisle, I went home, thought about maiming myself but decided against it and instead got high on a cup of coffee. Finally, I came to the conclusion that I am femme, yes, but weak, no. I decided my femme is about strength, about flirting outrageously with a woman and teasing her cool, false indifference into open interest. It occurred to me that I had initiated the seduction, seduced her into seducing me into no passive receptivity but an assertive opening up of my body to hers. Sure, I had run away, but the point had to be that I was free and strong enough to do so.

I like being seduced. I like being seduced into seducing, playfully coaxed into teasing, into leaning over, kneeling down, adjusting my bra, my lipstick at just the moment she deigns to glance in my direction. And I like the way the grocery store dyke recognizes the dyke in me and responds by running her hands through her hair and looking me over. I like the way she says, "pretty," how she makes of it the word that signals our difference. As handsomely beautiful as she is, as gorgeous and sexy as she is, "pretty" is the word she uses to mark my body in its difference from hers, and I am so pleased she noticed. I am both like and unlike her, and she noticed. I am that beautiful word, lesbian, and, not incidentally, I am that strong-bodied, sweet word, femme. I am beautiful, complicated in my new name, a pretty tomboy in my baseball cap, tee-shirt, shorts and red lace underwear; a sexy woman, tall and taller in my heels and slim in my short black dress; a teacher, playfully made up in my butch drag of jeans, a white oxford shirt and a blue silk vest, smiling as I swagger from one end of the blackboard to the other discussing self in terms of body and a nondeliberate, performative becoming; a writer on break, searching the grocery for chocolate ice cream and lipstick and finally running into butch, running into my self.

This piece describes an unlikely, playful yet decisive coincidence of chocolate, lipstick, and self-revelation. Better yet, it makes of an everyday event an other-revelation: my femme never offered my child's body to the man who is my father. My femme took that child in her arms and woke her to the strength of a woman's body. Femme is as femme does, and my femme saved me. She is my own extraordinary excess, that which tumbles out of the (too often) inflexible subject position of lesbian, not to mention feminist. She has born in me the body with which I might finally be strong and sexual, a lesbian body that refuses the normative masculine/feminine construct, not by refusing gender altogether, but in producing and performing the poetics of my self, my other, and our sex: the femme-butch dance. It's really really (pause) hot .

Notes

1. Caryatis Cardea, "A Question of Family," *Sinister Wisdom* 55 (1995): 58.
2. Joan Nestle, ed., *The Persistent Desire: A Femme-Butch Reader* (Boston: Alyson Publications, 1992).
3. Gwendolyn Bikis, "Cleo's Gone," in *The Persistent Desire* 344.
4. Gayle Rubin, "Catamites and Kings," in *The Persistent Desire* 467.
5. Karen Augustine, "Joe/Rape Poem," in *Loving in Fear: An Anthology of Lesbian and Gay Survivors of Childhood Sexual Abuse,* ed. Queer Press Collective (Toronto: Queer Press, 1991) 19.
6. Madeline Davis, Amber Hollibaugh, and Joan Nestle, "The Femme Tapes," in *The Persistent Desire* 267.
7. Jan Brown, "Sex, Lies, and Penetration: A Butch Finally 'Fesses Up," in *The Persistent Desire* 411.
8. Inga-Britt, "Just Listen," in *Loving in Fear* 11.
9. Jean Noble, "Red Running Shoes," in *Loving in Fear* 37.
10. Diana E. H. Russell, *The Secret Trauma: Incest in the Lives of Girls and Women* (U.S.: Basic Books, 1986) 25, 199–200.
11. *Loving in Fear* 10.
12. JoAnn Loulan, *The Lesbian Erotic Dance* (Minneapolis: Spinsters Ink, 1990) 88.

A WOMAN'S PREROGATIVE

Marcy Sheiner

I went through my sexual identity crises rather quickly, and am no longer obsessed—or even terribly interested in—the question. Perhaps this is because I've undergone several permutations in orientation: straight to lesbian, lesbian to bisexual, bisexual to . . . what? I still use the label bisexual when forced to self-identify, because it's the only one that even remotely describes me. But as the monogamous partner of a female-to-male transsexual, I am perceived as straight by many gay people and most heterosexuals, who find reassurance in my painted fingernails and his dark beard. Young lesbian friends tell me I'm beyond categorization and therefore ultra hip, while some older lesbians are, I suspect, intensely uncomfortable about my situation.

Frankly, my dears, I don't give a damn. I have never felt the need for an immutable sexual identity, and I most certainly do not crave membership in any one "community," because I treasure and guard the autonomy that comes with detachment.

It's not that I'm a stranger to the concepts of identity and community. There are certain aspects of myself that I feel down in my bones, characteristics that define me to myself and to the world. I am a woman. I am a mother. I'm a writer. I'm a feminist. I am Jewish. No matter where I go, I will always be a New Yorker.

And now that I'm taking a stand on the side of butch or femme, I'm indisputably the latter.

My femmeness can be studied from three different perspectives: in relation to genetic men, in relation to butch women, and in relation to a transsexual man. This, of course, begs the question: what constitutes a femme identity separate from my partner?

Is there a femme identity without butch or male to define it? While it would seem a point of honor to answer in the affirmative, I'm not sure if *any* identity exists without its counterpart. My now-intense Jewish-New York *schtick*, for instance, didn't emerge until I was in my forties and moved to California, where I was teased or asked about my "accent" and ethnicity almost daily. In the face of my sudden difference, I chose to make New Yorker and Jew nearly synonymous, and to cultivate the image that had been thrust upon me.

The first thing that comes up for me as I analyze femme identity is fear, fear of promoting stereotypes, fear of being perceived as anti-feminist. After all, my femmeness manifests itself in an intense aversion to all tasks dirty and physical, a bewilderment of all things mechanical, a fondness for order and beauty, and a compulsion around housework: I cannot *be* in a kitchen without cleaning it. My femmeness is, in short, feminine, and the 1970s feminism on which I cut my political teeth taught me to abdicate the femininity within.

I tried. I cut my hair, donned jeans, flannel shirts, and hiking boots; I never let a man open a door, change a light bulb, or pay the check. I even took an auto mechanics class and for one grimy year did my own oil changes and tuneups—resulting in frequent highway breakdowns.

Such practices have vanished from my life like the passing trends they were, and these days I feel much more connected to the young suburban housewife I was in 1968 than to the rabble-rousing feminist I was in 1975. Sometimes this troubles me; I worry that I may be "regressing." Received opinion has it that radicals and liberals dissolve into conservatives with age. As I stand on the threshold of fifty, am I simply following a life pattern I deplored in my youth? Given the experiences I've had, the people I know, the opinions I hold, and the work I do, this doesn't seem very likely.

Still, the concept of femmeness as an intrinsic part of who I am, rather than solely in relation to sexual partners, eludes me. Perhaps by examining my femmeness in relation to those various significant others I'll somehow uncover an identity separate from them.

My first "date," an afternoon movie with chubby freckle-faced Billy Peterson, occurred when I was eleven. Before I left the house my older sister lectured me on how to behave. She told me to ask him questions about himself, to listen politely, and not to talk about myself at all. Appalled, I rebelled; I spent the entire day babbling, and at the end of it Billy kissed me on the lips.

Why argue with success? To this day I talk a blue streak with potential and actual lovers, though by now I've acquired some basic techniques to keep them interested and aroused. Are my conversational and seduction techniques characteristic of femmeness? I'm not sure. I couldn't even tell you what they are, so ingrained have they become in my personality. I'm told that I'm "entertaining," and I frequently make people laugh. I'm told that I'm sexy and seductive.

But while I refused early on to stroke the male ego, in most matters I stepped right into my prescribed role around men. They drove, they paid, they initiated sexual contact. Though my own orgasm was several years in coming, I made sure that my partners always climaxed. When I told one boyfriend that my satisfaction was secondary to his, he asked me to marry him.

Now, I wasn't *lying* when I told my future husband that I derived pleasure from his climax. In part I was evading an embarrassing exploration of my own path to orgasm; in part I honestly did derive satisfaction from the ultimate proof of his passion. I certainly never intended to set up a dynamic where his pleasure and needs dominated our entire marriage, yet that is exactly what happened. The pleasure I felt in the nurturing role neatly dovetailed with (some would say originated from) cultural expectations, and was exploited. Like a lot of women, I got typecast, and, like a lot of women, I came to resent it.

Some of my housewife friends, I noticed, were able to get more for themselves through cunning and coyness. But I never quite got the hang of manipulating men, so I had to find other ways to protect myself. I did this by shutting down my femmeness. No longer would I play helpless helpmate to some man; from here on in I decided to be absolutely independent, to rely solely on myself. Inwardly I toughened up, determined to need nothing from anyone, male or female. This attitude not only rendered me less vulnerable, but was also a badge of honor, a political act even, coinciding as it did with the emergence of the 1970s Women's Liberation Movement. Killing off my femme looked and felt pretty much the same as throwing off the shackles of patriarchy.

This led, of course, to divorce and single motherhood: raising kids alone in near poverty (in the spirit of the times I took minimal child support and no alimony), working at lousy secretarial jobs, and still doing all the housework, now along with all the hated "male" tasks.

To say that I was somewhat misguided, or that my choices created an extremely difficult situation for me and my children, is not to negate or trash feminism. I would not be writing this were it not for the women's movement. Still, adjusting to the sudden switch of female role expectations has been, to put it bluntly, an absolute mindfuck.

To this day I carry around two diametrically opposed belief systems. The first was formed in childhood: memories of my great-grandmother, a long silver braid hanging down her broad back, rustling up vast quantities of food for her family; my grandmother, cooking fresh chicken soup for her husband every day of her life; my mother, throwing boiled potatoes and canned vegetables onto the dinner plates, resentfully, yes, but she performed her wifely duties nonetheless. As backdrop to these memories float images of Donna Reed and June Cleaver, models of womanhood embedded deep within my consciousness.

But I also carry equally powerful memories from young adulthood: marching down Fifth Avenue with thousands of newly energized women; sitting in circles spitting out our oppression; writing down my rage in cramped apartments while my kids slept in the only bedroom. From this time period the faces of Gloria Steinem and Betty Friedan replace those of television housewives as role models.

These opposing values and models are constantly at war within me. The example set by my foremothers instilled in me a hefty load of woman–guilt, easily triggered by a dusty table, a sick friend (who will die without my homemade chicken soup), a hungry partner (ditto), or a phone call from one of my grown children navigating life's routine obstacles. But if I continually heed the call of the sick and dusty, it's at the expense of those "self-actualization" values that are part and parcel of feminism. And as the years creep up I'm discovering yet another legacy of feminism: a sad sense of failure, formerly reserved for the Willy Lomans of the world, about not having "made it." I cringe in bookstores at the plethora of new coffee-table tomes profiling accomplished older women, extolling only the positive aspects of aging. Why don't *I* feel wise and energetic? Why aren't *I* at the peak of my career? This aspect of mid-life crisis is certainly unique to my generation. My mother and foremothers were not expected to excel in the public sphere, so were spared this particular agony. My daughter and her peers, who had less female conditioning shoved down their throats, just *might* be spared the compulsion to take care of everyone within a twenty-mile radius. But my generation got sandwiched between two sets of values, a position in which we're damned if we do and damned if we don't.

Is it any wonder then that I have trouble unraveling feminine, feminist, and femme? I know that for many women, lesbian relationships have provided the key to that unraveling, but for me this wasn't the case, primarily because my first and most significant lesbian relationship occurred within the context of 1970s feminism, when I was trying so hard to cleanse myself of retro femininity.

She was butch, except I didn't call her butch, I called her "androgynous."

Now we both laugh at the succession of lovers she's had since me—soft fleshy femmes all—but at the time I was in my flannel-shirted phase and considered myself—or at least aspired to be—"androgynous" as well. We were in complete denial about who we were and the roots of our attraction to one another.

Looking back, I see that I was intensely ashamed of, and attempted to hide, my femmeness, or was it my femininity? I'm still not sure. What I *was* sure about, though, was that feminist was synonymous with butch, or at least androgyny. I saw my lover as far more feminist and competent than I; she could do things like change the spark plugs and rewire lamps, while I could only ladle out the lentil soup. In theory we were sisters who shared the same values, so I believed philosophically that we ought to be mirroring one another's behavior. But secretly I *wanted* to dish out the soup, I *didn't* want to change the spark plugs—and that's what made me feel so ashamed. The femininity that had run for cover around male exploitation retreated even further around feminists.

How I ever managed to find that girl again is a miracle, but twenty years later I have.

Because my current partner was once anatomically female and was treated as such, I immediately felt, on a visceral level, that I could trust him. I sensed that he would not perceive feminine behavior as weakness and use it against me. From the very start of our relationship I felt myself letting go, relaxing into such behavior without shame or apology. In the early days, whenever James opened the car door for me, I actually felt a rush of sexual desire. His embrace of masculinity devoid of superiority enabled me to embrace femininity without feeling inferior.

I've always been drawn to extreme situations as a path to enlightenment, and my attraction to a transsexual man was fueled by a yearning to experience gender from an entirely fresh angle. In this situation the concept of masculine and feminine as complementary and not inherently unequal flashed as brightly as a neon light.

Here was a person who felt his male identity so securely that no amount of anatomical evidence to the contrary, no amount of social conditioning or pressure, had ever been able to convince him otherwise. When I met James he was post-surgery and two years into hormones, so the world perceived him as male. But I caught the butch dyke mannerisms, and watched them gradually recede. I witnessed the adolescent-boy face mature into that of a man.

I experienced myself as an essential ingredient in this transformation: it was clear to me that my femaleness served to enhance and reinforce his maleness. I felt this most acutely in bed, where I surrendered more swiftly and completely than with previous partners. I tapped into my sexuality as a source of power that I could share with my partner, power he could borrow to assist in his transformation. There's a line in the song "You Are Woman" from *Funny Girl,* "You are smaller/ so I can be taller than." Yes, of course, this can be read as sexist propaganda, but it can also be read as "Opposites attract," or "*Vive la difference!*" At any rate, it's the best reference I can come up with to describe our dynamics.

I do not experience these sexual dynamics as a form of exploitation, but as self-empowering. I believe this is because the distrust that I harbor towards genetic men simply doesn't come into play here. Rather, our male-female dynamics seem to create a magnetic circle, a field of energy that's rejuvenating to us as individuals and as a couple.

Additionally, my experience has been strongly informed by a queer sensibility, because when I met James I was editor of *On Our Backs,* the lesbian sex magazine. I lived and breathed lesbian/feminist/radical sex analysis; dialogue around butch/femme was the stuff of my daily existence. Most FTMs are loathe to liken their sexual relationships to a lesbian paradigm, and the parallel probably doesn't apply to all. But my initial reference point for this relationship was butch/femme. I formed an understanding of James based on my understanding of butch, and I gained insight into myself from dialogue around femme.

At the same time, my relationship is undeniably informed by my own heterosexual history as well as by the predominant culture. Ironically, I can now better understand and relate to my friend Angie, who's been married for over thirty years. She's an Italian matriarch who looks like Sophia Loren and runs the world—or at least her extensive family and circle of friends—from her kitchen. For years I couldn't relate to the issues Angie faced in her relationship with her husband, or to most of the accouterments of her daily life. Yet now that I'm in a monogamous relationship with a man, we're talking about our lives with the same kind of synergistic understanding we shared when we were fourteen.

This kind of acceptance by straight people has been called heterosexual privilege. Indeed, my family does not know James's history; they're ecstatic that I've finally "settled down" with a "normal guy." I admit that I derive a certain sense of privilege from "passing," and you can bet your sweet ass that I intend to wring every last drop out of it. I've lived enough years as an outcast; I don't need to make my life into some kind of statement to satisfy *either* the mainstream *or* the opposition of the moment.

Still, I owe a debt of gratitude to the current opposition, namely, queer culture. While history and experience tell me that the concept of femmeness may eventually be distorted and/or ossify into yet another oppression, right here, right now, the reclaiming of femmeness on the part of mostly queer women is a source of validation. It's clearing a path for me to navigate these menopausal years compounded by the uncharted territory of feminist mid-life crisis. Additionally, this deconstruction of femmeness is heartening in that it proves feminism to be an ever-evolving process.

Earlier I posed the question of whether or not femmeness exists apart from butch or male partners. For me the answer is yes; but, like other identities, it's taken years of experience, and different kinds of lovers, to learn about it. I was not always comfortable being obviously Jewish; I had to learn to appreciate my history and culture before I could laugh at and enjoy the way that Jewishness manifests itself in my personality. I did not always feel secure calling myself a writer; it took consistent work, getting published and paid, before I was able to announce this as my profession and not as a wacky hobby. For a long time I couldn't say I was a feminist without defensive fury choking my vocal cords. So too it has taken time and a variety of relationships for me to feel comfortable as a femme.

On the surface my current lifestyle resembles my years as a housewife. When I think of how I fought to claw my way out of that existence, I worry somewhat about embracing it now. But the truth is, I'm becoming more relaxed with it every day. I don't feel like I'm caving in; I feel like my natural self is emerging. It no longer seems so imperative to achieve fame and fortune and/or transform the world, and that's an enormous relief. Some of this mellowing, of course, comes inevitably with age. And I would not so gently retire into housewifery were I not also writing, which remains a constant in my life.

Feminine qualities were forced on me as a girl, adolescent, and young woman. Because they were mandatory and restrictive, they were oppressive. Feminism was a rebellion and a way out of the oppression, but certain aspects of feminism turned into a new form of oppression. My rediscovered femme identity feels neither oppressive nor rebellious, but integral to who I am. Choice is the crucial element that makes the difference.

ON BEING A
BISEXUAL FEMME

Leah Lilith Albrecht-Samarasinha

At four, when my 1970s hippie feminist mom tried to make me wear overalls so I wouldn't grow up with sex roles, I cried that I wanted to play dress up. At nine my best friend was Gwen Wilbur, the other working-class, dark-skinned scholarship student. When we played make-believe, she was the husband and I was the wife. At twelve, I loved to swirl around in long hippie skirts and sneak on my mom's makeup and Chanel Number Five every chance I got. I had moments, hormone-filled ones, where I would sway and sigh and think how much I liked being a girl. I also didn't shave my legs, was the smartest kid in my class and a budding lesbian-separatist, and beat up the boys who tried to feel me up on my way to home-room. I wasn't anybody's stupid little girl, and everyone knew it.

Twelve was also the year I told my mama that I was bisexual and all she said was, "Fine. As long as they don't look like truck drivers." There was so much wrapped up in that statement. On the one hand, she was showing how scared she was of butch/femme, saying that it was okay for me to be queer only if I was a "straight queer": someone who was conventionally gendered and partnered monogamously with another conventionally gendered woman. But I also think she was trying like hell to prevent something she already knew was going to happen, but didn't have the words to express. That is, that I was a queer femme girl who was going to grow up to desire butches—queer sexual deviants—no matter whether their dicks were biological or bought at Good Vibrations.

Growing up, I always felt like my gender and sexuality were unexplainable, un-namable. For starters, I was a feminist nerd who had a subscription to *off our backs* when I was fourteen, and I knew there was something weird about me saying I was queer but not being a baby butch. I also longed to be a correct woman-identified egalitarian lesbian feminist in junior high; the "women's culture" I was reading about looked like a sweet refuge from my abusive passing-for-white family and equally abusive and racially terrorizing school and town. But I knew I was still attracted to some boys, and that it was too strong to just go away. As I threw away my weird feminist past for anarcho-punk in high school (a counterculture that was a wee bit more accessible), in between creaming over the butch girls slamming in the pit, I dated a lot of boys. All of those boys identified as bisexual or gay. All of them were transgendered to some extent, being either effeminate fag-boys or trannies. People regularly thought we were both women when we kissed on the sidewalk. I also fell in love with my first girlfriend, a bitch-queen femme girl who was a whiter twin to me.

Looking back now, I see those loves as me loving people who affirmed my unsure identity, who knew where I lived as a femme and could help me come to be it fully, even if none of us had the words to say just that. In college, as I came to some kind of adulthood and began to live my femme self on the street out loud and strong, I found my deepest passions lay with butches. I found the word femme for myself when I was nineteen, when I borrowed my roommate's copies of *The Persistent Desire* and *Stone Butch Blues* and everything fell into place. Femme was a word that invited me inside, that let me know I was part of a historical category of women, not a sexual freak. Femme described who I am as a strong, loud, take-no-prisoners-take-no-shit woman-identified woman who feels the most powerful when I have on eyeliner and lipstick and am wearing my red silk garter belt and little black dress. It named who I and other women are as the positive side of being feminine, the shameless hussy, the bitchy mama, the nurturer, healer. But, throughout those two years of coming out, I kept on fucking boys as well as girls. I desired butch queer men and women who were of color, preferably mixed-race like me, working class, culturally hybridized, and sexually besotted. The sexual identity I have constructed is of a femme woman who desires in a queer, not solely lesbian context, where my lover's race and class are equally a factor of my desire.

It makes sense to me. But I have been told, by some classically identified butches and femmes, and by "queer theory" lesbians of all genders, that I am betraying the femme identity by sleeping with men. They have told me that femme women are supposed to stand by their butches, that the difference between femme women and feminine heterosexual women is slim, and ultimately lies in their clear choice of butches over masculine heterosexual men. This argument says that real femmes are not bisexual; all the many, many femme girls who started out by fucking boys had horrible experiences with them. They just didn't know what they were missing and, once they discovered girls, switched loyalties and never went back, they argue. I understand this argument as one used by butch-femme communities in the 1970s and 1980s as a defense against attacks by lesbian feminists and straights who assume that butch-femme is the same thing as heterosexuality and that femmes are all bisexuals or confused straight women. As a bisexual femme in the 1990s, I understand the struggles of femmes in the seventies and eighties to be seen as real lesbians; but now, for me, I want to expand the definition of femme to one that names my life powerfully.

What the above argument tells me is that I should simplify my sexuality because the revolution hasn't happened yet. Erotophobia and homophobia can easily extend it to mean that I'm a freak and a slut. Either way, the argument means that my whole self can't come to the revolution. What scares me about the argument is how closely it parallels two of anti-porn feminism's ideas. The first, in the words of Dorothy Allison, being that "the only way to accomplish change is to make hard bargains, to give up some points and compromise on others; in the end what that has always meant is trading some people for another."[1] Allison did not want to do that, and neither do I. I do not believe that the revolutionary social change we need will come out of anything but all of us telling, and living, the full truth of who we are.

The second argument is trickier. It is the argument that has raged since the publication of "The Woman-Identified Woman"[2] and the beginning of lesbian feminism and modern Western anglo lesbian culture over the boundaries of the lesbian community . Lesbians of all flavors have argued over whether bisexuals exist and to what degree we should be "included" in the queer community. Even those dykes who support bisexual inclusion have argued that there are fundamental differences between "the bisexual experience" and that of lesbians, and have reacted negatively to bisexuals who claim a lesbian identity. Much of what underpins these feelings is a belief that lesbian communities must remain "safe space" free from the influence of patriarchy and compulsory heterosexuality. The white cultural feminist belief that all women, no matter what their race, class, or sexuality, share common values and cultural traits and thus a bond that supersedes all others, also underpins the arguments of those who do not want bisexually behaving people to fully claim queerness. Towards this end, proponents of this belief work to exclude men (no matter what gender or sexuality), and women who sleep with men.

Proponents of these beliefs draw a cultural-feminist line in the sand between "men" and "women." But if one sees the world from a transgendered feminist perspective, the view gets more complicated and also makes more sense. To simply say that as feminists and lesbians all women are our allies and all men are not is, in the words of transgender activist Leslie Feinberg, "[to] lum[p] John Brown and John D. Rockefeller together as enemies and Sojourner Truth and Margaret Thatcher together as allies."[3] If one speaks from an anti-racist, anti-colonial feminist perspective, it is impossible not to understand the stupidity of making such a statement. In doing so, one posits that men or Euro-immigrants are born sexist or racist, instead of being taught to oppressively wield the privilege a material system gives them for those traits. What makes more sense to me, as an anti-racist, anti-colonial feminist, is to make political and countercultural alliances with people of all genders, races, and classes who share my political perspective.

The theory I have learned from the transgender movement understand "butch" and "femme" as meaning two kind of gender practices that are oppositional to colonialist patriarchy. I see biologically male, female, and intersexual people living butch-ness and femme-ness, which I would define as the positive aspects of masculine and feminine gender roles performed in a queer context. Many butch faggots I know live their masculinity far differently from straight heterosexual men. Like butch women, they feel that their gender spirit is something they were born with, and is significantly different from the way heterosexual patriarchal men perform their gender. Most butch faggots I know came up into their gender using butch women as role models.[4] On a parallel track, I have come to feel that femmes share more with drag queens and MTF transgendered people than we do with straight women.

Issues of visibility and the privilege of passing are complicated to negotiate if one is solely bisexual or femme, never mind being both. Many argue that anyone seeing me or another femme on the street holding hands with a genetically male partner will see a boy and a girl. The argument goes on to say that my femininity allows me the privilege of passing as heterosexual in general, at all times in which I am not with butch women or in queer spaces defined by their presence. These people define queer as butch women or femme men, people who they saw as gender rebels, whose gender choice was an inversion of hegemonic standards. But this equates "dyke" with "butch" and "queer," something that's common and wrong in queer communities. In her essay "Femme-Dyke," Arlene Istar writes:

> In the lesbian community, butches are our image of dykes. . . . Lesbians are never described as women who wear dresses and high heels, or have long

nails or hair. . . . Oh, we all know there are lesbians like that, but somehow they are different, not like "us," somehow not authentic.[5]

This ideology of dykeness conflates "femme" with "heterosexual feminine" and "not *really* queer."

Well, I'm sure as hell nobody's "spritzhead girlfriend," as Hothead Paisan would put it. Femme *is* queer. Drop a femme into a straight bridal shower and she'll stand out as much as a drag queen would. Femme in the working-class, often colored, contexts I have experienced it in is brassy, ballsy, loud, obnoxious. It goes far beyond the standards of whitemiddleclass feminine propriety. Femme women, like MTFs, construct their girl-ness, and construct it the way it works for us. At our strongest, we are the opposite of feminine heterosexual women who are oppressed by their gender and held to impossible media standards designed to foster hatred of one's body. According to those media standards, I am ugly. I am a racially ambiguous woman who is small breasted, small hipped, has glasses, "frizzy" or "kinky" hair, and dark, fairly heavy body hair including long hairs on my nipples. But the more I come into my strong femme self, the more my beauty shines.

Writers like Michaelangelo Signorile and some activists in the Queer Nation and ACT-Up of the late eighties and early nineties have imagined that being "out" is the strategy to end all strategies of fighting homophobia. In doing so, these overwhelmingly white and male activists created a uniform standard of out queerness. In my experience, this aesthetic was a punk/skin look of shaved heads, piercings, tattoos (often "tribal" ones ripped off without context from First Nations cultures), leather jackets, and Doc Martens. The look was softly to moderately butch for women, sometimes femme (especially among men of color), but mostly the same for men. Again, butchness became the signifier for queerness. It also became implicitly white: a white, punk aesthetic that read to many people, especially of color, as Nazi skin. This idea doesn't cut it for me. I think it's an idea that comes from a place of unexamined privilege, where one can be shielded from knowing the limits of individual, personal strategies for change. I believe in the necessity of *talking* to people, and doing mass political organizing to counter their homophobia. Mostly, I want to challenge the idea of a uniform standard for being "out." To many white middle- to upper-class people, this "queer aesthetic" may be "shocking," but to many working-class and of color people I know, me and my butch are far more radical. We are queer *and* we come from home, at the same time. The security guard who harassed me and my Latino butch fag lover for kissing while we were waiting for the elevator knew something was queer about us, even if he didn't know just what. I believe in outness as a strategy where one walks down the street looking like what one is as a gender rebel, no matter what that is.

Femme sexuality, especially if one is not solely a femme top (as I am not), is far from a neutral category. For me and many other femmes, the core of femme sexuality lies in femme hunger, in a particularly femme strength of sexual openness, vulnerability, and need. For me, it can be summed up by the image of "her fist/slams into my cunt up through my cervix/and grabs my heart/I don't mind."[6] When I have sex, no matter what the gender of my partner is, I need to feel the touching burn through the layers of numbness I have wrapped around myself. I need intensity; I need to get filled up and fed. To open up, give it all up and be loved, not hated, for my intensity, for how much pleasure I can feel and how vulnerable it makes me. It is a vulnerability that can be both incredibly powerful and incredibly terrifying. I must choose who I lie down with very carefully.

I used to feel that there was no way I could trust a genetic man with this vulnerability in a world of institutional sexual violence against women. I thought that when I continued to desire queer male partners that it was a sign of my internalized homophobia. Even six months ago, when I still believed that all women, for instance, have common interests unmediated by politics, race, class, or sexuality, I used to believe that in a world where the slut, the whore, and the shameless hussy are pissed on, it was much saner to give that gift of womanhood to a butch woman who won't hate me for it than to give it to a man I may never be as sure of. Again, what I have come to is that drawing a line against all who claim manhood does not work. I man-bash sexist oppressive men as much as the next dyke. But the butch fags, FTMs, queens, and nancy boys in my community, especially if they are of color and/or working class, are as much my allies as the queer genetic women of my community. I may have much more in common (which then becomes a basis for attraction, trust, and healing) with a gay South Asian man than I do with any number of white dykes itching to exoticize me into the lotus blossom of the week. I have found that disrespect as well as disgust for high femme sexuality can be found both among all facets of queer communities, including butch women.

I want a world liberated from the blood and shackles of imposed false sexes and genders and the differences in power and privilege awarded those genders. People would play with gender there, but one could choose one's own gender, switch after a while, make it up as s/he went along. What sexual organs one had would have very little, if anything, to do with one's gender expression. In that world, I could fuck partners who might have penises they were born with, might have ones they'd gotten surgery for, might have bought, or who might not have one at all.

The truth I have discovered of my desire, in this South Asian-mutt's passing-slut 1996-New York-body, is that my femme is an attraction to butch queerness in any form that satisfies hunger. I believe that understanding this is crucial to opening up femme identity to independence from butch identity, as standing separate from our more visible partners. Femmes need to work to explore and define who we are—who we have always been—apart from our butch women partners. We need to explore—just as butch women have explored their similarities to daddy faggots and FTMs and their desire for other butches, for drag queens, for faggots—our connections to other femme members of the gender community. In doing so, in asserting the similarities and explaining the differences, we will be able to explicate the difference between our feminine gender expression and our sexuality. And we will come to see that, as long as we fuck who we want, in ways that empower, inside the world of queerness, we are no betrayers, no weaker vessels of lesbianism.

So this is the beginning of a new story. It starts like this: me saying that no, honeygirl, fucking girls and boys in silver platform heels and liquid eyeliner doesn't make me a traitor. It means I'm continuing in the tradition, taking the sexual and gender rebellion of my femme foremothers one step further, to what I need it to be.

Dedicated to Marie and Daniel, my two best butches, with deep love and gratitude.

Notes

1. Dorothy Allison, "Public Silence, Private Terror" from *Pleasure and Danger: Exploring Female Sexuality,* ed. Carol Vance (New York: Routledge, 1984) 108–109.

2. Radicalesbians, "The Woman-Identified Woman," from *Out of the Closets: Voices of Gay Liberation,* eds. Karla Jay and Allan Young (New York: Douglas Books, 1972) 172.

3. Leslie Feinberg, *Transgender Warriors: Making History from Joan of Arc to RuPaul* (Boston: Beacon, 1996) 110.

4. Daniel Rojas-Orrego, conversation with the author, September 1996.

5. Arlene Istar, "Femme-Dyke," from *The Persistent Desire: A Femme-Butch Reader,* ed. Joan Nestle (Boston: Alyson, 1992) 103.

6. Leah Lilith, perf. *Don't Fuck Anybody You Wouldn't Want to Be* by Leah Lilith Albrecht-Samarasinha.

FISHES IN A POND
An Interview with Jewelle Gomez

Heather Findlay

When I arrived at Jewelle Gomez's airy, hilltop San Francisco home, Gomez greeted me warmly, promptly stripped off her skirt, and then ironed it in preparation for the class she was teaching that afternoon. If it weren't for the spectacular views, Gomez's informal gesture might have caused me to flash back to grade school, to one of those formative femme experiences otherwise known as the pajama party.

Gomez wields a mean iron. But thank goodness this stately, sharp, yet oh-so-nurturing *grande dame* of feminist and African American letters is more dedicated to composing her memorable fiction and essays. Gomez's writings have appeared everywhere from *On Our Backs* to *Pleasure and Danger* and her vivid novel *The Gilda Stories* will soon be the basis for a dance performance by the Urban Bushwomen in New York. ("My name," sparkles Gomez, "appears on the same flier as Barishnikov's!") Her lucky neighbors and students in San Francisco have benefited from her many speeches and writing workshops. Her latest collection of poetry, *Oral Tradition,* is not to be missed, and she is currently working on a young people's biography of Audre Lorde for Chelsea House.

I wish I could transcribe the texture and volume of Gomez's laugh. Especially when I quoted the top five anti-femme myths to her, a wicked look would appear in her eye and a huge guffaw would build up in her ample breast. Then she'd burst out laughing, a rich sound combining both scorn and delight. It was as if she were saying, "That may be true, but they don't know *what* they're talking about!"

Say what you like about yes-means-yes and no-means-no, but it's a femme's prerogative to be both affirmative and negative at once. And when Jewelle Gomez laughs, her graying dreads dangling, she's the picture of the beautiful monster described by French feminist Hélène Cixous in "The Laugh of the Medusa." In between howls we talked about passing, naming, beautifying, fucking, and of course the politics of lesbian femininity.

HF: There's an assumption in the gay community that it's harder for butches than it is for femmes because we can pass. It's butches who face street violence and that kind of overt homophobia. But I think we don't have the proper language to describe how femme oppression happens. It may not be as spectacular as butch oppression. We don't have Brandon Teenas among us who get murdered because people find out they're sleeping with women. But we get all kinds of subtle messages from the day we're born until the day we die that have a way of undermining our self confidence. For example, "You don't *look* gay."

JG: [Laughs] I think it's interesting that at this point in our movement—and I'm still uncertain what the movement is right now, but [let's say] civil rights for lesbians and gays, that's general enough—we feel the need to do the exact same thing that other oppressed groups do to us, which is to say, "Our oppression is more important than your oppression." It's kind of ridiculous. Each group gets oppressed in its own specific way. Butches have always been to me a kind of heroic figure because they were the lightning rods for attention. Because of the way they looked—they were so explicitly gay—they bore the brunt of overt bigotry. To me that made them heroic.

But then to hear, "Well, femmes are accepted because you can pass as straight," is ridiculous and mindless. So I tend not to make those kinds of distinctions in how [much] we get oppressed, as much as insist that we examine how the various ways we get oppressed as lesbians, whether you're butch or femme, make us all vulnerable. [Butch and femme oppression is] really different. And I think people's responses to it are different. There are some butches who think it's amusing that they get hassled for going into the women's room. They think it's kind of funny. There are other butches who find it offensive . . .

HF: Or traumatic!

JG: Yes, traumatic. And then lesbians who look more femme have to deal with sexual harassment a whole lot on jobs. We have to deal with men's presumptions—even when it's not harassment—that you're heterosexual and therefore available. And you have to deal with the social issue of having to come out practically all the time.

HF: So passing isn't always the most beautiful experience in the world.

JG: Right. It raises its own issues. If you think about our civil rights struggle as kind of a guerrilla warfare, you can think about what our specific positions can do to aid that struggle.

Gomez runs her finger over the tabletop.

God this table is dusty! Anyway, if you can ask, "How do we raise or make inroads into people's consciousness with our self-presentations?" and then use that . . . I find that much more interesting.

HF: Can you expand on that in the case of femmes?

JG: Historically for me it has always been first a conscious and then an unconscious tactic just to be present without explicitly saying, "I'm a lesbian," when I'm in professional or social situations. Oh! There's the tea.

HF: This interview is going to be interrupted by table cleaning, tea getting, and ironing!

JG: [Laughs] It's so stereotypical!

Much fussing over the peppermint tea, Gomez protesting that it's her lover's job to dust.

HF: So, you were saying that you don't usually come right out and say . . .

JG: Oh, yes, well. Now that's kind of impossible because everywhere I go people know I'm a lesbian. But in the first years of my career, when I lived in New York, I usually never said anything until I got to know people. I found that very helpful because then people had to make a decision about whether they wanted to continue in their relationship with me, or whether it was too much for them.

HF: So is it the femme as a "mole" kind of thing?

JG: Uh huh.

HF: You get yourself into the straight community, they learn that you're a cool person, and they like you. Then they find out you're a lesbian and it's like, "Oh! Hello, I guess I have to deal with this."

JG: It didn't start out as a conscious strategy, but it developed into one when I realized that it really made a big difference to people to know me first, and then decide.

HF: I bet it's a different thing for you, too, the whole "you don't look gay" problem. I bet that happens to you not only because you're a femme, but because you're black. People don't think that you can be black *and* be gay.

JG: Exactly. It's an interesting phenomenon. You become a very precise "other" that people don't know how to integrate into their world view. I had this weird experience around being black. Years ago the apartment building that I used to live in in New York City started becoming a little upscale. It was a really funky old apartment building, and these bankers started living there while they were waiting for their condos. It was the eighties and everybody was making a lot of money. I came in late one night, around midnight, and I was waiting for the elevator, and this young white woman came up. When the elevator came, I got on it, and she wouldn't get on with me. And I realized that clearly somebody had told her, "Don't get on an elevator alone with a black person." In her mind, I was a mugger because I was black. The same thing happens when people see me as a black woman; they can't see me as lesbian.

I was talking with some people I was working with once about a comment a man had made in the room. I was the only lesbian in the room, and there were four other black women who were heterosexual. I said, "Well, I found his comment a little offensive to black women, and as a lesbian I definitely found it upsetting." This woman said to me, "If the black women weren't upset about it—" and I said, "Well, *I'm* a black woman!" Somehow, to this other black woman, I wasn't black because I identified as a lesbian.

HF: So you immediately dropped out of that category.

JG: Right.

HF: Back to these insidious messages we get as femmes, messages that take such a huge psychological toll. Next is, "Femmes are sell-outs because they've bought into the beauty myth."

JG: [Laughs] How old are you, may I ask?

HF: Thirty-one.

JG: I'm forty-six. I only ask that because of historical placement. Because I think that there are a lot of different questions that come up around the beauty myth. As someone who went through the sixties and seventies, [I] really experienced a complete makeover as a woman. First, in the sixties, going from having straightened hair to an afro—people just don't realize this today. This was a reason for families to stop speaking to you. For a black woman not to straighten her hair was a major trauma in a family and in your job. Black women were being fired from jobs at airlines for not straightening their hair. So I *know* about the beauty myth.

And then [I went] through the seventies when women decided, "Okay, we do not have to be in full make-up and full drag in order to be beautiful," and [we] consciously rejected it. I went through several years where I wore nothing but plaid flannel shirts and jeans. That was a real conscious choice to re-find myself as a woman. Once I did that, it became clear to me that the option I was seeking was not to say, "Any woman who wears lipstick and a dress is a sell-out, or not a feminist," but to have the option of saying, "I get to choose when I want to go in drag, and when I don't. Either is fine."

So it ends up really being about choice. That's really what it means for me. For someone to say, well, if I don't have six piercings and five tattoos and my hair half-shaved, then I'm not a feminist, or not a lesbian, is kind of retro to me. We did that already, and now we have a choice. And the choice is, if I want to have a shaved head, five tattoos, and six piercings, I get to, and I don't give a damn about what anybody says about it. I've only gone as far as the five tattoos so far. [Laughs]

HF: And you're only up to five piercings?

JG: Actually, I have six piercings if you count the ones in my ears!

HF: God, those don't count anymore. Have you noticed that?

JG: I know! It's got to be piercings in the places you least expect!

HF: I think also that there are some femmes who dress in feminine clothing but who have not bought into the beauty myth because of something *different* about their feminine get-up. Like their androgynous sisters, or even their butch sisters, they too are reinventing femininity—in their own way.

JG: Right. I like what you said about reinventing femininity. I think that's what being femme really means. It means to take things that you appreciate from historical feminine traits, and to repackage them, redesign them for your own practical as well as psychological use.

For example, I always carry a handkerchief. When I was a kid, my grandmother—who was a high femme, the incredibly glamorous type—always carried a handkerchief, and one of the things she always used to say to me was, "Never go out without a handkerchief." I have come over the years to always carry a handkerchief because it's always practical. You never know, in New York there might be a bullet wound and you might need to help somebody out! The subway was always hot, you were always patting and fanning, and as I get into my middle years, with hot flashes, I now understand why women always carried handkerchiefs at a certain age, because they were always overly warm. So I have used that, and it's become almost a trademark for me. Now people always imagine me dangling a handkerchief from my hand in public. It means something to me because it's very utilitarian, and it reminds me of my grandmother—

HF: And it's pretty!

JG: [Laughs] Yes. So I like this reinventing femininity.

HF: Negative message number three: "Don't date a femme, because she'll leave you for a man."

JG: [Laughs] I do think that's funny. Until recently, when the lines became more blurred between lesbians, heterosexuals, and bisexuals, I don't think that was much of a question. Twenty years ago, the line between being a lesbian, that is, a woman who only slept with other women, and a bisexual, a woman who slept with both women and men, was a very definite line. In my day, a bisexual was a woman who only slept with women, but did not want to say that out loud, so she called herself a bisexual, although I think that identity has changed. Switching back and forth between a man and a woman was such a major, major deal, it hardly ever happened. Or if it happened, it was a life change of great proportions. It was not a casual sliding back and forth.

I don't have any statistics on how many lesbians leave their lovers for men. I will say, that if you're dating a woman who's bisexual, what's the big deal if she leaves you for a man? It should not be an issue, so why are you bringing that up? It's a red herring.

HF: I think that the fear that your lover will leave you for a man stems more from personal insecurity, than it does from general femme behavior.

JG: Right. Here's an article you should do sometime. Among bisexual women, how many are butch and how many are femme?

HF: That is an interesting question.

JG: I mean, this is really a generalization, but it seems like the bisexuals who represent bisexuality [publicly] are either femme or somewhat androgynous.

HF: I think it's also a myth that femmes have slept with more men, or spent a longer period of time in their lives sleeping with men. It's true in my case that I did sleep with men before I came out. I haven't since, not because I have some sort of policy against it, but I just haven't had the desire. But I know tons of butches who have slept with guys, and for some reason there's not some big stigma attached to that. That doesn't threaten their membership in the lesbian community, but with us it does.

JG: Right.

HF: Negative message number four: "Femmes are ditzy."

JG: Ah hah. [Laughs] Let me just say, that's buying into a whole anti-feminist, anti-woman position. I don't even think that's worthy of comment. It's like, who are these lesbians who think that? They are not feminists, and consequently they have no ground for discussion. Anything in society that is identified as male is better, smarter, stronger. Quite frankly, to me, making a discussion around butch and femme, you have to acknowledge that being butch does not mean you want to be a man. It means that you are a woman who has particular characteristics which in this society have been called male. We could just as easily call them yin and yang, and I think we'd have a more accurate depiction.

HF: Yes, there's definitely a lot of work to be done around certain feminine characteristics that are so stigmatized because of, well, two thousand years of thinking that anything that has to do with women is bad. And ditzy is one of them.

I am ditzy on occasion. But I demand the right to be ditzy on occasion without that meaning I am an idiot, or that I deserve to be paid half of what men get, or something like that.

JG: [Laughs] I think that a lot of these issues come back to [the fact that some] lesbians have not found a philosophical–political interpretation of who we are. As a feminist, that's a ridiculous conversation and I wouldn't even have it. But for someone who is just a lesbian and not a feminist, they think that's a topic of conversation. For me, it's like, it's twenty years after the second wave of feminism. Get real.

HF: Last negative message: "Femmes are passive in bed."

JG: Hmmm.

HF: Yeah, that's a tough one. I think we've kind of got the same problem with that, as we do with the myth that femmes are ditzy. It's like, well, I bet some are . . .

JG: Yeah, some are!

HF: Right. But I want the right to be passive in bed and not have that prove that I am powerless in general, or even that I experience being passive in bed as being powerless.

JG: What do people mean by passive? That would be my question. Do they mean receptive, which is one of the reasons why butches find femmes attractive? If they mean receptive, then I would say, "Oh, yes we are!" If they mean we don't initiate, I don't know who they're thinking of. In some cases, some femmes are less apt to initiate, in some cases they are more so. But again, that's one of the things that butches are drawn to. You have to take the whole package. "Femme" means certain kinds of things. Sometimes it means that our way of approaching is less direct, more circuitous. I think that's one of the things that makes us attractive. The reality is that some femmes wouldn't even qualify for the word passive under any circumstances, in bed or out. I certainly wouldn't say that I qualify as a passive person socially, or politically, or publicly. I haven't slept with that many femmes, so I can't really testify. But from my discussions with femme friends about sexuality, I would say that it varies. It could be as variable as passive butches. And I've *certainly* had my share of passive butches, socially and sexually.

HF: Right!

JG: And that doesn't lead me to generalize, to say that all butches are going to be "femme in the sheets," as we say. Pejoratively.

HF: I know! That's another negative message, that the flipped butch is somehow, "Oh, what an embarrassment. She turned into a femme! How horrible."

JG: Yeah.

HF: And it's so hard for femmes to say, "I like to get fucked," and not have that suddenly be a general statement about their whole personality. I remember that great story in Joan Nestle's *A Restricted Country*, about that femme she remembers from one of the old bars she used to go to. This femme always went to the bar with her little purse. It was a little satin purse. She carried a dildo in that purse, and you could see it . . .

JG: Yes! [Laughs]

HF: I'm sorry, that is not a sexually passive woman. She went out to that bar, and she was letting everybody know that she wanted to get fucked and how she wanted to get fucked. To me, that's very assertive. For a number of reasons, that "femmes are passive in bed" thing really pisses me off. Not so much because it doesn't describe us—in a very literal sense—but because there's so much stigma attached to it.

JG: Yeah.

HF: Butch-femme has a really long tradition in the black community. Are you familiar with Ethel Sawyer's research? She wrote this great piece of historical research on butch and femme in the black community. She also talks about the different language that blacks used to name butch and femme. She claims that a very common way to name butch and femme among blacks was "stud" and "fish."

JG: That's before *my* time!

HF: Of course all the anti–butch-femme people are saying "Oh, that's horrible. Stud and fishes. That is such a sexist thing to say about a woman, that she's a fish." Because obviously that's a reference to the negative idea that women's genitals smell like fish. But I don't know, I think it's kind of . . .

JG: I think it's cool! [Laughs] Taking back things, reclaiming things, I think it's important, and that women have to do it. We can't reject everything, because it will leave you with nothing. And there have been a lot of interesting and colorful phases in our lives as lesbians.

There are a lot of reasons that butch-femme was such a standard way of behavior in the black community, and I think a lot of it has to do with class. People frequently denigrate butch-femme because it was a working-class response to lesbian life. But the truth is, butch-femme interactions happen in all relationships, male or female, gay or straight. If you look at the emotional and psychological make-up of couples, you will always find behaviors that will fit into this kind of—I prefer to say at this point—yin-yang dynamic. That's the nature of human relationships. Actually, some of the best relationships are made up of parts that fit together and complement each other. Which means that [the partners] would be in some ways quite different from each other.

I don't understand that sort of wholesale rejection of our past. I'm really more interested in re-examining the past. That's why I think that Joan Nestle's books have been really really important. They've given us a good perspective on what it means to be a femme in this society, and how we can use what [femme] means, rather than reject it.

See, another important thing about butch-femme is it's a statement about sexuality. When you see a butch-femme couple, their whole demeanor screams, "We have sex."

HF: Yes. And that's why I, personally, really like the term fish. It may very well be part and parcel of a long tradition of sexist jokes about the way women smell but—unlike the term femme even—it's a specifically sexual reference. Imagine that, walking around with a name that announces your sex parts! I dig that. Seeing that we're on the topic now, tell me what's femme about the way that you have sex.

JG: Hmmm, that's a tough one. Like most people, femmes are a combination of contradictory impulses. Rather than passive, I guess I would describe myself as receptive. That leaves room for the divergent ways of being that are natural to most of us. Just because I like being on my back doesn't mean that I'm passive. For example, I really love to go down on my lover. So how does that fit in?

HF: Right. Me too. Actually, that's been a point of contention lately, because the woman I'm with right now doesn't like it. We'll have totally great sex, where I am completely the center of all sexual attention—which is the way I like it these days—and afterward we'll be lying there all happy and exhausted, and I'm thinking to myself, "When was the last time I went down on her? Months ago!"

It's not because I think sex should be a totally reciprocal, you-do-me-then-I-do-you kind of thing. That's so stupid. That kind of thinking can't recognize that some lesbians' desires are completely different from other lesbians' desires. I gave up worrying about "reciprocating," and what does that mean anyway? Am I not reciprocating when I let her fuck me? When I scream and yell and whisper dirty things in her ear? Anyway, I gave up on that reciprocating bullshit long ago. But I do hope I get to sleep with a girl soon who lets me eat her pussy.

JG: [Laughs] I think all of it goes back to how we interpret our identities and our actions. If we decide that being on your back, being a femme, being receptive—all those things ascribed to femmes—if we decided that's negative, as men have decided about women historically, then we're taking an anti-feminist stance, and refusing to acknowledge the power that's held in those positions. We're deciding that only things that are identified with male qualities are powerful. As a feminist, I absolutely don't believe that. I believe that lying on my back, in a receptive position, I have as much power as anyone else, whatever position they're in. Physically, emotionally, psychologically I hold a lot of power in that moment of receptivity.

And *that's* what's wrong with the world today! The idea that only in the hard thrust—read bomb, read gun, read attack—only in that mode of action does anything happen. I think that's foolish, and it's a mistake that men have made traditionally. We should not make the same mistake. The reality is that there's more than one way to do anything, and certainly there's more than one way to have sex. If problem-solvers in our country would think about it more, avoid the attack, and think about the roundabout or receptive ways that [we] can problem solve, we might be in better shape, quite frankly.

HF: Yes. A whole lot more needs to be said about the political power of femme receptivity. I think, too, that femmes need to get together with gay men to help articulate that. Because, of course, "passive" gay men get the same kind of crap that we do, where people think that getting fucked is the same thing as being totally powerless.

JG: And I think that it's something that we really need to discuss more with each other. Because I fear that wedge that comes between groups, [the idea] that suddenly butches and femmes are in competition somehow. Politically, that's death. Culturally and socially, it's a bore. We already have a struggle with our patriarchal society. We need to think of how, as women, we can act in concert as butches and femmes. And where we fill in with the other is where we can help each other, rather than recycle the same old tired labels about what femininity means.

I was on a butch-femme panel as part of a conference in New York about three years ago called L.U.S.T., Lesbians Undoing Sexual Taboos, and a woman got up and made a comment about how hard it was for femmes to be friends. I was completely taken aback.

HF: That's not true in my experience at all.

JG: Not in mine at all. I thought that maybe she was having a particular experience having to do with where she was politically. She was with a femme group up in the Bronx. It may have had to do with her age, because she was much younger, so she was dealing with a lot of people without historical context. I don't really know, but I found it completely bizarre, because I feel like femmes will go out of their way to be friends. We may be tough with people we don't like, but I feel that we go out of our way to be friends and to maintain relationships.

For example, I tend to have good relationships with all my ex-lovers. I know that's supposed to be a big lesbian thing and I'm actually very proud of it. In the heterosexual community, if you break up, you usually cross the street to avoid each other. A man would usually rather drop dead than call his ex-girlfriend and say, "How the hell are you? It's been a year, and I've been thinking about you. Are you okay? How's the dog?"

HF: [Laughs] Right. *Click.*

JG: Yeah, right. So I'm really proud that lesbians have that as a thing. I am close friends with both butches and femmes, because I have maintained friendships with a lot of my ex-lovers. And some ex-lovers of my ex-lovers and I are friends. [Laughs]

HF: It's absolutely essential for me to be friends with my fellow femmes, because to whom else would I talk about butches?

JG: That's right! Exactly!

HF: I also have a long standing love of talking on the phone. Femmes seem to be the only people I can get on the phone for as long as I want them to be on the phone with me.

JG: But you can always get a butch on e-mail!

HF: [Laughs] That's so true! This is a bit of a non sequitur, but Diane Anderson, who is *Girlfriends'* managing editor, commented the other day that being a femme is kind of like being a person of mixed race. In other words, you can't tell from looking that a femme's a dyke, just like you can't tell from looking that, say, a half-Latina is a woman of color.

JG: Hmmm. Like Paula Abdul or Mariah Carey.

HF: Yes. So she made the point that femmes and women of mixed race are located in this kind of liminal space.

And I think that some of the negative messages that get thrown at femmes also get thrown at people of mixed race: "You don't look Hispanic," or, "You're a sell-out because you could be a model," or, "Don't date or marry a mixed-race person, because she'll leave you for a white guy."

JG: Oh, sure. When I was a kid, shopping malls first came into being. First there was no such thing as shopping malls, and then they got shopping malls. And it was this whole big deal. You would drive out to the suburbs to go to these huge stores. I remember the first time that I went to a shopping mall—it was a Saturday afternoon—I saw all these butch women, and I was so excited. I thought, "So this is where lesbians are!" I was maybe fourteen, fifteen, but I thought, "This is where all the lesbians are; they all live in the suburbs." Well, of course, as I grew older I came to understand that those were not all lesbians. They were suburban housewives who dressed like butch women. They had short cut hair. They wore pants or pantsuits. And they were in their middle years—Hey, Buster!

Gomez's cats were tired of not getting her attention, and one of them was climbing onto the back of my chair. Gomez put him in his place.

Get down from there! She doesn't want you climbing on her. So anyway, they looked like butch women to me. In fact, some of them probably were butch women in their heterosexual relationships.

So how we make the identification is dependent on so many cultural factors. It's really impossible to pin someone completely with a word. This is what I find: I find that a word is a door that lets you into who I am. It's not a total thing. It's how you start to know me. It's helpful to consider ourselves in that way. If I say "I'm a black lesbian writer," I'm not saying that I'm only a black lesbian writer. I'm giving you the first step into knowing who I am so that you can know all these other things.

HF: So what have I not asked you that you want to tell me?

JG: We haven't talked about clothes!

HF: We talked about clothes when I came in. You were very nice. You complimented me on my outfit.

JG: That's true. But it is interesting to think about how we compare to different animals, to different species. You know, plumage, and what that means. In certain species the males are the ones with the plumage. In ours, females are the ones with the plumage. We have to look at ourselves within a larger picture, not just the here and now. I would be very interested in knowing how some young lesbians who don't particularly manifest what I think of as butch-femme attire, who look more androgynous—how their behavior would track along butch-femme lines.

HF: Yeah, or how they have reinvented butch-femme for their own generation.

JG: Yes.

HF: Actually, the truth is, the reason I haven't asked you about clothes is because I'm bored with all that.

JG: Ha!

HF: I'm bored with talking about how femme means that you wear skirts and make-up. Not because it's not true. It's just that I'm bored with hearing about it. I've never primarily identified as femme because of what I wear. Besides, I know some butches who are much more meticulous about their clothing than femmes I know.

JG: Oh, yeah. Like my girlfriend.

HF: [Laughs] My girlfriend has her standard Levis and T-shirt underneath a button down, which she wears to work every day. So she's not a big clothes-monger or anything. But I went out to the opening night of the film festival with a friend of mine—she volunteers for *Girlfriends*, actually—and she just looked stunning that night. There was something really exciting about that night because both of us had got so dressed up.

JG: Yeah, isn't that great?

HF: I *love* that. But she definitely deserved the prize for her couture. I guess I did drag out my fur coat—fake fur, so no animals died—but she had these wonderful wool trousers, perfectly cuffed at the bottom.

JG: Mmmm.

HF: And then she had this jacket, that was kind of a cross between a smoking jacket and a regular coat with lapels and the whole bit. It actually had a tie around the waist. She looked *great*. But the long and short of this is: The good thing about butches is that they have inherited the tendency in other species for the male to wear all the plumage. And there's another difference for you between butches and men. Butches are basically better dressers than men.

JG: Yes they are! [Laughs]

HF: They're like peacocks.

JG: Yes, and butches actually talk, as opposed to men. You can actually have a conversation with a butch. I find that very helpful.

HF: Yep. Anything else?

JG: One of the things for me, as a femme, is that I've always felt—and I'm glad that this has been relieved to a certain extent—I felt the burden of articulating what it means to be a lesbian. Historically, it always felt like it was the femmes that were running the magazines and the publishing houses, and the femmes that were writing the books that said [who we were]. Now this isn't an absolute, but there always seemed to be this sense that we had to speak for lesbians. We *had* to. So I'm relieved, in the nineties, to find so many more butch women willing to be identified as butches, out loud, because I've found that frequently that has not been true. They're willing to talk about that, and to talk about it in the context of being a woman. I think that this is a nice political change in the nineties, a change I really appreciate. Just like we need all the different voices in the lesbian community—in terms of ethnicity, race, and class—we need butch and femme and androgynous voices as well. For a long time, a lot of us [femmes] felt responsible for that.

HF: I'm glad that Leslie Feinberg was asked to speak at that college graduation this spring, for example. She's identifying these days more as a transgendered person. But that's cool, that someone who was at one point so strongly identified as a butch got up and talked about movement politics. We can take a break.

JG: I would like to see more of it. I teach writing, and I could tell you how many of the women in my writing class are butch identified. They're always the smallest number. Always. These women really need to be writing all this stuff down, and talking about it.

HF: What have you thought about the recent collections out about butch identity, like *Dagger*?

JG: I have problems when things are ahistorical. It's interesting that you've discovered something, and it's interesting for your particular group, but when you're not writing within a context of where it came from and what it means, it's not that interesting to me. Don't get me wrong; I thought it was sweet that [*Dagger*] was done. It was good because all these young women don't have a place to put this stuff, their feelings about being butch. But the historical context is what I think is most important. When we put the things we're feeling and experiencing in a larger context—social, historical, cultural—we're creating a political analysis. That gives our experience more resonance, makes it useful for others. I missed that sometimes.

HF: But the pictures were great, huh?

JG: The pictures were fabulous. [Laughs] And I think it's a generational thing. I worry about the future a lot. One of the ways that we make a path to the future is to examine where we come from and how it works with what we're trying to do now. I'm more interested in writing that does that.

Part 3

FUTURES
"The Queerest of the Queer"

FOREVER FEMME
A Soap Opera In Many Acts
And An Agony Of Analysis

Madeline Davis

1958: I am eighteen. I walk into The Chesterfield, a gay bar, for the first time. She—I didn't know it then—behind the bar. Blonde, slicked back hair, dark liquid eyes, a cigarette in the corner of her mouth. Tattoos running up one tanned smooth-muscled arm and a white t-shirt with one sleeve rolled around a cigarette pack. A gold watch worn with the face on the inside of her wrist. An ache in my thighs, knees weak and shaky, my heart loud enough to be heard over the juke box. I have never had this reaction to anyone. Bobbi tells me it is a girl. I can't believe that this devastating image might bear any similarity to myself. It would be five years before I would dare to approach and find out. I am working part time as a folksinger and waitress in coffee houses. I have long hair and a guitar. I write songs about how much life amazes me.

1963: I learn to be loved by women, women like that first woman behind the bar. Short hair, men's shirts, aftershave on their smooth faces. They lead me for nerve-shattering hours into soft dark nights. I do not touch them. It is not done and I do not dare to ask why. The neighbor woman questions me about our noises. She is concerned that I am being beaten. How could anyone imagine that pain could be a part of such love? That realization was still many years off. I perform on stage with an all-male rock band. I write romantic songs for women and brazenly sing them before straight audiences.

I wear outrageous glittering gowns. I love sex. After a shy adolescence, it liberates me like nothing else.

1972: I am sharing in the love of strong, beautiful women. I have dared to ask the questions, push the barriers. I am rewarded with presents/presence I did not know were possible. I am gifted with their satiety as well as my own. We are bold and blatant public sisters. Gay rights is on the move and I become a politician. I speak before thousands. Still, I rouge my cheeks and line my eyes with kohl, trying to enhance whatever I believe is my real self. My lovers still button their shirts left over right. We move into the fullness of our lives together: different and almost equal. The playing field is more even and I am full of questions about who and what we are.

1973: I have become a professional woman and an activist. I am a femme and as prescribed I dress appropriately and love butch women. One day I am on the job, standing behind the circulation desk at the public library. It is mid-summer morning when she walks in. Her hair is honey blonde, curling on her shoulders. She wears a leather mini-skirt over wide hips and a close fitting black sweater that hugs her full thrusting breasts. Her legs are encased in net stockings. Her lips are deep coral and full. She smiles and nods as she proceeds to the shelves of new books. My reaction is completely unexpected and unnerving. Not in years have my knees liquified like this. Not in years has such pain shot through my thighs. Never in public have I become so wet. I excuse myself from the desk and leave the clerk in charge. I rush to the ladies room, lock the door, and press my back up against the cold tile wall, staring at my face in the mirror. I am as red as an angina attack. I am damp as a raging fever. What is this about? It is not appropriate for this kind of woman to evoke such a reaction in me. Am I not who I thought I was all this time? I feel so . . . "queer." In the years that follow I will be too afraid to explore this incident with my flesh; yet it will not leave me and I will think about it every time I consider who I am.

1976: I am in love again. She is boyish and beautiful. She is strong in her body. She fixes things. She can build a fire in the woods in any weather. She teaches me to canoe. She says she is not butch. I think I have finally come to the end of my search. A woman with the physical attributes I so admire but one with whom I can share the intimacy of equals. I am lying to both of us. I search inside her for the butch she simply does not know is there. I make us crazy, searching. There is nothing to find. We begin to fall apart. But we have come to love each other, so we stay together much too long. In time to come, we would be best friends. But we did not know it then. We only knew the perfect formula didn't work. I made us both mad. My activism turns to writing. Liz and I begin the book. It will be a hard road. Somewhere on that road I cut my hair. My image changes. I look like a "grown-up."

1985: After ten years, I am single again. I do not leave time for healing between "marriages." I become involved with a woman who wears lipstick. Kissing her reddened mouth is exotic. It is cultural, this look. Most of the Hispanic women I know wear lipstick. Still, she is tough. She wants someone to submit. I try. It doesn't happen. I need to be in charge. How femme is that? Perhaps completely. Perhaps it is all illusion.

1986: I find a writer. We share our words, our poetic histories, our sense of wonder. We establish an easy familiarity and make each other laugh. Our love is joyful and with me she finds her gender. But I am gone too much. I leave to write and edit, and under the stress of work beyond my control, I leave my body, retreating into a dream world where someone can take care of me. She doesn't know. She doesn't ask. I don't tell her. She takes note that I am gone and slips away. Six years later we have loved each other, and have failed. We share the blame and continue to love each other, apart. The book is published. We have done well. I am tired and sing myself to sleep.

1994: I attempt to relinquish control, to become a bottom. Perhaps the euphoria of giving up, going under, will heal me of too much dead-end labor and too many losses. It lasts eight weeks. I get angry. So does she. We don't like each other. In other parts of my life I am focused. I play drums. I write stories. I have become a body worker. My hands have learned wondrous things and I use them to bring comfort and healing.

I have become an actress. My performances bring some tears and much laughter. I have the lead in a new play. The part calls for no make-up and tattered army clothes. I portray a strong independent older woman. In the end, I win. The reviewer says I am a type not seen or appreciated in the heterosexual world. I am large and powerful. He compares me to a couple of prominent male actors. He likes my performance but describes me as someone I am not sure I know any longer. I look into the mirror. My persona has changed. My hair is short and curly—and grey. And inside there have been other changes. I take home bouquets of flowers and the memory of applause. I have always been an actress.

1995: I stand in the middle of a soft-lit early spring evening room. A black lace peignoir barely hides a leather body harness, spandex panties and a studded belt. In my hand a soft leather whip swings in the light breeze that blows through the dark window. On the bed a paddle, a crop, and my lover on her knees, asking for a discipline she has worked hard for and richly deserves. I hear her breathing, and my own. I will marry this woman who carries my instruments, takes care of my needs, and adores me. I ask her how much of the time I turn her on. She says eighty-five percent and it is too much, but she can't help it. We laugh. I say it is perfect for me.

Over thirty years. How many persons have I become? The memory of that first night at the Chesterfield still makes the flesh of my arms prickle and burn. And the long-haired shy sweet singer of songs is still alive. Through all of the changes in myself and in the myriad worlds around me, I have discovered facet after facet and still, I have become more and more what I was that first day. Always, inside my soul, in the way I look out of my eyes, in the way I ache for the right kind of love, in the way I position myself in the world, the lesbian in me is forever femme.

Perhaps the act of naming ourselves is one way not only to recognize our separateness or difference from the "others" but a way to verify our actual existence as lesbians. If we do not have a unique definition, a definition that stands on its own rather than in relationship to, are we, as some of the old butches have said, not really lesbians? Are we like the tree in the forest: if no butch is around to see or hear the raging of our desire, does it still exist?

In *Women Who Run With the Wolves*, Clarissa Pinkola Estes describes the dual nature of the feminine, what she defines as "an outer being and an interior *creature*, one who lives in the topside world, one who lives in the world not so easily seeable."[1] She depicts them as opposites which are fluid and ever present in every woman, the strength of one balanced by the opposite strength of the other, "separate but conjoined elements which combine in thousands of ways."[2] This duality of the feminine is often related to the phenomenon of twins who are held in sacred awe and sometimes feared by many cultures. Woman, when recognized as embodying this dual nature, is assumed to be terribly powerful, deserving of both reverence and dread.

I would like to posit my vision of the two sides of the feminine, what I wish to call the "civilized" and the "wild," and how she presents in the lesbian femme. The civilized feminine has learned well the parameters of appropriate social behavior. She is the arbiter of taste, fashion, rules, codes, organization. She is caretaker as nurse, as nanny, as teacher. It is she who makes the world flow smoothly and gracefully. She is careful, and passes on the roles and functions of her gender to those of the next generation who will utilize them in the appropriate manner and will refine them according to changes in the social order. She is lovely. She wears delicate pink pearls.

The wild feminine operates on her instincts, her needs and her passions. She laughs loud, dances wildly, and dreams big. She is anarchistic and follows regulations if they suit her. She is both healer and destroyer. She is mother as nurturer, as seductress, as disciplinarian. She is effusive, and pours out her pro/creative energies upon the earth for all to see and use. She is beautiful. She wears audacious red rubies.

Of these two, the femme lesbian may appear as either; she may be able to utilize the attributes of either, but in her heart of hearts she is ever tipped towards the wild. She has learned her lessons well and has decided to follow her own path.

Perhaps the moment this persona is forged is the moment we (femmes) stretch our tiny girl fingers into the world, the moment we speak our first words, the moment we are faced with a culture that tells us we can or can't, should, or shouldn't. In that moment the hair on the backs of our necks stands up, our blood races, our fists clench, and something feline and feral growls low and menacing far back in our throats. Some untamed thing that shares its voice only with its own kind bares its pearly teeth, reapplies its lipstick, checks the mirror, and asserts its particularity.

The old butches say that my heterosexual past, coupled with the fact that I love being made love to, makes me, not straight, but not a "real" lesbian. The fact that I would not willingly have sex with someone whose penis was attached by something other than a leather harness seems to cut no ice. The fact that my fingers are wet with the musky juices of a woman who writhes under my touch, makes no difference. The fact that I am at home only where women gather, where women labor, where women play, where women's histories/herstories, women's lives, women's desires, women's spirits come together to do the critical task of running the universe, has no bearing. Well, I say, I have loved you, old butches, and I am mightily offended that you give me so little credit for my choices. You bet I'm real. Yes, I have had choice, and have used it. I have chosen, freely in the core of my heart, women for my life.

And the feminist lesbians, guardians of the Left's political Right. For how many years did you tell me my long hair and mascara were inappropriate? How often did you issue dictums that "role playing" was a "game" we no long needed. That the way I loved and wanted to be loved was excessive, exploitative, base, degrading, and much too sweaty. How many times did you lead me half way down a path that became alien and rigid and so unforgiving that I ran away as fast as my high heels would carry me! What did you really mean by "the personal is the political"? Authors Joan Parkin and Amanda Prosser have noted that: "The feminist project of valorizing the personal has not included sexual desires such as ours [femmes, butches] that refuse to participate in their own coy partial effacement."[3] I was outraged when I realized that, at least for you, political passion and sexual passion were incompatible. And so I opted to retain the latter and became an outlaw. Audre Lorde has said that recognizing and living in accordance with knowledge of the erotic is an act of empowerment, and that "Of course women so empowered are dangerous."[4] A femme who recognizes her erotic power and resolves to live within it fully is formidable indeed.

In my late teens I was introduced to the concept of sado-masochism. Contemplation of scenarios of dominance and submission were fascinating, and in my imagination I became the one pleased. All acts were executed for my delight and satisfaction and, although in some fantasies I was bound and restricted, it was always with my consent. Those who dominated me serviced me, and could sense what would be pleasing without being told. I was young, and having been raised a proper femme, could not venture, even in fantasy, to take hold of authority and demand my satisfaction. And then I grew up. I found I was a competent teacher and could demand of my students the pleasure I sought for myself.

It was difficult in those early days to reconcile being femme, which I had equated with passive or reactive, with being top, which is assertive and active. Although I made attempts at bottoming, assuming that one can only be a good top if one is willing to experience the position of the other, I was not altogether successful. The physical experience was a delight. The emotional experience collapsed with a resounding thud. I did learn, however, that to be femme is to be powerful in many ways, and that as either a bottom or a top, a femme can be one who guides the action, molds the circumstance, sets the scene and even "calls the shots." This perspective was further validated during the research conducted with Liz Kennedy for *Boots of Leather, Slippers of Gold*. We discovered that there have always been femmes who have been teachers of sex for young butches, and that they have asserted their desires and preferences at least as far back as the 1940s.[5] I realized I come from a rich tradition of femme sexual dominants.

There is nothing like the beauty and strength of femmes. I have found it in wonderful places. When Joan Nestle and Amber Hollibaugh and I sat before a tape recorder in the dining room and wept for the unbearable love we felt for the women in our lives. When Lamar Van Dyke, Seattle flesh artist, pierced my labia and added a feather to my tattoo and we spoke for long hours into the night about active/submissive feisty women who came to us to regenerate their strength and thereby renewed our own. When Danish historian Karin Ludsin and I reclined in the lounge in Amsterdam and ogled the woman with the short black hair and blue eyes, and years later shared our lovemaking secrets lying on the grass at Vassar, fascinated by the changes and the unchanging.

I look at young femmes and marvel. They have sprung into the world like Athena, fully armored and stunning in the proud uncompromising strength of their spirits. They are the warriors I worked so hard to become. Their eyes are clear. They see a future in which women are brave and purposeful and take what they want. A future in which the femme of the species is the hunter, the most vicious, the most protective. They work their muscles with martial arts, inappropriate for most girls of my generation. They apply color to their eyelids like ancient courtesans who seduced leaders and ruled empires with strong hearts and iron wills. They fling their long hair over their shoulders and laugh gently at the awkward advances of young butches who bow before them and shiver in their presence. I watch these young femmes and sigh with delight that they have been born into a world I have helped to create. And they wear their surroundings so easily and beautifully.

I do not always recognize us, femmes, even though I see us every day. We often look like our straight sisters, but when our eyes meet there is a mutual recognition that we have ventured beyond, that we have pushed barriers and made choices that for some may have been very hard, but for all were what we needed to do to remain true to ourselves, to our lovers and to our culture. We have been fortunate enough to have escaped some of the ugliness heaped directly upon butch women, yet in sharing public space with our partners and in the quest for our own particular sovereignty, we have put ourselves in the line of fire and have borne our portion of brutality. We have grown angry and defensive and stronger for having helped to fend off an uncompromising world. We are brazen and resilient. We have learned to talk back, to not put up with, to stake out, to defend and protect territory, and to forge a fairer place where we can live in community and beauty with the women we love.

Notes

1. Clarissa Pinkola Estes, *Women Who Run With the Wolves* (New York: Ballantine Books, 1992) 119.

2. Estes 119.

3. Joan Parkin and Amanda Prosser, "An Academic Affair: The politics of butch-femme," in *The Persistent Desire: A Femme-Butch Reader,* ed. Joan Nestle (Boston, Mass.: Alyson, 1992) 442.

4. Audre Lorde, "The Uses of the Erotic," in *The Lesbian and Gay Studies Reader,* eds. Henry Abelove, et al. (New York: Routledge, 1993) 340.

5. Elizabeth Lapovsky Kennedy and Madeline D. Davis, *Boots of Leather, Slippers of Gold: The History of a Lesbian Community* (New York: Routledge, 1993) 216–221.

PASSING *LOQUERÍA*

Gaby Sandoval

> Living on borders and in margins, keeping intact one's shifting and multiple identity and integrity, is like trying to swim in a new element, an "alien" element. . . . And yes, the "alien" element has become familiar—never comfortable, not with society's clamor to uphold the old, to rejoin the flock, to go with the herd. No, not comfortable but home.[1]

I have crossed the Mexico–U.S. border countless times. As a child, my mother would drill me on two sets of addresses, schools, teachers, and historical facts; one in Spanish for the trip to Mexico, one in English for the trip to the U.S. I don't know why I didn't have a passport. Instead, my mother would sit anxiously, squeezing my hand in hers while the border patrol of either nation climbed onto the bus. She was scared I would use the wrong language or tell the Mexican inspector I was born in the U.S. or the American agent I was Mexican.

I've crossed the U.S.-Mexico border countless times. The last time, I forgot which identity to foreground. This was my mother's nightmare come true only she wasn't around to help out. I told the luggage inspector I was born in California. He asked for my visa or passport and I realized my mistake. Images of deportation from Mexico to the U.S. raced frantically through my head. "My mom has them with her in Chihuahua," I lied, "she will meet me at the next checkpoint." At the next checkpoint, I was a Mexican national again.

I am at home in my discomfort. I am a queer child; never quite fitting in,

but always passing. I am a femme who exploits the confines of gender perceptions. I negotiate my "shifting and multiple identity and integrity" not
always to the satisfaction of others but always as honorably as I can. These
abilities are definitely telling of a life lived on the border, with all of its con-
tradictions and confusions.

When I say the border, I do not privilege one physical place over another.
I do not speak of nation-state boundaries, but rather of "the psychological
borderlands, the sexual borderlands and the spiritual borderlands . . . not particular to the Southwest."[2] These spaces are neither here nor there, not easily
defined and even more difficult to document. They are like the rivers along
which national borders often run. They are always in motion, fluid, usually
tumultuous. They may seem calm on the surface, but the pull of conflicting
currents within is constant, as evidenced by whirlpools of activity. Anything
built upon them can be dismantled, whether by force of nature or of human-
ity. They are perpetually in a state of redefinition as are the identities created
in the borderlands.

Gloria Anzaldúa's analysis of the border and border identities has been
instrumental to the understanding of these ambiguous spaces. She defines the
borderlands as any place where two or more cultures meet.[3] More importantly, however, Anzaldúa describes their function: "to define the places that
are safe and unsafe, to distinguish *us* from *them*."[4] Borders mark distinction,
but not always as expected. I believe that certain difference stand bare at borders, whether physical or metaphysical. The eye can see where the "third
world" meets its overdeveloped exploiter, where poverty greets decadence
and scarcity yawns its hunger at excess. But when difference is more subtle,
like a light-skinned Chicana or a feminine lesbian, identities become blurred.
The line of demarcation widens and its edges fray, and *them* and *us* become
progressively harder to categorize.

Visually, I am not always perceived as colored, immigrant, queer, or working class. I have learned to switch codes and adapt to other cultures so well
that I am confident I can create home anywhere. This has the tendency to
lead people to define me with reference to what I am not. I came into my
identity as Mexican because the eyes of white children at school glared "for-
eign" and they taunted my difference when I spoke. I am *not* American. But
I am American to every Mexican immigrant more recent than my parents
because I was *not* raised in Mexico and my English is near perfect when I
concentrate. I became *pocha* every time I had difficulty completing a full sen-
tence in Spanish over summer vacations spent visiting family in Chihuahua. I
was obviously *not* really Mexican, but no one would vocally disrespect my
parents' child-raising skills by accusing me of being *gringa*.

My ability to reshape identity has taken me as far as accepting a Colored identity from Namibian children whose concepts of white meant the blond hair and blue eyes I do *not* have and black meant a race I do *not* belong to within the context of Namibian society.[5] With reference to what I was *not*, I had to be Colored. Chicana was not a part of their consciousness. Similarly, femme is not always a part of straight consciousness. Butch or masculine women are often assumed to be queer. Therefore, with reference to the fact that I am *not* butch, most straight people assume I am straight.

More recently, others saw me as femme with respect to the butch woman on whose arm I stood. I was, yet again, identified by default. This is no longer the case. Do not misunderstand, I am still femme. The physical markers have not changed. I groom long brown curls, wear dresses, and enjoy the creamy feel of lipstick on my lips. The difference is that I own my femininity. I have reclaimed it. I no longer have to be on the arm of a strong butch woman to be femme, just as I do not have to be sleeping with any woman to be queer. Despite the misreadings of others, I claim myself as femme.

I choose my femininity; it does not choose me. We have been taught (at least subconsciously) that femininity is a weakness, that anyone feminine is worthy of our contempt. I take what I know best, what I was taught best, and I work with it. Cosmetics, for example, have been used to keep us consuming, to maintain gender roles and to define conventional standards of beauty. I use makeup on occasion, not because I am not beautiful without it. I will not spend any significant amount of money on it. I am also wary not to allow it to become a mask to hide insecurities behind. Instead I wear it strategically to widen the space others' perceptions of me have constructed. I can change my appearance so dramatically with a small, healthy dose of vanity, the right clothes, and just a touch of color that people tend to look twice before they recognize me. I like the "wow-I-didn't-know-you-could-look-like-that" expression that creeps onto their faces. It is always about playing with other people's perceptions of who I am; this keeps them on their toes. It is a skill I would not have picked up if I had not grown up between cultures; it is a skill that is invaluable to surviving on the border.

Identity is also tangled in physical markers and the visual cues we use to categorize along gender lines. A woman, and in my experience, a Chicana, may never know the significance of long hair until the day she cuts it off. Before I owned my identity as a femme, I would invest substantial amounts of time and money in the length, shine, and placement of my hair. Eventually I realized that all of this effort was really expended in attempts to hide what I felt was not right with me, everything about me that differed from the faces that smiled blankly at me from the other side of the television screen or the glossy, colorful magazines in the racks at grocery store lines. Looking at these images, it was not hard for me to understand why I did not like myself. I learned that self-hate is like the smell of smoke in your hair after a night at a club; it clings. But unlike smoke, it does not wash out. Every insecurity I had ever had, from the time the ends of my hair sprouted from my scalp, were tangled in my locks.[6] When I cut it off, I learned new definitions of beauty and self-appreciation. It is amazing how much of my identity was curled up in that mane, as evidenced by the number of people who did not recognize me when it was gone. Cutting my hair had nothing to do with coming out of the closet. It was an exercise in self-love. I forge my identity as a femme out of this love coupled with subversion.

None of this has been easy. The border is a complex space to negotiate. Femme—like this border site—is never static. It is often dangerous; its fluidity slips through your fingers and can easily make you believe you have lost yourself. Writing about lesbians of color, Anzaldúa phrases it well: queerness is "an interesting path, one that continually slips in and out of the white, the Catholic, the Mexican, the indigenous, the instincts. In and out of my head. It makes for *loquería*, the crazies . . . It is a way of balancing, of mitigating duality."[7] I would say that my path has been a way of "mitigating" multiplicity. It is about assuaging the pain of belonging to one community but being perceived as belonging to another. Femme is *loquería*. Having your identity constantly under question, who wouldn't risk losing their mind, and their identity along the way? Because I am light-skinned, Chicana/os question my loyalty. Likewise, because I am femme, not only is my identity questioned by a straight community that does not understand femme femininity, but it is also questioned by those to whom I could be the strongest ally, butch lesbians.

Women who assume masculinity are popularly believed to be the "real" lesbians. They are seen as the strong women, the face of queerness, and therefore are more often slapped with the injustices of heterosexist society. If I do not actively identify as a lesbian, if I do not hold my lover's hand at the park, if I do not love her openly, most of society would assume I was waiting for the right man. So I do not blame butch women for being wary that a femme woman may use her privilege at their expense. We know how to oppress each other because we are oppressed. I cannot get rid of those privileges society lends me; however, I do hold myself accountable for the ways in which I manipulate them.

I have learned well the art of manipulating identity. It has often been a painful process of growth, but invaluable to a life lived on the border. I know that I, unlike others, am not always forced to fight against the currents of border rivers. My fair *güera* hide allows me not to be brown or be held in contempt in our racialized society. My femme femininity allows me not to be perceived as sexually deviant. I exploit the structures in place hoping that whatever injustices I may not be able to eradicate, I can subvert. Yes, I am manipulative, but always remembering those who do not have my choices.

Notes

1. Gloria Anzaldúa, *Borderlands/La Frontera: The New Mestiza* (San Francisco: Aunt Lute Books, 1987).

2. Ibid.

3. Ibid.

4. Ibid.

5. Colored denotes a mixed-race identity in Namibia and in other parts of southern Africa.

6. Laura Jiménez, conversation with the author, Sept. 1995.

7. Anzaldúa 19.

HOW DOES SHE LOOK?

Rebecca Ann Rugg

Writing about femme identity catalyzes a fashion crisis of the intellect. I long to be smartly turned-out for this femme reckoning, up on all the right theories, able to model that I'm a right-on white girl, that I am down with the lesbo/homo cause despite (or I'd say because of) my long hair and makeup. Underlying this fashion crisis are two constant problems for a nineties femme: invisibility as a dyke and how to authenticate herself as one despite doubt and rudeness from others.

Analysis of the circulation of femme as a sign in 1990s lesbian culture reveals femme functioning most commonly as the poster child of Lesbian Chic, promoting the vile assimilationist politics of what I mark as lipstick-lesbian culture, in which being seen as "straight-acting" is taken as a high compliment.[1] Announcing oneself as a proud femme dyke is especially complicated here in Los Angeles, where the largely white lipstick-lesbian culture is assimilationist and butch-hating. There are thriving communities of lesbians of color in Los Angeles some of which are fiercely butch-femme, but in the mostly white lesbian world of glossy magazines and West Hollywod, most personal ads come with the caveat "no butches" or "no drugs, no dykes."

These strings of exclusions in personal ads echo a long-standing practice in the gay male personals: "no fats, no femmes," "straight-acting only," and now, of course, "HIV negative only."[2] Among both gay men and lesbians the personal ad exclusions proscribe any deviation from a supposed norm of gender expression. The difference in the lesbian personals is that instead of being effeminophobic—or femme-phobic—they are just the opposite—butch-hating. The equations implicit in these strings are indicative of trends in nationwide conservative lesbian and gay identity politics.

175

Recently in LA's *Lesbian News* I saw "straight-acting only, discreet" in a lesbian personal ad. The equation of femme with straight-acting (not to mention discreet!) in the mainstream lesbian imaginary makes identifying as femme carry an extra liability of explanation. Femme circulates as a term of derision particularly in what I call the pomo dyke scene, home of the daddy-boy dyke and much genderfucking.[3] It is often framed as a matter of taste that these folks are not femme themselves or into femmes erotically. In an effort to reveal as artificial the equation female–equals–feminine, the desirable parameters of a woman's gender have become either masculine, androgynous, or "fluid." The feminine woman is vilified here, and it seems to me at least partly a matter of sexism that some pomo dykes cannot imagine that a femme could be down with the cause.

I undertake this analysis and circulate under the sign of femme myself, cruising terms (as well as butches) in bars and personal ads. Although my erotics are grounded in butch-femme exchange, I do not mean to suggest that butch-butch coupling is necessarily anti-femme, nor to suggest that femme-femme coupling is inherently anti-butch, or that both are always anti butch-femme. I am interested in opening up possibilities for resolution of the deadlock in which femme is caught between being perceived as the face of assimilation and being exorcised from a pomo dyke community. This essay attempts to continue the recuperation of the sign femme and of the identity category itself, thereby showing off femme dykes as both radical and desirable. This recuperation is an ongoing project undertaken by many women; especially important to note is the work of Joan Nestle and the many writers in her anthology, *The Persistent Desire: The Femme-Butch Reader.*[4] The excavation and writing of femme histories is one way of showing off femme dykes, and without the work of writers like Nestle, Madeline Davis, and Elizabeth Kennedy, stories of nineties femme would be written in a vastly different climate of understanding, if written at all.

Daily lives lived femme constantly require negotiating problems of visibility; thus, there are innumerable examples of radical and subversive performances of femme in every imaginable context. The live stage performances of the brilliant femme actress Lois Weaver stand out as particularly important to include in the discussion of how to show up as a radical and subversive femme. Longtime off-Broadway performer of the group Split Britches, she also graces the cover of *How Do I Look?* and co-stars in Sheila McLaughlin's film, *She Must Be Seeing Things* (1987).[5] As a femme Stella in *Belle Reprieve*, Split Britches' drag version of *A Streetcar Named Desire,* Weaver performs femme visibility in a number of ways.[6] Weaver's performance in *Belle Reprieve* suggests tactics by which to gain a "femme reprieve" from invisibility. This femme reprieve is performed onstage, but Weaver's performances can also be a means to understand the performance and reception of femme in worlds offstage. I do not mean to posit a simple relationship where "life imitates art," but to point out that Weaver and her butch partner, Peggy Shaw, purposely endeavor to blur the differences between on- and off-stage. As Sue-Ellen Case has noted:

> Weaver and Shaw . . . slip easily from one narrative to another. . . . The instability and alienation of character and plot is compounded with their own personal butch-femme play on the street, as a recognizable couple in the lower East Side scene, as well as within fugitive narratives on-stage, erasing the difference between theater and real life, or actor and character. . . . [7]

In the spirit of fugitive narratives, then, I slip from Weaver's "femme reprieve" to stories of femmes in bars, and back again to the stage. The circulation of femme around me in various offstage contexts sets the scene in which I analyze Weaver's work and her contributions to the negotiation of femme visibility.

Famously Femme

When I bought *How Do I Look?* I wondered about the blonde on the cover. I had seen *She Must Be Seeing Things*, but didn't make the connection to the film. I had recently seen Lois Weaver with Peggy Shaw in *Lesbians Who Kill*, then Split Britches' latest production, but I couldn't place her. I didn't make the connection to the butch-femme couple without the butch: Weaver is alone on the front cover of *How Do I Look?*. The shot is a still from *She Must Be Seeing Things*, in which Weaver sits, presumably in a movie theater, and looks off to the side of the book's cover toward an unseen screen. "How do I look?"—the question whose many different valences are glossed so marvelously by Teresa de Lauretis in her article in the same volume—is thus posed to Lois Weaver as well.[8] She looks straight, perhaps, which is the problem around which the film revolves in a number of ways; she looks blonde and white and alone. But she doesn't look like lesbian chic as seen on the cover of *Newsweek*. Her hair is bleached, she's not a twenty-something. She doesn't have the shiny gloss of the rich. That she is beautiful, even without that gloss, pushes at conventions of beauty. She looks at the unseen screen, rather than at the viewer who sees her on the cover. The ways in which she does not look (like a lesbian/rich/directly at the camera) put two questions to the viewer: How do I look at you? how do I look to you? This is a perfect picture for the cover, a shot whose ambiguity embodies questions of looking. This is also a perfect femme picture, as femmes invite (or command!) looking.

Lois Weaver's solitary presence on the cover embodies questions of femme (in)visibility as well. In order not to read her as straight, one must know of her, so her status as a femme dyke depends on extratextual knowledge. Even knowing her work as an actress, this connection may be hard to make. By contrast, her picture with Peggy Shaw on the cover of Lynda Hart and Peggy Phelan's *Acting Out: Feminist Performances*, registers much differently. In this publicity photo from Split Britches' play *Anniversary Waltz*, the butch-femme couple embraces; Weaver wears a ripped wedding dress and dark veil and Peggy Shaw sports a dark suit with white fringe. Lois clearly reads as a femme dyke here, but, as is typically true, femme requires butch to signify as lesbian. The cover photos beg the question of what kind of solitary pose will signify femme as independently lesbian?

A Girl Walks Into A Bar, Part 1

A beautiful brash maybe working girl or "pro" white femme struts into The Palms, a lesbian bar in West Hollywood, on a Saturday night. She works the runway, sweetie. A friend of the friend I came with whispers, loudly, of course, "She's *a little* dressed up." This is meant to indicate that the femme looks like a prostitute. Femme as prostitute is not exactly an original idea, but one in fact with a long and important history. What is perhaps newer is the way this equation turns insult, the way class inflects femme so that the expression of a feminine style is only acceptable or useful inasmuch as it furthers the assimilationist project, a politics of "we're just like you." Without brand-name clothes or when not classy enough to blend in, when the heels are high enough to call attention, then femme acquires a fallen woman status and is used as a pejorative term. "She's a *little* dressed up, don't you think?" Since I am also more than a little dressed up, I wonder why this rude question is asked of me (and why *my* friend likes this rude woman). It has to be the asker's presumption of my middle-class status allowing her to distance me from the femme in question and to assume that I would join her in femme-sexworker bashing. "Actually, I'm happy not to be the only one here anymore," I say, serving attitude which apparently doesn't register, because she keeps trying to talk to me. I want to approach the other femme and ask her where she gets her nails done, but sometimes I hesitate to approach other femmes, because when it goes wrong, I find myself viciously disappointed.

For instance, at a local bar the other night, I see two six-foot-tall femme ladies on the dance floor together. Both wear tiny miniskirts, one black leather, the other hot-pink satin. I get excited, thinking maybe they live nearby, maybe I could have two new femme friends. Then I wonder if they're a couple, or if maybe they aren't lesbians at all. Being uncertain of other femmes is one by-product of femme's association with assimilation: my ambivalent disassociation from women who look the way I do is lonely and crazy-making.

When a friend introduces the tall mini-skirted ladies, they both reach down to shake my hand, and then my butch date's. When they find out she's not a gay man, the handshakes stop awkwardly in the middle and turn into horrified stares at and whispers about this person I love, a transgendered butch dyke, in their eyes an embarrassing stereotype. From this encounter it is clear that femme as a certain type of feminine aesthetic is exactly the expression of assimilationist politics.

In some lipstick-lesbian communities, femme is expressed as a counter-stereotypical aesthetic designed to change the way lesbians are perceived by straight people. What hovers around this desire to change perception is the promise that *all* gay people will blend in, be "just like you" (the "you" of the address is always straight). The politics that insist upon all lesbians being feminine support this project of blending in, or assimilation. Though assimilation at first glance may seem innocuous, this promise of blending in is supported by embarrassment at the "obvious" (stereo)types in the gay community, like butch dykes and drag queens; from the encounter at The Palms this list could be extended to include working-class high-femmes.

The embarrassment that assimilationist gays feel at the presence of such (stereo)types is often coupled with the wish that these folks would disappear altogether. Expressions of this wish abound; for instance, gay magazines such as *OUT* regularly feature letters to the editor in which assimilationist gays urge that drag queens and dykes-on-bikes be kicked out of pride parades. Colonel Margarethe Cammermeyer, heroine of the recent TV-movie biopic *Serving in Silence*, encapsulated the project of assimilationist politics in a 1995 *Advocate* column:

> Discrimination against gays and lesbians continues—whether in the military or in society at large—through the perpetuation of the same stereotypes, such as the notion that homosexuals are mentally ill, unstable, effeminate or butch, and preoccupied with sexual activity. To put an end to these stereotypes should be the goal of all gays and lesbians, and this is why those of us who have challenged the ban have risked family and career to speak out.[9]

The notion that those who challenge the military ban are doing so in a counter-stereotypical effort is strange amidst so much talk of rights. Far more troubling is Cammermeyer's language: "Put an end to stereotypes" she says, can be all too easily translated to mean, "Put an end to butch dykes, effemi-

nate fags, the mentally ill, and all those preoccupied with sexual activity."
Quite a program.

The irony is that Cammermeyer herself certainly can be perceived as butch.
Serving in Silence stages butch-femme erotics between the military Cammermeyer (Glenn Close) and her artist lover (Judy Davis). The *Lesbian News* fea-
tured Cammermeyer on the cover standing close to Barbra Streisand, who
produced the movie, with the caption "Joining Forces." This cover flirts with
portraying the two as a butch-femme couple. The dissonance between
Cammermeyer as butch and her butch-bashing political program shows
stereotypes to be an extremely complex phenomenon. Cammermeyer, quoted
as being "against" stereotypes while embodying one, exemplifies the ambivalent vacillation that allows the stereotype to have cultural currency in the first
place.[10] Here the butch's words contradict her butch body.

Assimilationist politics have a long history, are now gaining strength, and
will not vanish if ignored; these are the people about whom the movies are
made, and the ones who own the glossy gay magazines. Because these folks
have the dollars and can get over, they are the ones who set political agendas
that will decide the very boundaries of how we are allowed to live. The
struggle for liberation must include the liberty to express identity in a great
variety of ways. Those of us perceived as acceptable by an assimilationist
politic must constantly show our alliance to people marked as stereotypical.
Thus, the problem for the femme dyke who is not assimilationist is not only
distinguishing herself from straight women, but from those femmes who
consider straight-acting a compliment.

How to distinguish oneself becomes the question. Must such distinctions
be made verbally; that is, instead of keeping our collective mouth shut, must
we open our individual mouths constantly? If the only way to be fierce is to
make noise, either by being articulate or a loudmouth, this means that fierce-
ness is exclusive. This definition of fierce excludes femmes for whom silence
is powerful and multifaceted, or who are just shy. Certainly there must be
ways to act and look femme without speech that are radical and subversive.
In order to investigate acting and looking as well as speaking, I now turn to
stage performances *meant* to be looked at (instead of constantly ripping off
performances of strangers in bars without permission). Lois Weaver's presentation of herself as a fierce femme dyke self-consciously stages these issues of
femme visibility. I identify Lois Weaver's tactics for foregrounding femme: as
outrageous femme flirtation; fierce iron femme exteriority; and a "something
wrong with the picture" strategy. These strategies overlap, all of them working against a reading of femme as heterosexual and showing off femme as
desirable and powerful.

Femme Flirtation

Lois Weaver's first entrance into the world of *Belle Reprieve* is a great show of femme strength. As she struts slowly and purposefully downstage, my friend's friend at The Palms would probably describe her as "a little dressed up" in her floral print dress. She directly addresses the audience, asking a series of questions:

> Is there something you want? What can I do for you? Do you know who I am, what I feel how I think? You want my body. My soul, my food, my bed, my skin, my hands? You want to touch me, hold me, lick me, smell me, eat me, have me? (5)

She turns sideways, ignoring the audience, and throws her head back to drink down almost a whole glass bottle of Coke. Her pleasure in the drink is palpable. The juxtaposition between the girlish Coke drinker and the beauty with breasts thrust out, head back, in search of liquid pleasure, cuts an extremely erotic profile. She comes up for air and turns to look directly at the audience. She asks, "You think you need a little more time to decide? Well, you've got a little over an hour to have your fill" (5). She flips her skirt while turning to walk upstage, hips swinging, nonverbally dismissing the audience.

In the first set of questions she signals that she knows the audience wants her, and that she is in control of their desire; in her response to audience laughter at her sexualized drinking, she solidifies her position as arbiter of desire. She gets to do whatever she wants about the spectatorial desire for her, all the while looking back and speaking words of invitation. By ending with a reference to the rest of the play in which she's about to act, she gives a wink to let the audience know that she knows they'll be watching her, and for exactly how long. Through her camp femme flirtation with the audience, Weaver performs agency from an objectified position. Kate Davy explains Weaver's strategy this way:

> the masculine gaze which objectifies the feminine is played out with a vengeance and a twist: the apparatus is made aware of itself: the woman looks back. And she is femme.[11]

Weaver's opening monologue acts out what Davy describes here, as Weaver invites objectification and puts a femme twist on it. The femme twist in this case is that woman as traditionally objectified—blonde and busty—takes power in a gazed-upon position: the visual economy is now under the control of the flirtatious femme.

Iron Femme and Aching Butch

Iron femme Lois Weaver is the expert director of spectatorial desire as she performs a sultry torch song in *Belle Reprieve*. As Stella/Weaver sings, Stanley/Shaw comes up to the stage out of the audience clapping loudly, to say, "Any moment this dame spends out of bed is wasted, totally wasted"(23). Vivian Patraka notes that Split Britches is able to "insist that a central part of theater is the spectators' desire to look at bodies. It is as if the eye were the sex organ of the spectator (and that includes women, and even feminist, spectators)."[12] Peggy Shaw makes this sex organ of the spectator active, strapped-on. She acts out audience desire, flaunts her border crossing, her transgression. Coming up out of the audience, she implicates spectators in this movement, penetrating the stage to kneel before Lois Weaver/Stella. Split Britches' staging of the femme as desired body does not leave Weaver playing a wimpy or dependent femme, but instead quite the opposite.

As Shaw comes up out of the audience, she not only acts out the audience's desire to touch as well as see, but also invokes her offstage relationship with Weaver. They play both their characters and themselves here, which helps to make them signify as a butch-femme couple, rather than as a pseudo-hetero Stanley-Stella. The Kowalskis as cultural icons are certainly invoked by the characters onstage. But the story of Stella Kowalski, battered wife, is referenced and then left behind as the play moves in a direction which imbues Stella with agency and power. When Shaw straps on the audience's desire, saying "Any moment this dame spends out of bed is wasted," she doesn't endow Weaver with lesbian visibility, but radically, differently, brilliantly, she queers the audience's desire.

In this moment of Stanley/Shaw's strapped-on desire, Weaver performs femme somewhat differently than in the flirtatious femme scene discussed above. Reviewing for the *Village Voice*, Mim Udovich called *Belle Reprieve* the "ultimate role standoff of iron femme and aching butch."[13] If Weaver performs femme's flirtatious power when alone onstage, Udovich's adjectives suggest that when onstage with a butch, Weaver's femme is performed and read somewhat differently. Investigating the description of Weaver as "iron femme" when onstage with the aching butch Peggy Shaw yields another tactic for the performance of visible femme lesbianism. Split Britches inhabit the stage together without making femme read as dependent on butch. Weaver and Shaw disarm the normalizing processes of signification, where femme-equals-feminine-equals-weak-equals-dependent.

Picture Perfect

In one scene in *Belle Reprieve*, Weaver and Shaw create a stage picture that quotes the famous scene from the film version of *A Streetcar Named Desire*: Stella faces towards the audience embracing Stanley who kneels in front of her. "His" ripped T-shirt exposes a rippling back. Kneeling before Stella, in this scene, Shaw as Stanley asks Weaver, "Are you saying I'm not a real man?"(24), which gets a huge laugh. Weaver replies, "I'm saying you're not real. You're cute. Could be much cuter if you weren't quite so obvious" (24). This obviousness has a number of subtle layers: it is a reference to Shaw's "obvious"/caricatured portrayal of the obviously tense Stanley, made famous by Marlon Brando, who played the role almost obviously as a caricature of himself. "If you weren't so obvious" is also a camp gesture to a homophobic cliché familiar to so-called obvious queers. Stella/Weaver reclaims the clichés of butch and femme, making them something to laugh at and laugh off. The obviousness—the excess femininity—of the woman who walked into The Palms "a little dressed up" is here played out in the reverse in Weaver's calling attention to caricatured qualities of butchness.

Obvious as well in this scene is Weaver's departure from and simultaneous camp engagement with a narrative which seeks to position her as dependent, weak, and invisible. When Weaver talks back to Shaw, gets a huge laugh, and invokes subcultural humor all at once, she sharply departs from the narrative of the iconic Stella she supposedly plays. Her sharp departure from this story by answering back is the strategy of femme performance I identify as iron femme. Performance of a fierce exterior, accomplished through either the strategy of iron femme or flirtatious femme, has the radical power to disrupt the signification of femininity as weak or as always straight. I can imagine that the "dressed up" dyke at The Palm would answer back the comments from my friend's friend, give her a quick lesson in fashion and manners, and then walk off to join her friends. These femme performances of fierce, iron exteriority show up equally well next to aching butch as alone; these are examples of scenes on- and off-stage that don't leave a femme looking like she needs a butch to complete her.

A reading of this scene comfortably within *Streetcar*'s narrative of heterosexuality is also confounded by the presence of whipped cream smeared all over Weaver's face, left over from a pie-in-the-face number a couple of scenes earlier. Because of the pie, audience attention is focused on Weaver, particularly on her feminine body, and it is clear that there is "something wrong with the picture." Without pie on her face, Weaver would be a perfect picture of beautiful heterosexual womanhood. This "something wrong with the picture" brilliance in Split Britches' work uses the feminine lesbian body to play with conventional codes of heterosexuality. The pie throws the perfect picture into relief, which both questions the perfection of that heterosexual picture in the first place and allows lesbian sexuality and iron femme strength to show up.[14] *Belle Reprieve* explicitly requires attention to what's wrong with the picture; "something wrong with the picture" is, then, not only a strategy for enacting femme identity, but for reading femme as well. Reading with this strategy, the fishnet stockings of the "dressed up" woman in the context of a dyke bar might appear in this lesbian context to be the "something wrong with the picture."

Moving from these examples of "something wrong with the picture" to citational practice, the desired feminine body as a place of power—Weaver as iron femme—is redefined in the context of the original play in which the desired feminine body—Stella as battered wife—is usually a site of violence. Staging departures from the original context is a critical strategy of snapping back, iron strong. All three of Weaver's strategies for performing femme onstage inform and are informed by offstage performances of femme lesbianism, an identity of potential danger and violence. Unfortunately, it seems to me that I catch the most fever for my feminine gender expression from other dykes, the people with whom, for me, the stakes are highest. The risks a feminine person takes in a male dominant culture should not be replayed within dyke communities. It is with other dykes that being able to play hard-as-nails iron femme has become my best method for snapping back.

A Girl Walks Into A Bar, Part 2

A white dyke I just met tells the story of a weekend outing. It's a get-to-know-you story; she's explaining her politics this way: "I found this great bar this weekend in Long Beach. Except this femme girl started hitting on me, like, grinding up to me and I was so scared because, I mean, couldn't she tell I was a queer dyke?" Queer dyke here describes what I call in this essay pomo dyke: often into leather, owns a motorcycle, usually dates other pomo dykes. In conversation months later, I found that the woman's frustration was not so much at being hit on by a femme, but at being taken for butch. The frustration the storyteller feels at her identity's invisibility is a problem with which I have a lot of sympathy.

Truly, butch cannot express all the ways masculine lesbians identify themselves, just as femme is hard pressed to encompass all feminine lesbians. But in this moment, because she makes it about her disgust at the femme, I think that she looks butch to me, and that she should feel lucky to have a fine femme hitting on her. Clearly my employing a strategy of camp femme flirtation will not work to show off femme to this woman, so I choose to make a show of iron strength. Though deeply angry, I am gentle in telling her how wrong and sexist she is, explaining that I know the white lesbian scene in LA is very lipstick lesbian. My queer-dyke acquaintance says she hadn't thought of how her story "sounded" misogynist, and goes on to say, "She was, like, a mall-chick, with huge permed blonde hair, though, you know?"

In this encounter, femme-bashing was supported by a display of classist logic that stunned me into silence. Pomo dykiness is often synonymous with a downward mobility that looks like a politics of class but is in fact a politics of style which can dishonor the very working class whose fashions it appropriates. The queer-dyke still thinks it was acceptable to be scared because the girl was, like, a mall chick (read working class). Essentially, what this means is that she wouldn't be scared if the girl were cool-looking, pierced or tattooed as well as femme; or that if she were a glossy rich-looking lipstick lesbian, it would be somehow acceptable to be grossed out by her femininity itself because those femmes are okay to bash. In the case of the working-class femme, it's said to be about her big hair, not her femininity as such, which is how misogyny hides in the already closeted classism of the downwardly mobile. I wonder if I not only let the queer-dyke get away with this but even facilitated it by disclaiming the white LA lipstick lesbian trend.

Genderfun

Pomo dyke culture is not something in which such femme-hating or otherwise messy politics necessarily inhere; it's great for people to have sexualities that turn them on, and styles that make them feel stylish and hip. But style isn't always neutral: styles signify politically and sometimes the significations are based on exclusions of groups of people. As with the stereotype, the problem is that certain people can't be whatever is in style. Being stylish and hip can come at someone else's expense, by inappropriate appropriation.

For example, fun with gender can come at the expense of those for whom gender is not fun but carries the weight of a constant threat of violence; not victims or sad cases, but fierce transgendered/transsexual folk who live on the boundaries of gender usually in ways that endanger their lives, people for whom the stakes are infinitely high. Fun with gender must be respectful of those whose full-time, or part-time, or even just-more-than-occasional fight it is. If genderfucking pomo dykes learn that gender is complicated, the next step is standing up for transgender expression. This connection would seem to be obvious; however, I commonly witness pomo dykes dissing transpeople's fight to inhabit gender in a way that feels appropriate for them because this fight takes identity too seriously.

Genderfuck and daddy-boy dyke identifications, which I'm calling pomo, can sometimes value masculine or androgynous attributes at the expense of femme dykes as well as at the expense of the transgendered, and here the categories overlap, as categories tend to. Of course there are many male-to-female (MTF) transsexual/transgendered dykes who identify as femme, and also many daddies and their boys who identify as transgendered or FTM. The femme-phobia of some pomo dykes is probably inadvertent, often simply an elision of femme from their erotics. Maybe there is no accounting for taste, but I have heard many of these women talk about their aesthetics in extremely femme-hating language, saying things about their desire for butch/masculine women because they're strong, while femmes are whiny or indecisive. At its worst, this femme-hating is combined with classism and femmes are also called uneducated tacky stupid loudmouths. Statements like these remind us that taste is never created in a political vacuum. The way pomo dyke taste can effect an exorcism of femme from this community is troubling and an example of sexist politics.

The erasure of femme from the pomo dyke community also results from privileging fluidity in identity expression. The privileging of fluid or changeable identity has become, ironically, extremely rigid. Not only am I uncool because I am full-time in one identity—so perceived anyway—but also because I have long hair and nails which is perceived as sexually disabling, rather than a proud display of bottom orientation. If full-time means rigid, then the fluidity with which I decide which parts of me to foreground—white, woman, student, teacher, femme—disappears. I must somehow mark myself to be seen as a member of the pomo crowd that doesn't "limit themselves" by taking gender/identity seriously. It's OK to be "femmey" in pomo dyke culture as long as one's hip signifiers (tattoos, piercings) are more visible than one's femininity. A femme might choose visibility based on this style, employing a "something wrong with the picture" strategy similar to that seen on the Split Britches stage. "Something wrong with the picture" in this case is a bit problematic, because it is enforced rather than chosen: in pomo dyke culture it is only acceptable to be femme if more visible in other ways.

Put another way, all this suggests that femme only participates in this pomo aesthetic when it is an "act": the performance has to be foregrounded *as performance* to be considered hip. It all sounds like a bad reading of Judith Butler that has become so familiar that Butler herself had to go back and clarify what she meant about performativity. She writes,

> if I were to argue that genders are performative, that could mean that I thought that one woke in the morning, perused the closet or some more

open space for the gender of choice, donned that gender for the day and then restored the garment to its place at night. Such a willful and instrumental subject, one who decides on its gender, is clearly not its gender from the start and fails to realize that its existence is already decided by gender.[15]

I quote her here not to rehearse her entire argument, nor to argue that pomo dykes are "bad theorists." Rather, I want to point out how privileging so-called fluidity in gender style can sidestep larger discussions of what is at stake in the notion that existence is decided by gender. In many cases, at stake are bodies unwillingly subjected to violence. This is not to say that pomo dykes do not face violence in their lives. I risk homogenizing anecdotes here in order to make a point that for transgendered and transsexual people—FTMs, drag queens, transgendered butches, MTFs, effeminate men, and especially queer high femmes—fucking with gender can never be simply cool or fun, but is always a matter of bodies and lives at stake.

Just Like A Woman

Belle Reprieve suggests a number of ways to perform independent femme visibility. The "femme reprieve" from invisibility is a moment in which the femme takes a powerful stand in the spotlight and acts out. Another strategy suggested by the play is that of parodically staging the supposedly natural, whether it be stage sex or binary gender. Offstage this tactic might look like dressing up and going out to a lesbian bar. As for what kind of solitary pose would signify femme, one answer is posing itself, a theatrical foregrounding of identity. Theatrically foregrounding identity might look like wearing the props of pomo in order to identify oneself as a dyke. Visibility as hipster—making "something wrong with the picture"—is thus one solution to the feeling of what Tracy Morgan describes as being "plagued by our invisibility—especially when we are butchless femmes."[16] However, privileging this strategy of visibility or this style might come at the expense of fierce foremothers who I for one am not willing to relinquish as heroes in any way, certainly not by regulating these ladies to some older-less-than-hip shelf.

The work of Minnie Bruce Pratt, for one, is indispensable to me. I sink into her deeply poetic stories of femme life in her latest book *S/HE*.[17] Her vignettes speak to my life, bespeak me, point out options I hadn't thought of yet. One in particular, *Frostbite*, moves me each time I read it. She writes of a walk home through snow with her lover, wearing flat flimsy low heels:

> When I peel my stockings off, I see patches of frostbite, and am furious with myself. A mocking internal voice says: *What silly shoes to wear in a blizzard. Just like a woman. . .*

> Now I remove the layers. I strip down to the power in the gestures of my hands, the sureness of my step, the way I turn my head and ask a question. I know that clothes only shadow me. This evening I decided to walk out with vanity in my lady shoes on the ice of the worst snowstorm in decades. This evening I wanted the power of showing my feet almost bare, my hips and breasts free under thin silk clothes. Now I sit on the bathtub edge, my feet in running water that stings and burns.

This is the physical fashion crisis: to wear what appeals, to look how you want, because props do matter; they can be a means to power. The mental fashion crisis is in what style to tell the truth. The possible price for either is frostbite, getting burned. The challenge is stopping the hateful voice in your head. *Just like a woman?* Yes, that's right, just like a woman, and a fierce femme lesbian one at that!

So, dress up, ladies, objectify yourselves. In order not to be perceived as the face of assimilation, speak out to say you're a big dyke even as you paint your nails and get out the fuck-me pumps and turn heads. In order not to be exorcised from the pomo dyke community, keep up (or begin) the dialogue, because in the end, these folks are potential allies in many ways. In order to fight the new gay right, answer a personal ad and get a glossy assimilationist lipstick lesbian to pay for an expensive lunch and drop the 411 on her (that is, give her the information) about why her politics suck. Get "a little dressed up" and go out to a club with some femme friends. With wild hair and a fierce iron attitude, play the flirtatious femme with a queer dyke. By running in loudmouthed packs, we will give each other strength to put forth politics that work against assimilation and for a vision of a future that includes us and those (stereo)types we love.

Notes

This paper has benefited enormously from careful readings by Douglas Crimp and Sue-Ellen Case, without whose support I never would have attempted this project in the first place.

1. The question of what to call women involved in femme-femme lesbian subcultures has been raised. For the purposes of this paper, I need a way to draw a distinction between femmes in a butch-femme subculture and femme-to-femme lesbians, and so have come to the uneasy compromise of calling them "lipstick lesbians."

2. For a discussion of effeminophobia in a gay male context, see Eve Kosofsky Sedgwick, "How To Bring Your Kids Up Gay," from *Fear of A Queer Planet,* ed. Michael Warner (Minneapolis: University of Minnesota Press, 1993).

3. I choose this term to gesture at how "pomo" as the title of an era or a type of queer can invoke an understanding of (gender) identity as fluid.

4. Joan Nestle, ed., *The Persistent Desire: A Femme-Butch Reader* (Boston: Alyson, 1992).

5. *How Do I Look?: Queer Film and Video*, ed. Bad Object Choices (Seattle: Bay Press, 1991).

6 Bette Bourne, Peggy Shaw, Paul Shaw, and Lois Weaver, "Belle Reprieve," from *Gay and Lesbian Plays Today,* ed. Terry Helbing (New Hampshire: Heinemann Educational Books, Inc., 1993). Other textual references cited parenthetically.

7. Sue-Ellen Case, "Toward a Butch-Femme Aesthetic," from *The Gay and Lesbian Studies Reader,* eds. Henry Abelove, Michèle Aina Barale, David M. Halperin (New York: Routledge, 1993), 302.

8. Teresa de Lauretis, "Film and the Visible," from *How Do I Look?* 223–264.

9. Margarethe Cammermeyer, "Taking the High Ground," *The Advocate* 21 (February 1995): 43.

10. For a discussion of stereotypes and colonialism, see Homi Bhabha, "The Other Question: Stereotype, Discrimination and the Discourse of Colonialism," from *The Location of Culture* (New York: Routledge, 1994).

11. Kate Davy, "Reading Past the Heterosexual Imperative: *Dress Suits To Hire,*" *The Drama Review* 33:1 (Spring 1989): 157.

12. Vivian Patraka, "Split Britches in *LITTLE WOMEN The Tragedy*: Staging Censorship, Nostalgia, and Desire," *The Kenyon Review* 15:2 (Spring 1993): 12.

13. Mim Udovich, "Brass Menagerie" rev. of *Belle Reprieve*, *Village Voice* 5 Mar. 1991.

14. See also Kate Davy, "Reading Past the Heterosexual Imperative," 158, 161.

15. Judith Butler, *Bodies That Matter* (London: Routledge, 1993) x.

16. Tracy Morgan, "Butch-Femme and the Politics of Identity," from *Sisters, Sexperts, Queers,* ed. Arlene Stein (New York: Plume, 1993) 46.

17. Minnie Bruce Pratt, *S/HE* (Ithaca: Firebrand, 1995) 102.

PRONOUNS, POLITICS, AND FEMME PRACTICE
An Interview with Minnie Bruce Pratt[1]

M innie Bruce Pratt is a writer, poet, essayist, and public speaker. Her first photo of herself as a femme dates from the age of three. The release of *S/HE* (Firebrand Books, 1994), her most recent collection, discusses pleasures and strategies of femme-butch relationships, as well as the fluidities of sex and gender boundaries. Pratt emerged as an important writer within women's liberation communities with the publication of *Yours in Struggle: Three Feminist Perspectives on Anti-Semitism and Racism* (1984). Pratt has also published several works of poetry, essays, and prose that take a stance on issues ranging from lesbian desire to race and class to the complexity of gender expression. Minnie Bruce was interviewed one day in Greenwich Village, a short train ride from her home in New Jersey—where she has excellent rates on rent, lots of space, and a strong femme-butch relationship with activist/writer Leslie Feinberg, entering its third year. Over lunch, in an airy white shirt, purple floral scarf, and eyes with the candor of an experienced femme, Pratt discussed the ways in which women's liberation in the late 60s and anti-racist activism brought her closer to her own femme liberation. In addition, she spoke of how her femme identity works not only as a way to understand herself as a woman but also as a means of articulating her gender expression as a site of resistance.

The Pronoun S/he: Feminist and Gender Communities

Q: Let's start with the basics. I was wondering how you would pronounce the title of your new book, *S/HE*.

MBP: I am still in a kind of crisis myself about how to pronounce it. I realized this when I was doing another interview and the person kept saying "she" and so I would say "well, s/he is *s slash h-e*" or "s/he is *she-he*." Generally when I am introducing it to an audience I say "s/he is *s slash h-e*" and sometimes I say "the pronoun formerly known as "*he*." It shows what a crisis we have in language that we don't have gender-ambiguous pronouns. Twenty-something years ago, when June Arnold wrote *The Cook and the Carpenter* (1972), she experimented with "na" and it never caught on. I hear that there is a discussion going on the Internet, in the various gender bulletin boards, that people are experimenting with other pronouns like "hir" and "ze."

Q: Interesting. So did you title your book in response to a feminist rethinking of pronouns, or to activism in gender communities around this issue?

MBP: Well, this pronoun [s/he] was beginning to be used in feminist circles as an alternative to saying *he* or *she*. It wasn't being done in the context of a gender community. It was being done as a feminist-linguistic alternative to he or she without any complication of the *he*-ness or the *she*-ness of the situation. So I decided that [the pronoun s/he] bridges my position between having been part of women's liberation and now being part of the gender community. But I chose it as on-page rather than conversational.

Of course we're talking about social situations in which you do not know how people want to be identified. Even if they may live their lives visibly as one or the other—as an unambiguous maleness or unambiguous femaleness—that's not necessarily how they are experiencing life. The social process of getting to know someone well enough that they reveal the intricacies of their sex and gender realities to you, that is not instantaneous.

Q: Does it seem like there is a space, or more of a space, where other communities besides the gender communities are rethinking possibilities of gender identification?

MBP: I feel like it is happening when I do readings from *S/HE*, especially in gay and feminist audiences. People are really open to thinking about these things. They are uncomfortable in some ways but they're very excited by new discussions about gender/sex fluidity.

Femme Values

Q: In the first section of your book, the questions about your sexuality are coupled with questions about your femme identity. Was your coming out as a femme related to coming out as a lesbian?

MBP: Feeling my femme identity was really a very long process. In my upbringing in the deep South, femme identity had been assigned certain values: if you were femme, you're ornamental; you're not necessarily very smart, aggressive or tough. There were certain class values attached to femme too. To be femme in an ultra-femme way twenty-four hours a day . . . only people who had time and money could live like that. Meanwhile, I am working summers in the garment factory where you just don't femme up to run the gripper machine. In addition, a highly developed, stylized public femme quality was often linked to certain values which, when I came out as a feminist, seemed antithetical to values of women's liberation. At the same time, I did find mentors within feminism who claimed femme identities and said, "You know, this is really not in contradiction to fighting against women's oppression." So I didn't say to myself "I can't be a femme," but I did struggle with how to make a public presentation as a lesbian. . . . I felt to do that, I had to dress more androgynously than I had in the past. I quit wearing skirts.

Q: When you dressed androgynously, did others still perceive you as a femme?

MBP: I remember going to a national women's studies conference once, where I met a well-known lesbian-feminist scholar. I had on Army fatigue pants and a thin pink cotton shirt and a little orange ribbon around my neck. The scholar came up to me, and said, "Hi, you look nice today," then she reached out and flirtatiously touched my ribbon. So even in this more androgynous style, I still had my femme wiles. Of course being femme isn't just about the clothes; we know that.

Q: We sure do. So, what do you think about lesbian dress codes?

MBP: You know, this was very culturally limited thinking, within a group of mostly white, mostly middle class, mostly lesbian-feminist movement folks, including myself. This was not thinking that was influenced by Latina femmes, or African American bulldaggers. This was 1970, which was twenty-five years ago—pre-queer theory, pre-transgender theory.

Q: So during the androgynous seventies, were you in butch-femme relationships?

MBP: I was always attracted to the butchest women around. Absolutely. My first lover walked like a sailor. She had long blond hair, but her body language and her way of being was in distinct contradiction to that. She wore men's trousers and she actually dressed like a gay man. She came out when she was fourteen, pre-*everything*, so her path to trying to figure out her sexuality, her sex, and her gender identity was complicated.

Writing Femme: Generations of Lesbians

Q: Now that you have published *S/HE*, do you feel that your femme identification is more public? How does that affect your connection to different kinds of lesbians, for example, young lesbians or people in the gender community?

MBP: My [previous] work gets used in women's studies classrooms to talk about women's struggles, about anti-racist work, and about anti-Semitism. In some ways, I have felt like I am of another era, the generation of us who sought revolutionary change in the 1960s. This work [*S/HE*] connects me to queer young folks in a way that my other works often do not. I find that sad, because I would like to think that people feel the struggle against racism is not separate from an understanding of sexuality. One of the things I did consciously in this book is weave in issues around race. It seems so much of queer theorizing has been about gender and sex and not race. I couldn't have written about femme identity if I hadn't done the anti-racist work I have done. I wouldn't have requestioned the nature of sex/gender categories without first questioning race categories.

Q: Could you expand on that?

MBP: If you deal with race in this culture, you have to talk about the nature of categories, the way they are imposed and the politics of that imposition. This can bring you back to look at categories of sex and gender in a much more complicated way.

Q: As you speak to the categories of sex and gender, what do you think are the politics of these?

MBP: I believe that people should have freedom of gender expression. . . . But that is not the only plank in my political platform. I am interested in how sex and gender is structured by race and class oppressions. I am interested in liberating femmeness from all of the values assigned to it under a class-based economic culture. That is what I am interested in. I am not interested in just playing femmeness; I am interested in making it a site of resistance, too, because of the values imposed on femaleness and femininity by a class-based patriarchal culture.

Q: So, how do feminist and race politics influence the way that you think about yourself?

MBP: I am completely at peace with who I am. Part of being at peace is really having acquired, again by way of women's liberation and anti-racist work, an understanding of who I am. I finally acquired an understanding of the way in which I have been trivialized. It wasn't just that I was a woman, it was that I was a little femme girl trying to play softball; it was that I was a femme young woman trying to get hired at a university; it was that I was a white femme woman expected to let the white men run the world. I am at peace with myself because I have rejected those rules for being femme.

Q: But, as a little girl or a young woman, you didn't name yourself a femme. When did you start identifying as femme?

MBP: Well, it was only about four or five years ago. I had been thinking about butch and femme for quite a while. In 1982 the Barnard conference happened and that raised issues of sexuality in the community. Then Joan Nestle came out with her anthology *The Persistent Desire* (1992). That was really very helpful. There was a growing tide in the community of talk about butch-femme. I went through a lot of struggle in my long-term relationship in the 1980s around issues of butch and femme identity. It was very difficult. I definitely was living in a lesbian-feminist culture where the struggle for women's liberation was often expressed as a need to eliminate masculinity and femininity.

Q: So that was a drawback of lesbian-feminist politics at that time, but did feminism help you at all coming to terms with being a femme woman in this culture?

MBP: Certainly it is hard to deal with being a femme and a woman in this culture. When I say that I was a femme at three, I mean that I had the same gender expression then that I have now. But I had not gone through the struggle of liberating myself as a woman, as a sexual person . . . I had to grow up on a number of different levels. For instance, that I would grow up and support racial segregation and white supremacy was expected of me as a white woman. I had to liberate myself from that as a value.

What do I do within my femme identity? Do I use it to perpetuate oppressive values, or do I use it to fight them? I think that this question is true for butches as well. One of the reasons I have so much respect for Leslie is that she went through a period in her life in which she thought, "Which of my behaviors are really crucial to my identifying as a butch and which need to go as remnants of oppressive beliefs?" I have never been involved with anybody who respects me so completely as a person and as a femme and as a woman. That respect is linked to her respect for herself.

Q: So, has talking with Leslie and other butches facilitated your femme identification?

MBP: One of the things that has made it easier for me to come into my femme identity is that I had a number of conversations with butch women in which they expressed to me their appreciation for femme as its own separate way of being. It meant a lot to me to have that acknowledgment of my own reality instead of having conversations with people who undermined their own or my gender expression. I do not know what it would mean to come to self-appreciation in other ways because that is how I came to it. I can certainly see coming to it through femme-to-femme appreciation.

Q: When you say femme-to-femme appreciation, do you mean friendships? Are friendships with femmes important to you?

MBP: In earlier lesbian-feminist years, my closest friends were butch women. I didn't have femme friends. As I got to be more comfortable with myself as a femme, and began to appreciate femininity, I hung out more with people who identify as femme or high femme. It is not a sexual relationship; it is sensual. Recently, I have developed friendships with femmes who are younger than me, in their twenties or thirties. I love that. I really love that.

  I love looking at femmes in New York City. In *S/HE*, I wrote about walking on Broadway and seeing a femme who had braided her hair with copper wire, and ornamented herself with spiked bracelets and tattoos. I thought she was a goddess. The most beautiful woman.

Femme on the Streets

Q: Do you think that people see you as femme when you are out on the streets?

MBP: Every time I go out with Leslie, people stare. So I have a routine that I have developed. Just the other day, Leslie and I were walking down on the Jersey shore, on the boardwalk, and this guy who had a Marine T-shirt on, a big blond guy, was staring us into the ground. So I stared at him until he broke. I am really good at this; it's my southern ice-queen stare. My attitude is, "You want to stare at us? Okay. Let's stare." Leslie does it too. I think we divide up the chore of dealing with this. She takes on the teenage boys because my staring at them might be perceived as inappropriate.

Q: Do you and Leslie ever pass as straight when you are out together?

MBP: I don't think we pass. I think in a situation like the one in *S/HE* where we crossed the border to Canada, what we did was set up a visual moment so that someone who is only going to look at us for about five seconds would accept his initial perception of us as "normal." The fact that we had to set it up like that to protect ourselves from this authority is an indication of how very, very queer we look. We only appear straight for the first five seconds. Just walking down the street, in the diner, or at the boardwalk, we hear, "Is she a man? Is she a woman? If she is a straight woman, what is she doing with this gay man?" We check in with each other. "What do you think, is it okay? I think we should go. I think we should cross over to the other side. Danger." We very much go out as a team.

Q: In this butch-femme team, how do roles play themselves out? I am thinking of femmes I know who love to do daddy-girl or mommy-boy dynamics as part of their butch-femme erotic relations; do these mean anything to you?

MBP: In the past, when I've been with butch lovers who have been less sure of themselves around their masculinity and their butch identity, one of the ways I related to them was through mothering. That's not the case for me now. As I have come into my femme identity, I think I'm able to be more of a girl than ever before. Actually, there are ways in which I am an aspect of myself that I've never gotten to be, especially when I was an actual, literal mother. Now when I am my most sexual, I just feel womanly or girlish, not motherly. Coming into my femme identity has allowed me to be both a girl and a strong woman. One of the important events in my early relationship with Leslie is that we were wrestling, and she couldn't win even though she had taken years of karate. Finally she said, "Wow, I'm not going to worry about you on the street, because you are such a good fighter!" I have never had a butch lover tell me, "You are really strong; you are a fighter" as a compliment and with respect. It ended up as a tie. I loved that.

Q: Do you consider yourself transgendered in any way?

MBP: I don't see myself as transgendered. However, a man who cross-dresses in a very feminine way in order to pursue feminine desires might consider himself a transgendered femme. However, my birth sex and my gender expression are fairly congruent by the social standards we operate under. I do consider myself a part of the gender community. Partly because of my alliance with Leslie, but also because I consider myself an ally—now I am a conscious ally. It's no accident that I am with Leslie. It's not a fluke or a chance. My first girlfriend when I was five was completely transgendered. My first husband when I was nineteen was completely transgendered. Transgender is a place I find very liberating and exciting.

Q: So is femme desire then for transgendered bodies, or a place where gender isn't so clear?

MBP: I love the contradiction between gender identification and biological sex. I love having the simultaneity, the both/and. I am sure there are femmes who don't find that as exciting, for whom it is not as deeply a part of their lives.

Q: Finally, putting this all together, what does femme mean to you?

MBP: Femme means to me that I have a feminine gender expression as a site of resistance to old values. Those values say that I am not a fighter, I am not smart, I am not tough, or that I can't be sexual and be a mother too. There are a lot of these should-nots attached to the old way of being femme that I have cast aside. In making my life a site of resistance, I walk through life my own way and create a kind of power and defiance that says "You can't touch me unless I say yes." To me, femme means being powerful in myself, in my own body, with all her feminine ways. It means saying to myself I don't have to take care of other people or give myself up for somebody else. Femme means that I am conscious about what people are saying and doing around me, toward me, as a woman, and that I always maintain my dignity and power.

This is the way in which I feel women's liberation and current trends in queer and transgender theory overlap, because certainly women's liberation laid the foundation for my way of being femme. I do not think that femme means making your butch take the trash out for you. I do not think that femme means loving to shop. If loving to shop for clothes was femme, Leslie would be a femme. I don't think femme is having long fingernails. I don't think femme is not understanding how to deal with money. Those are old degrading stereotypes that establish femme on a foundation that is degrading to women. And I do not agree with that at all. For me, femme is a place of resistance to that degradation, a place to divest femininity of limiting stereotypes, and a place to assert the power and dignity of femaleness.

Notes

1. Questions by Harris and Crocker; interview conducted and transcribed by Tania Hammidi; edited by Harris and Crocker, and Minnie Bruce Pratt.

MARILYN, MAYHEM, AND THE MANTRAP
Some Particularities of Male Femme

Alex Robertson Textor

Lesbian Femme and Male Femme: Lived Similarities; Lived Differences

Recently, critical narratives concerned with lesbian femme identities and practices have seen the light of print. These narratives have questioned lesbian-feminist readings of femininity, sexuality, and gender. Among other writers, Madeline Davis, Amber Hollibaugh, Joan Nestle, and Minnie Bruce Pratt have participated in the articulation of basic tenets and continuing possibilities of lesbian femme. I would argue that these general characteristics—these tenets and possibilities—constitute a category of gender construction that is simultaneously queer and empowered. Also, I insist that to pronounce various practices and positions "femme" requires referring to the codes and frameworks of lesbian femme, that situate the emergence of femme as an empowered category of queer gender.

Conscious self-constructions of femme, at their most basic, involve, in Wendy Chapkis's words "self-display, whether in a quietly demure or sexually flashy fashion. . . . There is something about a femme-y style that in itself produces insecurity, a sense of vulnerability and exposure. The femme invites the gaze and it takes a great deal of feminine self confidence to risk that kind of scrutiny."[1] Self-display is one aspect of femme self-presentation. Another prominent defining feature of lesbian femme is the recontextualizing of femininity for queer seductive purposes. Sue-Ellen Case describes this element in her essay "Toward a Butch-Femme Aesthetic." While Case's analysis does not examine femme as a subject position unto itself, she does advance the following about femme performativity: "Beauty [the femme] is the desired one . . . the one who aims her desirability at the butch."[2] This femme *aiming of desirability* is also articulated by Amber Hollibaugh in the essay "What We're Rollin' Around in Bed With," co-written by Cherríe Moraga. Here, Hollibaugh understands femmes to be enablers of erotic exchange.[3]

The choice of a celebrity, an actress, or a specific character within a film as a model for femme gender self-creation is present in many individual lesbian femme narratives. Sex educator and writer Carol Queen recalls the evolution of her femme identity with a butch lover:

> My own womanness had frightened me until the night we did Quaaludes, and I arched back off the bed, dizzy with the drug and a kind of power I had never relaxed into before, and purred: "I feel like Marilyn Monroe!" To which she replied, hands full of me, "You *are* Marilyn Monroe."[4]

Queen goes on to invoke Marilyn Monroe as her "spirit guide," explaining that such a choice on her part, along with encouragement from her butch lover, allowed her to "reconstitute as a femme woman."[5] Lesbian femme self-modeling involves a shaping of identity that relies on yet betrays dominant cultural imperatives as it produces queer genders. Queen's invocation of Monroe's femininity reinterprets cultural codes for otherwise unforeseen purposes.

Lesbian femme conventions perversely deploy femininity. Self-display dislodges the cultural taboos that confine overtly sexualized self-representations to the pornographic sphere. Modeling knowingly reiterates sexual codes while navigating new erotic pathways. The role of lesbian femmes in enabling or mobilizing sex also breaks with the cultural myths that grant the position of initiating and activating sex to men. Femme queerings include: trappings of femininity (lipstick and other forms of make-up, feminine-gendered mannerisms); seductive, "mantrapping" sexualities which mobilize queer desires; and the tracing/modeling of self through spectacular representations of glamorous and powerful women. Most significantly, each of these conventions is appropriated within the terms of lesbian femme for purposes which queerly subvert heteronormative cultural regimes.

Though commonalities exist between lesbian femme and gay male femme, it is also clear that there are dissimilarities. Effeminate men, like butch women, dramatically reject gender normativity as assigned by the dominant sex/gender system. On the street, male femmes are often physically endangered targets of homophobic wrath. Male femme transgressions are identified as gender terrorism. Male femme identities can only emerge from these often terrorized positions of gender liminality. At the same time, male femmes by no means have the corner market on experiences of violent, invasive attack. As male femmes face homophobic violence, lesbian femmes confront the misogynist violence of threats of rape and other forms of sexual harassment.

Male femme is not *necessarily* queer in its desiring relationship, although it is unequivocally queer in its gender dysphoria. While lesbian femme self-presentations certainly can and do depart from culturally established gender norms and codes, it is in desiring relationships to other women—especially butch women—that femme lesbians often cite their queerness. On this point, Madeline Davis writes that femmes are: "Women who look and act like girls and who desire girls. We're just the queerest of the queers. It makes me laugh, but it also makes me feel so different. . . . We're kind of like those women in the 'lesbian' porn movies—long hair, lipstick—except we're real. We desire everything about our butches—even their womanness. I think that's pretty queer."[6] Here, Davis positions lesbian femme desires as queer, while she also suggests that femmes reconstruct heterosexually imposed and enforced categories of gender as *lesbian*. Male femme and lesbian femme share an enduring purpose despite the differences sketched out here, and despite also the vast socio-sexual differences between gay men and lesbians. However, it is crucial that male femme as well as lesbian femme practices and behaviors are recognized as chosen sites of oppositional agency.

Effeminate men have long been a visible subculture of gay men. Effeminacy, as I detail later, is just one identifiable category for femme male inhabitation. What I am extrapolating here as male femme is somewhat at odds with effeminacy, in that it requires a referencing, conscious or otherwise, of lesbian femme legacies of style and sensibility. I cautiously read engagements with *practices* socially gendered female by *bodies* genitally sexed male as femme. I stress caution because I don't want simply to generate a detachable "femme." Instead, I seek here to understand male femme as a gender category which shares with lesbian femme a collection of characteristics. This sharing places male femme in a position of referability back to lesbian contexts of reclamation and construction.

All too infrequently, gay men have not referred back to lesbian contexts, even during eras when lesbian communities have assiduously endeavored to pay close attention to gay men's cultural realities and needs. At times, gay men assume that the work of re-envisioning gendered structures, idioms, and artifacts is solely their domain. To quote one cultural worker very dear to me, the late Italian gay liberationist theorist, activist and drag queen Mario Mieli:

If Marlene Dietrich in her glitter is an emblem of the oppression of women, she is at the same time a gay symbol, she is gay, and her image, her voice, her sequins form part of a homosexual culture, a desire that we queens recognize in ourselves. . . . We are fed up with dressing as men. We ask our sisters in the women's movement, then, don't burn the clothes that you cast off. They might be useful to someone, and we have in fact always longed for them. In due course, moreover, we shall invite you all to our great coming-out ball.[7]

Here Mieli cites Dietrich as enabling and indirectly models his own self-presentation on Dietrich's persona. At the same time, Mieli contrasts his *ability* to celebrate Dietrich with the assumed *inability* of a feminist movement to do so. There is an assumption here that the agents who translate femininity into queerness will necessarily be drag queens, not women. What is missing in this account is how lesbians have refigured femininity throughout the twentieth century. What is also missing is Dietrich's own sexuality as a lesbian, and her status as a Hollywood lesbian icon.

In the 1990s, discussions of butch-femme among gay men don't contain the sort of embodied urgency that characterizes similar conversations among lesbians. For gay men, butch-femme conceptually lacks the distinctive pasts and reworked presents that exist for lesbians. In terms of plotting gender or sex, practical negotiations of gay male sexual activity are split into the top/bottom dyad, with those in between choosing the personals-ad position named "versatile." While lesbian butch-femme is also often organized around a top/bottom opposition, its accompanying codes of gendering exceed a mere description of desired sexual practice. Butch-femme expresses the transfiguration of sexual role into explicitly gendered social role. Such an elaborated social code is not present in the gay male community along butch-femme lines, no matter how explicitly individual relationships to penetration determine sexual roles and practices.

Yet both "butch" and "femme" have their own meanings and valences for gay men. To give one example, a hypermasculinity often named butch is deployed by many gay men for erotic purposes. This butchness is subculturally confined by its own tongue-in-cheek, muscle-bound hermeneutic. When the sexual constructs of butchness are extended less self-consciously to the social realm, another category materializes: the straight-acting gay man. In the personals, "straight-acting and appearing" are so central to the gay male ego-ideal that they come to stand in for "normative," which, among men, might be less euphemistically phrased as "not effeminate." Again in the personals, gay men confront a "femme" presence in the form of aversion to "fats" or "fems." Among men, the stomach-turning monstrosity of this imagined "fem" meets its opposite in the culturally normative "male" genders that most men, straight *and* gay, inhabit. To be sure, drag queens are celebrated by segments of the gay male community. But I would argue that femme men tend to be valued for their ability to generate humor and levity, and not taken seriously as social and sexual subjects.

For gay men, the femme exists in the disavowed figure of the queen. Whether s/he is in intentional drag or in a less consciously performative state of effeminacy, this (usually imagined) queen provides an invaluable gender barometer, especially useful for gay men eager to counter-identify their genders as normative, as not deviant. Because masculinity is coded so rigidly, the slightest gender-dysphoric mannerism marks its male agent as effeminate. I would argue that this stranglehold on representations of masculinity increases gay male insecurities about their own genders, setting up considerable stakes among many gay men to be read as anything *but* effeminate.

Some Possible Male Femme Identifications

The following four categorizations are meant to usefully plot different ways that men can be femme—not to foreclose the spaces for male femme identity. I read these categories as both *queer* and as necessarily *gay*.

Practice/Project/Position	Defining Characteristics	Binary/Counterpoint
1. effeminacy	male dysphoric gender; coded as feminine/ gender-crossing	"masculinity"
2. androgyny	dysphoric gender; coded in-between recognizable genders	"masculinity"
3. drag	transitory, temporary category of gender inversion	normatively clothed
4. bottom	anal-receptive (and otherwise *servicing*) sexual role	top

What we understand today as effeminacy owes much to the history of figures like Quentin Crisp, dandies whose self-presentation invoked meticulous and arch articulations of femininity. Until very recently, what passed in the straight imaginary for gay men was solely the effeminate queen. Unlike effeminacy, androgyny involves a crossing of codes that suggests neither the masculine nor the feminine. Androgyny might denote self-presentations that altogether dismiss ready understandings of either masculinity or femininity, through a process not of *mixed* coding, but of codings of gender that are simply *unfamiliar* or *unimagined*, as in the case of Boy George during his first media run (1982–1985). Drag does not signify sustained participation in male femme identity creation. Contemporary drag queens with considerable media presence include Joan Jett Blakk, Lypsinka, Lady Bunny, and RuPaul. The bottom is, unlike the three preceding categories, not necessarily a femme category. To return to the personals, the *butch* bottom label is a popular one. I include bottom as a possible femme practice because it has, in dominant culture, been over-associated with the feminine. In the analysis of Marilyn that follows, I am interested in the crafting of male femme identification at the point where a transsexual jump is played with but rejected. This would suggest yet another classification of male femme—*hybrid femme*—living within the overlapping terrain each of my categorizations supplies.

Marilyn's Hybrid Femme

"I don't know what you do, honey, unless you put Novocain in your lipstick."

—Dorothy (Jane Russell) to Lorelei Lee (Marilyn Monroe
in *Gentlemen Prefer Blondes*, after Monroe has
immobilized her fiancé with a kiss.

"I like people thinking I'm sexy . . . doesn't everyone?"

—Marilyn, 1983.

Male pop stars have been some of the few men in the twentieth century to challenge the orthodoxy of gender roles, in part because the iconography accompanying popular music (especially since the mid-1960s) has championed social transgression. In the early 1980s, a new breed of London-based male pop stars cropped up. They were dubbed "gender-benders," and three of them became especially well known. The most famous among their ranks was Boy George, lead singer of Culture Club, who reigned with Michael Jackson in 1983 and 1984 as the best-known pop star worldwide. Another, Pete Burns, fronted the band Dead or Alive. Dead or Alive had one big international smash at the start of 1985 and afterwards languished in the land of semi-hits. The third, always a solo singer, was named Marilyn.

For a brief time, beginning in the fall of 1983 and continuing until early summer of 1984, a man named Peter Robinson filled the pages of teenage music magazines in the United Kingdom. Mr. Robinson performed and lived under the name Marilyn, a nickname once given to him by taunting school-age bullies in response to his idolization of Marilyn Monroe. In a 1983 interview in *Rolling Stone*, he explained that he took the name Marilyn as a way of telling them off.[8] Marilyn was born in Jamaica, and grew up near London. In the early 1980s, he left London for Los Angeles, hunting fame. He returned to London in 1983 to pursue a pop music career.[9] In 1983–84, Marilyn's label released three singles, "Calling Your Name," "Cry and Be Free," and "You Don't Love Me," each with declining sales. His only album, *Despite Straight Lines*, was released in mid-1985. It spawned two subsequent singles, "Baby U Left Me (In The Cold)" and "Pray for that Sunshine." *Despite Straight Lines* flopped disastrously, failing to make even the British Top 100. Marilyn had already been eclipsed by other stars of the moment.

Marilyn's basic get-up was simple: pink lipstick; long, teased, bleached, and sometimes dreadlocked hair; some jewelry; and both men's and women's clothes. Sometimes he posed shirtless, other times in full sequined drag, but nearly always with his trademark lipstick and pout. His lipstick was at the core of his self-presentation. Cathy Griggers has called lipstick "a classic signifier of the social materiality of femininity's masquerade."[10] Lipstick, along with other make-up, nudged Marilyn toward the fullness of a sultry and intentional femme sexuality. It was his lipstick that spelled out girl trouble and predicted mayhem. With lipstick, Marilyn could leave his mark, on a collar, a jowl, a coffee cup, or a discarded tissue.

In *Vested Interests*, Marjorie Garber describes Marilyn as "Boy George's former boyfriend, the transvestite pop music figure . . . with his long blond hair and hairy chest . . ." and claims him as the epitome of celebrity imitation and regendering.[11] Drag has historically focused on impersonation of female celebrity figures. Monroe's continual emulation within popular and drag cultures, for example, shows her centrality to the modern construction of femininity.[12] Monroe's enduring iconicity reinforces this point. As Graham McCann points out:

> The initial series of prints produced by Andy Warhol after Monroe's death was an indication of the potential mechanical reproducibility of a multiplicity of "Marilyns" in the market place. . . . "Marilyn" is rubber-stamped and reproducible as a marketable image: blond hair, moist eyes, licked lips. . . .[13]

By wearing make-up and keeping his chest hairy, Marilyn made clear that he was not trying to "be" Marilyn Monroe, but was instead playing with gendered constructions of beauty. This is where Garber's description of Marilyn as a *re*gendered Monroe comes into play. Marilyn's drag made obvious his maleness as well as his femaleness. Marilyn idolized Monroe and took her name without attempting to look like her. He was a creature between recognizable genders, his name a marker for comparison and reference, not mimesis. Peter Robinson chose to live under the sign "Marilyn" in order to trigger the signals of modern feminine irresistibility. This he did as a man, never passing for a woman, let alone for Monroe. Marilyn couldn't be pegged as a drag queen: his gender-bending was not designed to solely imitate women; neither did it differ from his everyday demeanor. Drag and performance were permanent fixtures; one and the same.

Marilyn and his predecessor Monroe shared, vividly, the ability to pose as moving danger zones of temptation incarnate. Marilyn moved across genders to become what Paul Monette, among others, has named the "mantrap." In an effort to consolidate his adolescent obsessions with Elizabeth Taylor and Marilyn Monroe and his desire for men, Monette evokes this "mantrap":

> I'd think sometimes what it would be like to have the kind of body and raw power that made him reel. What it would be like to lure him onto the shoals of desire. I wanted to be a mantrap like Liz in *Butterfield 8*. A dark and twisted desire for sure, and one that was of no use. . . .[14]

What was of no practical use to Paul Monette in his boarding school hell in the early 1960s was the desire to transform his proto-gay desiring body into a mantrap. This transformation was as close to impossible as any. There were no guides, outside of the physique magazine media, of how men might appeal to other men, and *that* space, like the celluloid spaces of feminine conquest, was necessarily fictive anyway.

But what was impossible for Monette was for Marilyn the floodgate of possibility. In a 1983 interview with British maverick journalist Paul Morley, the catty discussion between the two ended with Morley asking the photographer to leave the room, so direct had Marilyn's advances become. In the interview, Marilyn edgily flirts with Morley, calling him "girl" and then "daddy" and then "darling," wondering out loud whether or not Morley is gay. Paul Morley manufactures a mantrapping portrait of Marilyn in the introduction to the interview when, discussing the accompanying photo shoot, he writes:

> The male's being photographed, and he's happily collapsing over soft furnishings, rubbing his body into his big baggy cushions, cheaply wetting his finger on his tongue, flinging his mane around his face, acting out his bor-

rowed name to a quick perfection, pretending with his sparkling eyes to a special, rising bliss. . . . The female's being interviewed, and he's telling big, small and awful lies, spinning out aphorisms that glisten with blatant contradiction—resisting, challenging, whining, losing, fluttering his eye-lashes, giggling, winning, snapping, rolling back into the soft sofa, sinking into the cushions, wrapping a big red scarf around his head and splicing the holy with the unholy.[15]

Morley, a journalist known for his acid critiques of pop stars, routinely tore into his interviewees. Here, he appears whipped into seduction, floored by Marilyn's advances. It is as if there is nothing he can do beyond accepting his position as the seduced. This is our picture of Marilyn, from his glory years 1983–85: lipsticked, flirtatious, mantrapping. As I pointed out earlier, these are all characteristics that lesbian femmes have cited as central to activizations of femme performativity.

In a February 1984 issue of *Smash Hits*, Marilyn claimed that all boys fan-cied him. Besides raising the ire of Boy George fans (the quotation came dur-ing a publicized tiff between the two) Marilyn's claim reveals that he saw himself as a sex *object* irresistible to men.[16] Simultaneously, Marilyn inspired intense fandom on the part of teenage girls. In the spring of 1984, following a publicized insult of Marilyn by rival singer Limahl, Marilyn's fans surrounded Limahl outside Radio One studios in London, passing him threatening notes and pulling his hair menacingly (39).[17] It was a slippage in gender codes that enabled Marilyn to pose as a site of transgressive homosexual desire yet also to bask in an explicitly female adoration that male pop stars have enjoyed since the post-World War II rise of the popular culture industries.

It is instructive to compare Marilyn to Boy George. Both emerged from the same club scene, where they had achieved limited celebrity. Both stepped into recording contracts as the specific values of the post-punk era were dis-placing those associated with punk. Neither had been trained as vocalists. Neither fit coherently into what Dick Hebdige has called the "noise" of a given subculture. Neither could be linked to existing social or aesthetic sub-cultures.[18] Both Boy George and Marilyn entered the music industry as already-created pop figures, as gender-benders primed for media exposure. Why then did Boy George become an international superstar, while Marilyn managed just three hit singles and suffered a lower profile?

Boy George was explicitly political, quick to make judgments and state-ments. At the height of his popularity, Boy George's politics seemed to push the boundaries of liberal humanism in gentle ways. His sexual politics recog-nized misogyny and candidly addressed gender ambiguity. He contested dele-gitimization based on race, gender, and nationality and opposed the proliferation of nuclear weapons. However, Boy George firmly resisted allegiance to any lesbian and gay community. In an oft-quoted moment, Boy George in 1983 explained to an interviewer that he preferred a cup of tea to sex. In a rude interview three years later, he craftily acknowledged that, in fact, this was far from the truth.

But Boy George in the early 1980s stubbornly pressed questions of his own sexuality away. In a 1982 interview, Boy George's take on a simple question about his childhood was as follows: "I'm not a transvestite. Everyone thinks I am, but I'm not. I wear Y-fronts! I'm a man! I'm quite manly actually. I don't think I'm as poofy as I'm made out to be. I'm not gay or anything like that."[19] Boy George's pop star persona was, very precisely, drained of sex. By desexualizing himself, Boy George abstracted himself from the messy matters of deviant sexuality. Such a distance was crucial for him. It permitted him to remain within certain limits of respectability while individually bending others. It is not a coincidence that a heroin-ravaged Boy George of 1986 began to talk about sex more candidly. Both involvement with drugs and acknowledgment of personal entanglement with queer sexual practices are infractions of bourgeois respectability. In short, Boy George in the early 1980s resisted identifying or allying with queers in order to avoid being written off.[20]

By way of contrast, Marilyn, as we have seen, could not believably claim celibacy or asexuality. Everything about his image was sexualized; he could *only* be read as gay. When we formulate the question of why Boy George became famous and why Marilyn did not, we need to consider how both George and Marilyn engaged with gender and sexuality. Boy George chose androgyny and asexuality (or "celibacy," a tricky and open-ended sexual identification), while Marilyn chose a highly charged sexualized effeminacy. While both men carved out cultural territory previously unexplored within mass media representations, Marilyn clearly posed a greater challenge to dominant imperatives of both sexuality *and* gender. Like Boy George, Marilyn called conventions of male gender presentation and performativity into question. Unlike Boy George, Marilyn did so without recourse to pop star exceptionalism. Marilyn's sexuality, unlike Boy George's, resisted collapse into the closet of idiosyncrasy by naming its desires and reveling in an objectified subjecthood.

Marilyn is an example of *hybrid male femme*, seriously invested in bodily articulating a femme gender. Borrowing from histories of effeminacy, Marilyn teased his audiences with sometimes androgynous gender code-bungling. By invoking the mantrap, Marilyn acknowledged his debt to the "real" Marilyn and paid tribute to drag culture's longtime Hollywood habit. A *hybrid femme* such as Marilyn invokes several of the four practices I mentioned earlier, projects and positions described: effeminacy, androgyny, drag, and "bottom" status.

Coda

In my analysis, situating lesbian femme as an empowering category of gender is a requisite context for responsively re-envisioning male "femme" as itself empowered; in short, as anything *but* denigrated.[21] Gay men influence lesbians and lesbians influence gay men along countless circuitries, including those of style, politics, sexualities, and language. Invoking camp dramatization, Lisa Kahaleole Chang Hall writes in her essay "Bitches in Solitude":

> I've caught myself waving my hands like a drag queen and stopped dead on the street, struck by the multiple layers of irony involved in my making the gestures of a man making the gestures of a woman that no "real" woman would naturally make.[22]

Here, Hall links drag queen constructions of femininity to a sphere of quasi-theatrical gender performativity. Although the femme I have discussed here depends on "real" lived genders—and as such is somewhat at odds with the above anecdote—Hall's story demonstrates the ricocheting of queer sensibilities across lines assumed to be fixed and stable.

Male femme is, at best, a tenuous category, suspended between established traditions of gay male effeminacy and lesbian femme. To map out examples of male femme exposes the distance between genders that we recognize as femme by default—by dint of their femininity—and genders whose formations bear more similarity to histories of lesbian femme. Though Marilyn may never have been aware of such legacies, the explicitness with which he worked the codes of femininity overloaded his body with queer feminine excess, with and as *hybrid femme*. New taxonomies of queer hybrid practices do, however, trace unexpected pathways of knowledge and inspiration, across legacies, histories, contexts, and environments. In the case of male femme, these unexpected pathways permit gay men to learn from situated lesbian histories of reclamation. It is these reclamations that have reproduced femme as an empowered and sustained category of gender in the first place.

Notes

I thank Liz Crocker, Erica Ganzell and Laura Harris for ongoing commentary on this essay, and Quang H. Dang for his unique and sil(l)y methods of supporting my work.

1. Wendy Chapkis, *Beauty Secrets: Women and the Politics of Appearance* (Boston: South End Press, 1986) 127.

2. Sue-Ellen Case, "Toward a Butch-Femme Aesthetic," in *The Lesbian and Gay Studies Reader,* ed. Henry Abelove, Michele Aina Barale, and David M. Halperin. (New York: Routledge, 1993) 294–306.

3. Amber Hollibaugh and Cherríe Moraga, "What We're Rollin' Around in Bed With: Sexual Silences in Feminism," in *Powers of Desire: The Politics of Sexuality,* ed. Ann Snitow, Christine Stansell and Sharon Thompson (New York: Monthly Review Press, 1983) 392–405.

4. Carol A. Queen, "Why I Love Butch Women," in *Dagger: On Butch Women,* ed. Lily Burana, Roxxie and Linnea Due (San Francisco: Cleis Press, 1994) 15–23.

5. Queen 18.

6. Madeline Davis, "Epilogue, nine years later," in *The Persistent Desire: A Femme-Butch Reader,* ed. Joan Nestle (Boston: Alyson, 1992) 270–271.

7. Mario Mieli, *Homosexuality and Liberation: Elements of a Gay Critique,* trans. David Fernbach (London: Gay Men's Press, 1980).

8. Kurt Loder, "London Calling," *Rolling Stone* 408 (November 10, 1983) 17–18, 20, 25–27, 89.

9. George O'Dowd and Spencer Bright, *Take It Like a Man: The Autobiography of Boy George* (London: Sidgwick & Jackson, 1995).

10. Cathy Griggers, "*Thelma and Louise* and the Cultural Generation of the New Butch-Femme," in *Film Theory Goes to the Movies,* ed. Jim Collins, Hilary Radner, and Ava Preacher Collins (New York: Routledge, 1993) 129–154.

11. Marjorie Garber, *Vested Interests: Cross-Dressing and Cultural Anxiety* (New York: Routledge, 1992).

12. An interesting parallel can be drawn between the status of Marilyn Monroe within gay male drag culture and the position of James Dean as butch lesbian icon/model. For an involved discussion of the latter phenomenon, see Sue Golding, "James Dean: The Almost-Perfect Lesbian Hermaphrodite," in *On Our Backs* (1988): 18–19, 39–44.

13. Graham McCann, *Marilyn Monroe* (New Brunswick: Rutgers University Press, 1988).

14. Paul Monette, *Becoming a Man: Half a Life Story* (San Francisco: Harper San Francisco, 1992).

15. Paul Morley, *Ask: The Chatter of Pop* (London: Faber and Faber, 1985).

16. In 1986, during the Boy George heroin scandal, photos of a barely clad Marilyn taken during a police search were printed by the *Star,* in a rare tabloid exhibition of male naked bodies. British tabloids have a tradition of featuring a topless woman daily, but men's bodies are never casually sexualized within its pages. Here, the *Star* represented Marilyn as he seemed to desire being represented: as a sex(ed) object. Marek Kohn, *Narcomania: On Heroin* (London: Faber and Faber, 1987) 153–154.

17. Linda Duff, "One Small Day," *Smash Hits* 6.12 (1984) 38–39.

18. Dick Hebdige, *Subculture: The Meaning of Style* (London: Methuen, 1979).

19. See Morley.

20. See O'Dowd 443, where Boy George discusses the reproaches he received from his manager vis-à-vis his decision to involve himself in more lesbian/gay community activism.

21. I thank Liz Crocker and Laura Alexandra Harris for reiterating this point.

22. Lisa Kahaleole Chang Hall, "Bitches In Solitude: Identity Politics and Lesbian Community," in *Sisters, Sexperts, Queers: Beyond the Lesbian Nation,* ed. Arlene Stein (New York: Plume, 1993) 218–229.

GENDER WARRIORS:
AN INTERVIEW WITH
AMBER HOLLIBAUGH

Leah Lilith Albrecht-Samarasinha

mber Hollibaugh is a powerful woman. When we were setting up
this interview, I joked about her being one-third of "the holy trinity
of high femme," along with Joan Nestle and Madeline Davis. And
she has been central to the struggle to reclaim and validate femme-butch
gender and sexuality during the feminist sex wars. She is also a lot more: old-
school femme, working-class woman, labor organizer, sex worker, writer,
and film maker. Most recently, she's been known as the founder of the
Lesbian AIDS Project, the first organization created to fight for the needs of
lesbians with HIV. She is a smart, passionate, and luscious survivor who con-
tinues to live the struggle. For me, a young femme, Amber is what I want to
be when I grow up. One afternoon, we talked real loud about femme identity, gender, sex, loyalty, AIDS, race and class, youth and age, whoring, and
everything else under the sun, as the straight women at the next table tried to
figure out whether we were drag queens or not.

A Lifetime Of Femme Identity

LAS: So has your femme identity changed over time?

AH: Oh, yes. You do change over time. The things that you considered fundamental to the way you constructed your femme identity when you were
twenty don't seem really important after a while. . . . It is intriguing to be in

your own life when you're not scared of it. That has taken me fifty years to get to. Now, I am no longer afraid that the choices I make somehow threaten an essentially important identity. I do not walk around saying: "If I do this, am I somehow more or less femme? Am I more or less the erotic person that I imagine myself to be?" I am. I am that person: I have been that person for a very long period of time.

LAS: I doubt myself like that all the time. I think, "I have been wearing pants a lot lately, so maybe I am not really femme."

AH: It is all a process of maturing and coming into yourself. But you do get there, even though it is a struggle. When the woman I was with for ten years and I broke up—and she was very, very butch—I was forty-five. I was a middle-aged femme. I didn't have a lot of preparation for what that was going to look like, and not very many people talked about it. Most of the middle-aged people I knew who were in butch-femme relationships were settling down, buying houses, just what we had done. Suddenly, in the midst of this coupled butch-femme world, I was by myself and not into the bars any more. And I said, how am I going to find lovers? How am I going to be a femme *here*? When I'm no longer young and sexually adventurous and out there?

LAS: Which is where I'm at right now—I go to the bar in a miniskirt and sit on a stool and feel like I can take home anyone in the bar. I'm enjoying it, but I also know it is for a limited period of time and I wonder about what comes next.

AH: It is a fabulous time period, but as a forty-five-year-old you don't really want to go and do it anymore. And even if you did, would you want to pick up someone who is twenty-six? That's the question when your body doesn't look the same, when you don't feel the same way about your body. I've got a long history now. I'm experimenting in different ways. My sexuality is permeated by age and how I feel about age. As femmes, I think, we get the same old shit that all women in this culture get. Butches get some of the privileges of men in the culture: "They age better."

LAS: So how do you handle this?

AH: Well, for one thing, I decided not to stay in that relationship when it was really in trouble, like I had seen femme friends of mine do. They stayed because they were so terrified. They had no alternatives; they basically waved their butch lovers off to go have flings because they didn't think that anyone wanted them as older femmes. I thought, I'll be single for the rest of my life, by god, before I'm going to wave anybody off.

LAS: Before you sell yourself short like that.

AH: If we decide to be non-monogamous, that's fine with me. But, by god, I'm not going to do something because I am so terrified about whether or not I have an erotic future. . . . I'd been in a relationship for ten years and I was confident about myself in a way I had never been. I no longer thought it was an accident that women desired me. . . . I'd been proud, I'd been cocky, I'd been like, "Yeah, honey, come and get it." [laughter] But I'd also been afraid. I had been afraid that once they discovered the real person, that somehow I would not remain that kind of instrumental fabulous hot femme that I like to put myself out as. Well, I lost that fear, and I could go forward.

LAS: I think that confidence in the reality of yourself is what femme is at the core. That confidence that your body is femme—but not "beautiful" in the killing way the culture and the ads put out there as an archetype—it is fucking gorgeous.

AH: That's right. That's exactly what happened to me. . . . As a femme, it is very necessary that you develop that arrogance, just so you can get by in the world and wear that really tight black dress down the same block everyday. That confidence is something you have to struggle towards and grow into.

LAS: If you're straight and looking in from the outside, butches may read as tough and femmes as vulnerable. But if you're in the life you know that femmes are much more ballsy—much more brassy—than butches. Something I say to my friends is that I am "a high femme with the heart of a stone butch." Under that really tough bitch-goddess exterior I have most of the time are all these vulnerabilities. I don't know how to show them to people, especially the butch in my life, who I get all caught up in taking care of and healing and making a home in my arms for. Do you see this dynamic playing out in your life?

AH: Yes, I do. I think that part of the magic between high femme and stone butch is precisely the understanding of that invincibility and that vulnerability, in combination. Although we present and project ourselves very differently, in order to have our integrity, we have a complicated set of standards around what we will and will not tolerate. I think that what that means for a lot of femmes is that we have a kind of integrity—if we survive—about holding onto your own erotic identity, refusing to give up any piece of yourself. . . . I know that's what butches do all the time, and also that it is visible on them in a different way. There was a point a few years ago when there was this button that said, "Butch in the streets, femme in the sheets."

LAS: They have one now that says, "Femme in the streets, butch in the sheets." We've come so far.

AH: Yeah, right, what progress. Part of what was so painful to me about that statement—besides that it was idiotic and completely demeaning to the way that people live butch-femme identities—is that it assumed somehow that being tough on the street was butch. It did not understand that the power you have to insist on as a femme to survive with integrity on the street is a real kick-ass ball-buster attitude. I don't think it is an accident that so many femmes I've known have histories of sex work, because we have the attitude to pull it off. It took me a long time to realize that I walked down the street very differently than other women, not because I was a femme but because I used to be a sex trade worker. I didn't drop my eyes. As a prostitute, if you can't make eye contact, you can't get a customer, so you really have to keep your head up. Once you've done that as a professional, you keep your head up. Part of the reason why men look at me is that I don't drop my eyes. If I dropped my eyes, it would be clear to them that I saw myself as a veiled woman, and that would create a kind of I'm-a-good-girl, I-don't-look-at-men identity.

LAS: When I was nineteen and living on Avenue B and wearing my mini and garter belt, that was one thing I learned. If I looked men in the eye, they would not harass me, which is the total opposite of the good-girl-ignore-it message that you are taught as the way to deal with being sexually harassed. I saw that my attitude freaked het men out even more than my young butch friends did. The men had no place in their heads for a woman in heels and a tight dress who wasn't scared or threatened by them, who was wearing all the cultural signifiers of sexual vulnerability, but was not someone who they could fuck with.

AH: To be a femme who cares about her erotic identity on the street, who does not drop her eyes, but who does not meet men's eyes for erotic charge, the question becomes: How do I keep my head up? How do I walk the way I walk, dress the way I dress, feel my body the way that I'm feeling, desire the women that I desire, and appropriate the street? How do I do that with the partners that I'm with when just the existence of our partnering is going to bring a concentration of hostility down on us? The butch because she's gender inappropriate, and me because I'm a *gender traitor*. I look like the right kind of girl, and I chose the wrong kind of . . . "guy."

LAS: It is very interesting when people get so furious that they don't know where to start. [laughter]

AH: I think about it a lot now, because I think about how to age, as a femme, and keep on being able to appropriate all that I need to. I want to address it in this interview because one of the things that terrified me as a younger femme was thinking about getting older. I didn't see femmes around me as they aged.

LAS: Did you see them defecting back to heterosexuality, or just not coming to the bar, or what?

AH: I just didn't know what happened to them. The only life I knew was within a certain kind of age period, bar life, and political life. But I do think it is very complicated to age with butch–femme sexual identities. Many butch women I've talked to have had real trouble trying to figure out how to navigate when they were no longer instrumental, when they could no longer open a door, when they had trouble making it up stairs, and when they couldn't be gallant with their girlfriend. That instrumentality was very compromised by aging. Femme identity, it seems to me, has many of the same permutations. As an older femme, you can't pull it off in the same way. I mean, you've got a backache, the sexual positions are just not as easy to get into when you're older, so what are you going to do?

LAS: Advil?

AH: Advil, and negotiation. The problem for me is that I don't see women older than myself who I can relate to saying, "This is what femme looks like at sixty. This is what you can do at seventy." And that's really hard. A negligée doesn't look the same on you at sixty. You may still *want* to wear it, and you may still wear it and your lover may think it is fabulous. But it is not fabulous in a culture that fetishizes youth.

LAS: You're going to have to completely renegotiate your relationship to your body and to all the femme style and artifice you've used all your life.

AH: We both know that butch–femme is something much more than style, but it is often negotiated through style; it is created through the appropriation of very specific gendered appearances. Butch–femme is created through playing with these artifices. So if that style is not as available to you, because aging modifies your own relationship to your appropriation of those symbols, we're really talking something that's complicated. Aging is about watching yourself grow old and that's not really very much fun. I mean, I'm sure some women have a fabulous experience doing it, but some women say they enjoy having their period. I have never found that I like my period; I didn't like it when I was twelve and I don't like it now. It surprises me every month; I don't celebrate it with the moon.

LAS: That's the thing about being femme; you don't enjoy *everything* about being a girl.

AH: That's right. You're always trying to figure out what part of female experience you're going to appropriate, and what part of it puts you in a compromised position. So you are *constantly* in an internal struggle: does this hairdo, this dress, this mannerism, this way of sitting, speaking, this eyeliner in any way compromise my femme position? Femme identity is as constructed as butch identity and not a lot of people talk about it like that.

LAS: Can you talk some more about that?

AH: The difference between myself and many of the straight women that I know is that they think that they are normal and natural. They believe in girl-ness, that girl-ness becomes woman-ness, and woman-ness becomes old-woman-ness. They believe in a gendered system that they flow through. . . . But my role models for being femme have been drag queens, because drag queens construct female identity. I look at drag queens and I think, *That's how I feel as a woman.* . . .

LAS: Drag queens and femmes both have that blatancy, that in-your-face outrageousness, and sense of being too much.

AH: My femininity is about irony. It is a statement about the construction of gender; it is not just an appropriation of gender. It is not being a girl, it is watching yourself be a girl. I go to drag queens as my mentors and my role models because they were the ones who believed completely and passionately in their femaleness. The better they were as drag queens, the more they were completely 120 percent girl when they were in persona. They knew exactly the work it took to get there. . . . They could take the dress off and be the messiest looking guy in a coffee shop, but in twenty-five minutes could be the most ravishing beauty. They made femininity make sense to me.

Femmes, AIDS and Activism

LAS: Speaking of outrageous women, do you see femmes playing a specific role in the lesbian AIDS movement? I see a lot of women I would call femmes in the AIDS movement—Lani Ka'aahumanu and Cynthia Astuto are two who come to mind—who have been key people because of their ability to talk very explicitly about sex. I see that as an extension of a typical femme role, the outrageously sexual woman who is not afraid to talk about it.

AH: I think that is true, and I don't think it is an accident. When you look at what the issues are for a lesbian dealing with HIV they are sexuality—often butch-femme—class, race, substance abuse, and incarceration. For HIV-positive lesbians, their histories are going to be already centered around butch-femme issues, such as the oppression of forbidden sexual desire, and questions of how to live their life without giving up their sexual community. Femmes have taken these issues very seriously over a long period of time, and long before HIV.

LAS: How do you see butch-femme and class playing out within the lives of lesbians with HIV?

AH: When I started doing the Lesbian AIDS Project, it was like coming home. . . . The women that I deal with in the Lesbian AIDS Project who are HIV positive and affected by AIDS are working-class women. Since my own personal and social life is constructed around those lines, when I look at lesbians with HIV, they're completely understandable. The question is how *you* lucked out and ended up not positive, how you avoided addiction or somehow avoided a dirty needle, or were a sex worker who used condoms enough to protect yourself, because you were in a privileged enough setting that you could do that, or had enough skill so you could do that, because there's a couple of ways you can pull that off.

LAS: Like a sex worker would learn to put some lube on her hand and slip it on real quick.

AH: Exactly. The women in Lesbian AIDS Project are often women who have been punished for enormous amounts of their lives for being gender-inappropriate. They are not women who have lived in the closet and were afraid to openly come out. Often, at least for the butches, they were women who were punished at twelve, at eight, at three, who always were different in communities that were very intolerant. . . . The issues of survival in these communities are *so* delicate that, if you have a daughter or a son who is too queer, you're terrified. . . . So when you look at the Lesbian AIDS Project, you see women usually with very strong sexual identities.

LAS: Because they were strong enough to survive?

AH: Right. But they are not necessarily comfortable with those identities: some of them feel that their butch and femme identities actually had something to do with their addiction issues, their lack of feelings. It is a complicated history. I don't want to present it like everybody is a happy butch or femme.

LAS: How do you, as the head of the Lesbian AIDS Project, deal with their butchness and femmeness in your work?

AH: My job is figuring out how to mentor women who have never been valued for the kinds of gifts that they bring around their identities. These are women who have never been praised for their sexual choices and have never been appreciated for how they desired women. Often, their story is that they felt ambivalent even if—at the same time—they were acting on those identities. They felt they were paying a terrible price. But once diagnosed, their attitudes often changed. They felt like, "I have got no time to fuck around here, so if my mother doesn't like my sexuality, my mother just doesn't like it."

LAS: So they think, "I've got five years left and it's just too bad, honey."

AH: Yes, and they want to . . . have an erotic identity of their own. That's a pressure on all women with HIV—to stop being sexual. There's a cultural weight that goes against all people with HIV. It says, "You're diseased, and you're contagious and you threaten us." That syphilis model is really at play in the subtext of HIV.

LAS: Also, specifically with women, the voices say, "You're a bad girl, and now you're paying for it."

AH: Right, and further, "You're a danger to me. You already have a forbidden sexual need and now you're going to complicate what's already perverse by insisting on that need even after your HIV testing." One of the really valiant struggles women with AIDS have fought is to remain sexual in the face of a life-threatening illness. The reason why I and a lot of the women in the Project are there is because we are committed to working to validate the rights of women with AIDS to community and to sexuality. We feel they have a right to work through the complex, maybe ambivalent relationships they have to identities, and not have to give up their desire to be sexual in the role that allows them to see themselves as powerful. If that's about being a butch or about being a femme, more power to you girl, you go. And if it is not, there's room in the Project to struggle through how this works in your life.

LAS: So, in terms of your work at the Lesbian AIDS Project, your political analysis seems to integrate race and class and sexuality and gender and everything else: you don't prioritize.

AH: I think the success of the Lesbian AIDS Project has been our refusal to reduce any one aspect of identity to the whole. It is not a project that's only about sexuality, it is not a project only about race and class, only about one kind of oppression. It is a project that actually tries to bring them all together, to value the integrity of the women who are at risk, and give them a space to find out what their priorities are in a culture that's never given them any room at all. It is about meeting other women like yourself, starting a dialogue about your lives and the forces that got you here in the first place. It is learning a set of skills you've never had in order to mobilize politically to reach other women. It is a place where you don't have to choose one part of yourself you can be. Women can be all of themselves at the Lesbian AIDS Project.

LAS: Is that why you got involved with AIDS activism? You started to get involved after the Barnard conference, right?

AH: AIDS activism as a movement valued my ability to do explicit work around sexuality. If you couldn't talk about sexuality as part of class and race in the beginning of AIDS work, you couldn't do the work. There I was, in a political movement—the sex wars, Barnard, all the controversy around butch-femme in the early eighties—and people were saying, "Why do you have to keep bringing this up?" You can only be in your own movement and completely oppositional for a while without feeling like a freak. Coming from a family that taught me never to cross a picket line, one of the worst times I ever had was crossing the only one I ever did: a feminist picket line of Women Against Pornography at the Barnard conference. I thought to myself, this is really telling. I'm crossing a picket line, with women carrying signs with *my* name on them, saying that I'm perverted, that I don't belong in this movement. I had to cross a collective line that should have been about rights and freedom but was restigmatizing me for my history. I decided that I needed to be someplace where I wasn't always saying, "Yes, but . . . " So, yes, AIDS activism looked to me like the place that brought together all the social injustices that were stigmatized. It was the place where all the culturally stigmatized secrets—which were what really put people at risk—came out, from race and class to "I suck men off and then go home to my wife."

LAS: One of those culturally stigmatized secrets is butch-femme—because butch-femme sexual practices like using dildoes and fisting without barriers are the ones that transmit AIDS the most easily from woman to woman.

AH: Yes, AIDS activism seemed like a natural world for me, a world that valued and demanded my skills. Finding this world has been one of the most fabulous things; instead of having to say "Yes, but . . . " I've been in the position to say, "Yes." The project has made race and class and sexuality visible. . . . And as a femme, it has been fabulous. It has been a way for me to go home—to go back to the women that I'm attracted to, that I love, whose histories reflect my own—and not be strange. We don't sit around all the time and talk about sex work; but, if it comes up, it is not strange. And because my position at the Lesbian AIDS Project is regular, I become valued. And if I did not have a handle on butch and femme—not just race and class—I don't think I could have done it.

LAS: Definitely. Cheers, honey. [laughter]

Femme, the Next Generation

LAS: What do you see as the next step for femme women who theorize butch-femme identities within radical gender theory? What do we need to do next?

AH: In the last few years, the transgender movement has insisted that there is another place for queer identity to be named. They have begun to explore what "butch" means in a transgender setting, and it is not the same thing as in a butch-femme setting. But what high femme means in a transgender setting outside of butch-femme, that needs to be taken on.

LAS: My god, thank you. When I went to see Leslie Feinberg read at A Different Light at the book release for *Transgender Warriors,* I really wanted to get up and ask her why she left out high femmes and butch faggots from her book. Because even though we do not cross from our assigned-at-birth gender to the "other" gender—the way transgender is often thought of—we still chose to live a different gender. If a high femme goes to a baby shower and *struts* her stuff, she will be read as being as queer as a drag queen would.

AH: You know that if you're doing high femme, your femininity is profoundly made up. Femmes make it happen in a way that is not at all natural—it is real, but it is not natural. As a femme, you have made decisions about how you will appear as a gendered person. And when you're doing it, you don't take a deep breath and say, "Ah, I'm finally me." Instead, you go, "Ha, I finally actually look like the way I think a girl who isn't a girl looks." When I look at drag queens—that's how I see myself—I like looking like a drag queen. It matters to me that I look that way. When I look to and identify with that construction, I am also transgendered.

LAS: I think that that is a very common high femme experience that is not often discussed. I cannot tell you how many times when I was eighteen my gay male friends would tell me that I looked like a trannie.

AH: Absolutely. I think that people have to be careful not to pose as part of a movement (like transgender) that they aren't primary players in, so I want to be very delicate about it. But for me, there is at least an aspect, as there is for stone butches, of transgendered experience. When you design girl-ness, when you make up the way you are female, that's a transgendered experience. . . . I think that transgender hasn't been mapped or named in the same way for femmes. That has bothered me because there is that transgendered aspect of high femme-ness that isn't about the erotic relationship, that isn't in relation to butches.

LAS: I think that's so important. Because unless we have that understanding of femme as trannie, there will never be an understanding of us as equally queer as butches.

AH: I think that a femme conversation with drag queens would offer some very interesting, very similar experiences. My fantasy has always been to have a femme panel that didn't assume that femme was lesbian. . . . I want us as femmes, where it is appropriate, to insist that we're part of that queer dialogue instead of what usually happens, where as we get more feminine we get perceived as straighter, rather than as transgendered. . . . I also think that femmes need to become each other's allies. If we do that, we will begin to make it truly safe to be a strong femme in partnership with a strong butch.

LAS: Our femme bonding will challenge that discourse where butch is the signifier for both lesbianism and butch-femme. There is no such thing in a lot of people's minds as an independent femme identity. If we battle that . . .

AH: But don't you think that that's what my generation of femmes has done? I think historically what people like Joan Nestle and myself and Dorothy Allison have done is to give the butch icon a run for its money. We have said that we are femme regardless of the butch that we are partnered with. That we are a free-standing sexual signifier that is as powerful an erotic voice on its own.

LAS: Yes, and a lot of women my age I know revere all of you—and Jewelle Gomez and Chrystos and others. . . . But it still it takes a long time to learn to balance vulnerability and toughness as a femme.

AH: It is very hard. I think we don't appreciate how complicated it is to assemble our identities, to let them become shaded and nuanced as we grow. Two things I have very much valued about S/M communities are: one, their members' ability to distinguish *play* from how one lives around butch-femme (among other complicated sexual identities); and, two, their understanding of how one constructs a sexual arena. I think that the S/M community doesn't have the visibility it should have. I have been—and continue to be—extraordinarily influenced by what I see in S/M communities especially around HIV, around safer sex, around gender, around sexual play and who tops and who bottoms. And what you call yourself when you're in that sexual play is different from what you call yourself in your life.

I think that more femmes, whether or not they see themselves as S/M, need to pay attention to the S/M community. . . . Most of us have a teensy tiny little arena to play in and no place to learn. . . . My sexual playground can be literally re-sculptured by a dialogue with somebody who has done something that I never imagined that I could do. I take their behavior and think about it and worry about it—try it, change a little bit over here, keep this piece of it, and so on—and end up with some new understanding that thrills me. . . .

LAS: I think it is important for femmes, especially, to learn from S/M communities about topping and bottoming. Power exchange is key to much femme-butch sex, in one way or another. To take one example, there's the classic femme bottom role, which can be a very powerful liberatory strong position. But if you're eighteen and you've struggled to the point where you know that you like being a girl and wearing stockings and a garter belt and being called a slut and fucked till you scream, but you don't know how to say "no" or how to negotiate your limits . . . My god, you're going into a minefield. If we're going to make the world safe for femmes, we have to know how to negotiate that minefield. I think back to what I went through when I was twenty, and I think it is a wonder I'm still in one piece. And that's a very common thing.

AH: The idea that you can't truly say "yes" until you know that you can say "no," is a very true one. You cannot make sexual choices until you know how to orchestrate and control sexuality, from every possible position. One of the things that happens in S/M that is very liberating for many women is that you have to be in your body no matter what. You are expected to participate. You really do call the shots: "No, don't do that" or "My wrists are numb" and "Don't hit me on the ass." So your needs, to the extent that you know them, really determine the content of the scene. Femmes need to talk to each other about sexual empowerment and historically remembering sexuality. So that we don't romanticize victimization, but we learn to use where it has left us, in our real bodies as we make love. So that I don't live in *or* deny my fear.

LAS: What do you see in the future for you in your femme identity and your life?

AH: Right now, I can actually arrange my world in alignment with what I think should be true. It is both a privilege and a challenge to be all the things that I am, to keep hold of them, remember them, value them, and figure out how to make them work. Even though it is a very difficult thing, we should keep choosing a bigger and bigger picture, even when people want us to be smaller. Femme identity really speaks to that, because it can not be reduced. It is a living, breathing thing that women are a part of, that women play, that many of us are not prepared to give up or make comfortable for anyone else, because we want to live it.

LAS: That's the bottom line: femme is always going to be walking down the street with a bullhorn in her hand yelling at the top of her lungs, "I'm here. Deal with it, goddamnit." Fabulous, huh?

AH: Damn straight.